ICT for Education, Development, and Social Justice

A volume in
Current Perspectives on Applied Information Technologies
Charalambos Vrasidas, Gene V Glass, *Series Editors*

CARDET

CENTRE FOR THE ADVANCEMENT OF RESEARCH & DEVELOPMENT IN EDUCATIONAL TECHNOLOGY

INSPIRE – EMPOWER – INNOVATE

www.cardet.org

CARDET is an independent, non-profit, non-governmental, research and development organization based in Cyprus with partners around the world. CARDET is becoming one of the leading institutions in the world for research and development in education, innovation, information communication technologies, and social issues. CARDET's mission is to inspire next generation education, and to promote research, innovation, and development through evidence-based practices, cutting-edge research, and empowered professionals. The CARDET team strives to offer the highest quality research and development services to benefit society.

The main goals of CARDET include:

- To conduct research and development on the links between education, training, information communication technologies, and social progress.
- To apply interdisciplinary approaches that improve and strengthen the role of civil society, democratic processes, equality, and social justice for all.
- To develop links with organizations and agencies around the world in addressing social, business, health, environmental, and education needs.
- To foster innovation and leadership for education and social reform.
- To provide research, evaluation, and training services to governments, businesses, and other agencies.

To achieve these goals, CARDET brings together an international team of experienced professionals with extensive global expertise in leadership development, innovation, e-learning, education reform, social justice, and evaluation. CARDET has collaborated with schools, education institutions, Ministries of Education, and corporations in Asia, Europe, and the United States. Members of the CARDET team has successfully completed projects in more than twenty countries, several of which were supported by the European Commission, the National Science Foundation, the U.S. Department of Education, Microsoft, The Commonwealth of Learning, the United Nations Development Program, The William and Flora Hewlett Foundation, the Cyprus Research Promotion Foundation, and several Ministries around the world. In the next decade, CARDET plans to enhance its contribution to education research and social development that make a difference in people's lives.

ICT for Education, Development, and Social Justice

edited by

Charalambos Vrasidas
CARDET and University of Nicosia

Michalinos Zembylas
Open University of Cyprus and CARDET

Gene V Glass
Arizona State University and CARDET

INFORMATION AGE PUBLISHING, INC.
Charlotte, NC • www.infoagepub.com

Library of Congress Cataloging-in-Publication Data

ICT for education, development, and social justice / edited by Charalambos Vrasidas, Michalinos Zembylas, Gene V Glass.
p. cm. – (Current perspectives on applied information technologies)
Includes bibliographical references.
ISBN 978-1-60752-021-4 (pbk.) – ISBN 978-1-60752-022-1 (hardcover)
1. Telecommunication in education–Social aspects–Developing countries. 2. Information technology–Social aspects–Developing countries. 3. Digital divide–Developing countries. 4. Social justice–Developing countries. I. Vrasidas, Charalambos. II. Zembylas, Michalinos. III. Glass, Gene V, 1940-
LB1044.84.I27 2009
371.33–dc22

2008043985

Printed and bound by CPI Group (UK) Ltd, Croydon, CR0 4YY

To Jenny

This book is dedicated to our late friend and colleague, Jenny Leach, Professor of Teacher Learning and Development at The Open University, who passed away in August 2007.

Jenny began her teaching career working in African schools and maintained relationships formed there throughout her life. It was fitting then, that the focus of her professional energy in the last years of her career was on researching and enabling teacher learning and development, particularly in Africa.

Jenny was co-director of the Digital Education Enhancement Project (DEEP) and the Teacher Education in Sub-Saharan Africa (TESSA) programme, as well as a number of innovative, large-scale teacher education programmes within the UK.

In all aspects of her work, Jenny emphasized respect for the identity of teachers, seeking to help develop with them professional knowledge, skills, tools, and networks. Much of her work explored the appropriate use of ICT to support teacher learning and practice, including computer mediated communication and mobile technologies.

In the words of DEEP project teachers and pupils, from a disadvantaged rural school in South Africa, "Jenny opened our eyes and our minds and we will always remember her."

—Tom Power & Rhodri Thomas
The Open University

CONTENTS

PART 3

ICT FOR INCLUSION

PART 4

ICT FOR CULTURAL UNDERSTANDINGS

FOREWORD

John Willinsky
Stanford University

This book's central and critical premise, namely that we have now to analyze critically how information and communication technologies can be better used to promote development and social justice, makes it especially timely now that the computer can be said to be part of a global system. Certainly, the ability to sit down with a computer and log into this system is still as unevenly and inequitably distributed as anything else that we tend to value on this planet. But at the same time, the network is becoming a part of an increasing number of schools and colleges, public libraries, and internet cafés around the world. Thus, this is the time to consider the potential, on a global scale as this book does, how these new technologies can be directed, not just toward gathering *information* and *communicating* that information, as the seemingly bland acronym *ICT* might suggest, but toward changing how and what the world learns.

The contributors to this book make it clear that what is made of these new technologies is by no means a given. What is to be done and undone by booting up, as we used to say, logging on, and clicking through, stands as a major challenge to the educational imagination. A global network of computers is indeed a powerful force, representing what is still, for many of us, a startling leap in the ability of people around the world to connect with others, to participate in social and commercial ventures, to access resources and materials.

ICT for Education, Development, and Social Justice, pages xi–xiv

Like print before it, ICTs can be turned to sacred or profane purposes. Yet it could as easily amount to more of the same—well, more of the same, only faster, more of it, and in more places. So in the case of education, it is wise to recall that computers had their start as "teaching machines," intended to be an improvement over teachers in the efficient and effective instruction of students. The famous behavioral psychologist B. F. Skinner built a rote-and-drill teaching machine in the 1950s, with IBM working at the time on turning mainframe computers to a similar purpose. This might have been the whole of the education endeavor for these new technologies, with each generation of the machines a little cooler looking, a little more compact, a little more adept at directing each step of the child's learning.

Only something else happened with ICTs. They did not remain simply a means of managing people, information systems, industrial, and military processes. People found ways of turning these machines into the most powerful of creative and expressive tools. The computer became a means, much as the press had, of subverting the official word, rewriting the given, and stating what had yet to be said. There were precedents, of course. Today's blogosphere carries forward the pamphlet wars of the Seventeenth Century. Networked cells of social activism, as well as of political terrorism, harken back to the printing press engines of revolution, hidden away in basements and sheds. Only this time with this new technology, the classroom is able to plug into this larger, often educational, sometimes dangerous, world. Educators are able to reduce the isolation and removal of the school from the world, sheltered as it has long been by the textbook-packaging of knowledge and the carefully culled school library. So now learners are able to take from as well as step into and contribute to that world, and this calls for some serious rethinking of educational possibilities.

This book is part of this refocusing of those possibilities, part of a critical consideration of how ICT can be used to advance ethical goals of social justice. The aim, as I see it at least without trying to summarize the whole of what this book undertakes, is to use this new medium to change the relations of knowledge and power, learning and education. What students must learn, to further this program of development and social justice, is how to use these new means of production to develop the basis for a more just society, and to begin to do that within the scope of the classroom. It begins with changing the learner's, as well as the teacher's, relation to knowledge and how it is produced, shared, and distributed.

There are many new models emerging for just such altered states of learning and knowledge production, with a sampling of such models presented in this book. Yochai Benkler has pointed out how such developments are demonstrating "the wealth of networks," in his book by that name. This wealth is distinguished by the "nonproprietary" and "nonmarket" basis by which people are creating the means for others to collaborate and share in the production of software (open source software), research and scholarship (open access), and learning materials (open education resources).

What I have come to realize, from working with the Public Knowledge Project on creating open source journal systems to help others publish, is that this interest in sharing is what might be identified as an *intellectual property of learning*, and one that we have only begun to explore in education. ICTs can help students participate, through their own work, in this mixed economy of proprietary and nonproprietary concerns with intellectual properties and knowledge economies. They can see how people are capable of transacting with the world in very different ways that have much to teach us about what might otherwise seem inevitable if not invisible about the order of things. These are lessons that have much to do with notions of social justice and development.

Yet to praise this creative and critical potential of ICTs is not to avoid the persistent digital divides that only frustrate such hopes for social justice. Still, there can be no waiting for such divides to somehow be overcome before starting to demonstrate how ICTs can be used to alter a world whose economic momentum, such as it is today after the recent meltdown, has been driven by economic inequities in wages, standards of living, and access to capital. It is simply not enough to acknowledge that access to print was similarly divided, and that inequity is the one constant of our lives. Rather, a better approach is to begin work on an aspect of such divisions where one can step in, as this book does. That in itself openly challenges what otherwise seems the immovable norm of inequality.

At the same time, the work that goes into changing any one aspect of this inequality must be inspired by a larger vision of what can be gained, in this case, by increasing access to ICTs, a vision that challenges the conditions and expectations of inequality. Part of what this book does is contribute substantially to the case for diminishing this digital divide, both in its demonstration cases and its realistic but still suggestive critiques. The book takes what the contributors do well, as educators and researchers, and makes it part of the moral imperative to reduce such inequalities, in ways that can only further persuade those in international agencies and elsewhere to take advantage of their position to change the material circumstances by which such resources as computers and Internet bandwidth are distributed.

The use of ICTs for education, development and social justice is, then, about turning students' learning, their questioning, their insights, into part of this greater, more public circulation of knowledge. Today, a student who makes the slightest correction to a *Wikipedia* article is contributing more to the state of public knowledge, in a matter of minutes, than I was able to do over the course of my entire grade school education, such as it was. There is a similar point of contrast with what John Dewey saw as the need for students to be prepared for "self-respecting, self-supporting, *intelligent* work" that can "affect the welfare of others," as he puts it in the *Schools of To-Morrow* in 1915, with his daughter, Evelyn Dewey.

Students today are able to do more than prepare for such work; they are able to experience what it means to contribute self-respecting and intelligent work (while learning how such collaborative efforts become self-supporting). For her part, Evelyn Dewey wrote in that book about schools that put carpentry tools and cooking utensils into the hands of students (if all too conventionally divided by gender), so that they could maintain their own schools and feed themselves. The students' learning took place through their responsible contributions to their communities. Today, students now have the tools to direct their learning toward contributing to the knowledge available about their community and their lives, especially as that relates to the development of social justice within those communities.

Yet for the Deweys, the student preparation of meals was not just about learning to cook; rather, "the kitchen becomes a laboratory for the study of a fundamental factor in human life." And in working within this knowledge economy today, students, too, need to see their work as a study of how knowledge relates to power, justice, and development. In that way, a book such as this is capable of directing learning toward a greater public good, leading to what Dewey called democratic education, in ways that will serve the democratic quality, expressiveness, and activism of people's lives well beyond their school days.

PART 1

OVERVIEW

CHAPTER 1

ICT FOR DEVELOPMENT

Challenges and Possibilities

Charalambos Vrasidas
CARDET and University of Nicosia

Michalinos Zembylas
CARDET and Open University of Cyprus

Gene V Glass
Arizona State University and CARDET

INTRODUCTION

In recent years there has been an increased interest in exploring the role of Information Communication Technologies (ICTs) in education in relation to development and social justice. Issues such as human rights, the eradication of poverty, freedom of speech, and equality are continuing discourses among international organizations, scholars, governments, and activists. Social and economic inequalities and injustices are evident in all countries, in all spheres of life. According to UN reports, we live longer than ever, and yet, life expectancy statistics show major differences from country to country. Poverty, famine, disease, and climate change are causing irreparable harm across the developing world. Although discussions of the use of ICTs for education reflect mixed sentiments among supporters and critics,

ICT for Education, Development, and Social Justice, pages 3–15

the purpose of this edited collection is to argue that if critically and systematically approached, ICTs and networked learning environments have the potential to promote both development and social justice.

It is useful to define some of the basic concepts used throughout this book. The first concept is that of *social justice*. Clearly, the meaning of "social justice" remains hotly contested. As discussed in the chapter by Zembylas (this volume), a number of important social theorists (Fraser, 1997, 2003; Young, 1990) underscore two fundamental dimensions of social justice: recognition and redistribution. That is, social justice is about eradicating the socioeconomic disadvantage that impedes individuals and whole communities from equal participation in the making of culture, in public spheres, and in everyday life. Education for social justice, then, entails those pedagogies and educational policies that improve the quality of learning and life opportunities of typically marginalized students (Cochran-Smith, 2004). Social justice theory calls for all aspects of education to be constantly interrogated and transformed based on the ideas of equity and justice. For example, a focus of social justice proponents in relation to ICTs is that educators need to examine critically not only who has ICT access in education, but also how ICTs can be used to promote a fair and just education for all students. Education for social justice, in general, encourages students and educators to deconstruct fundamental assumptions (e.g., about ICTs) which are often taken for granted. A more detailed discussion of the theoretical aspects of social justice and ICT is presented in the next chapter by Zembylas.

One of the most important areas of struggle for social justice is eradicating poverty, and thus a significant aspect is breaking out of the cycle of poverty. The cycle of poverty is the condition under which individuals are trapped in poverty as a result of a set of factors or events by which poverty began and would most likely continue for them, unless there is an intervention.

According to UNESCO (2008, 2003) reports:

- In 2004, almost 1 billion people lived below the international poverty line, earning less than $1 per day;
- 840 million people in the world are malnourished—799 million of them live in the developing world;
- 153 million of the world's malnourished people are children under the age of 5;
- Every day, 16,000 children die from hunger-related causes; one child every five seconds;
- 6 million children under the age of 5 die every year as a result of hunger;
- In 2005, about 10.1 million children died before they reached their fifth birthday. Almost all of these deaths occurred in developing countries.

Two other terms that are frequently used in discussions about poverty eradication, especially in relation to the role of education, are "education for development" and "development education." Although these terms are sometimes used interchangeably, they are quite different. Among Non Governmental Development Organizations (NGDOs) and activists, "development education" is a process which aims to raise awareness among people on development issues, enhance their understanding regarding the global and local challenges faced by developing countries, and promote people's engagement in action towards addressing these issues. According to DEEEP, "Development education is an active learning process, founded on values of solidarity, equality, inclusion and co-operation" (Source: http://www.deeep.org). Development education aims to empower people to address inequalities around the world and find solutions to overcome them. In this sense it challenges and encourages thinking to aid people to enhance their practical skills and confidence to bring about beneficial change locally and globally. In addition, it increases understanding of the economic, social, political and environmental forces which shape people's lives. Development education aspires to develop the skills, attitudes and values that enable people to cooperate in taking action to bring about change and take control of their lives. Finally, development education is focused on empowering individuals and communities to achieve a more just and sustainable world in which power and resources are equitably shared.

"Education for development," on the other hand, is education used to promote development and prosperity. The argument is simple: Education can improve the quality of life of the individual and of societies. Education can promote development and help remove the "unfreedoms" that prevent individuals and societies from satisfying their basic needs. Sen (1999) argued for a strong link between development and freedom. The deprivation of basic freedoms and oppression are realities for millions of people. As Sen wrote: "Expansion of freedom is viewed, in this approach, both as a primary end and as the principal means of development. Development consists of the removal of various types of unfreedoms that leave people with little choice and little opportunity of exercising their reasoned agency. The removal of substantial unfreedoms, it is argued here, is constitutive of development." (p. xii). This view of development, is not focused on the traditional view of the term, namely, on the link between development and the growth of the gross national product.

THE WORLD TODAY

Given that education is fundamental to efforts to promote social justice and development, one is forced to ask a simple question: Is education something enjoyed by all? It is ironic that in developed nations, the rhetoric on education focuses on lifelong learning, knowledge management, and e-learning, whereas in developing countries the focus is on ensuring primary education and basic literacy skills for all. According to the UNESCO (2007) report on "Education for All" (http://www.efareport.unesco.org), there are still more than 700 million illiterate adults, mainly from Sub-Saharan Africa and Arab States. Furthermore, four out of five births occur in developing countries, and people younger than 15 account for 42 percent of the total population in the least developed countries (UNESCO, 2008). Many of the developing countries that have yet to achieve universal primary and secondary education will face increasing enrolment pressure in the coming decades as the number of children in need of education rises dramatically. Primary education can help break the cycle of poverty (UNESCO, 2003). By providing children with basic education, we can facilitate the improvement of the quality of life for millions of people. According to estimates (Power et al. this volume; UNESCO, 2008), in low-income countries:

- with each additional year of education, the average earnings rise 11 percent;
- with each additional year of a girl's education, her eventual wages rise 10–20 percent;
- with each additional year of a girl's education, the death rate of her children under 5 years of age falls by 8 percent.

The second Millennium Development Goal by the United Nations states that by 2015, all children around the world, regardless of gender, will be able to complete a full course of primary schooling. According to the United Nations MDG 2007 report (http://mdgs.un.org), progress has been made in achieving universal primary education. More specifically, enrolment in primary schools grew from 80 percent in 1991 to 88 percent in 2005, and most of this progress has taken place since 1999. However, according to http://www.mdgmonitor.org, although 682 million children worldwide are enrolled in primary school, there are still approximately 77 million children who are missing out on a primary education.

To meet the increasing demand for primary education, one of the immediate needs is for more teachers. It is estimated that 18 million new teachers are needed to reach universal primary education by 2015. Ministries of education around the world are hiring contract teachers to save costs and rapidly increase the teaching force. However, because such teachers lack adequate training and work conditions, this practice has a negative impact on the quality of education that is offered (http://www.mdgmonitor.org).

According to UNESCO (2008), although the provision of pre-primary education for children ages 3 and older has improved, it remains scarce throughout sub-Saharan Africa and the Arab States. Furthermore, early childhood care and education programs rarely reach the poorest and most disadvantaged children (who according to research stand to gain the most from such programs in terms of health, nutrition, and cognitive development). On the other hand, some success stories give hope for the achievement of Millennium Development Goasl. For example, in Haiti, collaboration between the government, UN agencies and NGOs changed the lives of 4,300 of the country's poorest children, thanks to an education project that provided school materials and supplies to 33 schools. This project also promoted the right to education by supporting school attendance and teacher professional development.

THE ROLE OF ICTS

Recent developments in certain sectors of ICT have enabled more people to have access to education. ICTs can empower, under certain circumstances, educational efforts to promote development and social justice. It is these circumstances that this book explores by bringing together an exemplary collection of case studies, each of which addresses, through a critical lens, the use of ICT for education, development and social justice. These case studies from around the world—Argentina, Cambodia, Costa Rica, Cyprus, Ecuador, Indonesia, Israel, Kenya, Malaysia, Mexico, Singapore, South Africa, Thailand, Tibet, and the US—expose both the limitations and the opportunities from using ICTs in education to achieve the benefits of development and social justice.

Three major themes that are addressed in these case studies are poverty, social inclusion, and cultural understanding. Authors of chapters in this collection discuss how some of these themes can be addressed via a variety of ICTs including mobile technologies, Web 2.0 tools, online games, social networking software, and networked learning environments. These technologies have multiple dimensions including seamless integration in everyday activity, space and time independence, and they offer opportunities for unlimited interaction to millions of people around the world. These technologies can provide access to education and social services for the marginalized on a scale never before possible.

Collectively and individually, these case studies suggest that a critical view of technology is required if we are to leverage the affordances of networked technologies for promoting education, development, and social justice. For example, it is shown in practice how all stakeholders engaged in shaping the multiple ways in which ICTs can support development must be involved in the planning, implementation, and evaluation of programs. The "information society" rhetoric focuses on wide-scale implementation of ICTs without questioning fundamental assumptions that might unjustly exclude the disadvantaged. The purpose of this book, then, is to examine critically the relationship between ICT for education and issues of development and social justice.

ICT FOR EDUCATION

It is often argued that technology in education will make schools more productive and efficient, will improve teaching and learning, will provide authentic and engaging learning experiences, and will better prepare students for the workforce (Cuban, 2001). Although there is dramatic growth in the availability of technology to schools in developed countries, there is a great deal of evidence that teachers do not use technology as expected. Teachers are asked to find ways to successfully integrate ICTs into their classrooms, but often with very little preparation and support. Furthermore, researchers continue to struggle with the question whether ICTs can improve conventional teaching and learning. The evidence is at least inconsistent (Vrasidas & Glass, 2005).

Meaningful access and use of ICTs and networked learning is embedded in complex sociopolitical, cultural, and economic contexts. The problems faced by developing countries (e.g., poverty, famine, war, ill health) are multidimensional; and as such they need to be addressed systemically and systematically. Regardless of physical access, the ICT environment can be "exclusionary" to large groups of people. In this book, we attempt to unpack the assumptions embedded in the ICT rhetoric and propose alternative ways of articulating the relationship among ICT, social justice, and development. Examples and case studies of the use of a variety of ICTs from around the world are presented and an attempt is made to show the ways in which all these technological tools can be empowering and inclusionary for the underprivileged.

In general, the use of ICTs for education, social justice, and development can be approached from various angles:

- The use of ICT to promote access to education among the underprivileged. Examples include the use of online education programs to reach out to communities and individuals who, because of several constraints, cannot attend traditional schools.
- The use of ICT to promote awareness of development and the importance of education. Examples include the use of blogs, wikis,

social networking software, and e-newsletters to raise awareness of development issues.

- The use of ICT to build learning environments within which individuals and communities can learn about and take action to promote social justice. An example of such use is the development of 3-D virtual worlds within which students and teachers can actively engage in social justice activities.

Many critical theorists of ICT (Feenberg, 1995) argue that ICT alone cannot be the solution to the world's problems. There are multiple perspectives and views on how ICT can shape culture and influence developing countries around the world. Not all of these views are negative (critical) or skeptical. For example, observers from Palau and Scotland see the internet as a space where they can express, share, and enrich their cultural values (Zembylas, MecIsaac, & Vrasidas, 2002; Kitalong & Kitalong, 2000; Sloane & Johnstone, 2000). Burbules and Callister (2000) argued that in developing countries of Southeast Asia, access to online higher education is seen as an engine of growth. Therefore, such nations, will seek quality education, in any format, from whoever can provide it.

Fabos and Young (1999) argued that one must historicize and contextualize the use of ICT "in the framework of power and dominance, and...students are asked to tackle provocative questions [that] cultivate more critical or political sensibilities" (p. 242). They argue that:

> ... [W]e need to locate and highlight those projects which encourage young students to go beyond "seeing the world" as electronic tourists from the safety of their computer screen and a dominant American perspective. We need to celebrate those projects that ask troubling questions about local inequities, and even the economic role and impact of telecommunications on indigenous communities. We need to help students ask questions that consider why the sixth grade girl from the Midwest might never end up net-chatting with the same-age girl in Indonesia who may have sewed her overpriced Adidas t-shirt or Nike shoes. (pp. 249–250)

We turn now to the three themes identified earlier—development, social inclusion and cultural understandings—and show how the chapters in this book contribute to a richer understanding of these themes.

ICT FOR DEVELOPMENT

The first theme has to do with the extent to which ICT for education and development can contribute (if at all) to the "War on Poverty" or whether ICT fosters even further marginalization and poverty. The chapter by

Zembylas discusses the theoretical and philosophical aspects of the main themes of the book. The chapters by Leh and her colleagues, Power and his colleagues, Fischman and Romero, Daniel, and McIsaac and Moreira suggest that the issue is much more complicated than simply a matter of ICT as a solution or an obstacle to development. Rather, factors at both the macro (existing social structures) and the micro (quality curricular resources, differentiated professional development) levels need to be carefully considered. Macro-level influences are important in determining the differential access and use of ICT and micro-level influences are crucial in evaluating the effectiveness of pedagogical interventions to improve the opportunities and achievement of marginalized students. The aforementioned chapters deal with the intersection of development, education, and ICT in contexts of education needs of developing countries, and schools serving poor and disadvantaged students. ICT can indeed be used to enhance students' skills or teachers' development but if those interventions are not situated in the existing social structures and community challenges—that is, if the primacy of social inequalities is not recognized—then using ICT in education is unlikely to have any long term effects of reducing social and economic disadvantage.

Leh and her colleagues report on a project that was designed to improve student achievement in a high-minority, high-poverty school district in Southern California. The project consisted of a student program, parental involvement, and faculty development. Strategies used for the student program included data-based decision making, cues, timely feedback, visual and contextualized learning, synthesis of learning for deeper understanding and retention, accessibility to instructional support, and parental involvement. Strategies used for the faculty development involved coaching and mentoring to develop teacher expertise, assessment of instructional activities related to student achievement, access to differentiated professional development opportunities, and access to high quality curricular resources. The findings of this project suggest the need for combining quality curricular resources and teacher development with structural changes such as parental involvement and systemic efforts.

Similarly, Power and his colleagues explore the intersection of development, education and ICT in the contexts of schools serving disadvantaged rural communities in South Africa. These authors suggest that access to technological skills and tools is critical for tackling poverty, and thus ICT for education can constitute a powerful ally in the war against poverty. Finally, Fischman and Romero analyze the e-hopes from incorporating ICTs into education systems in Latin America, particularly in terms of access, equity, and fairness. The authors call attention to the fact that understanding the role and potential of ICTs in education cannot be accomplished without analyzing the impact of structural influences such as the neoliberal inspired educational reforms in the region. Recognizing the complex and uncertain effects of ICTs for social justice and development in this area of the world demands a critical view of ICT.

One of the key arguments of the book is that education can help people break out of the cycle of poverty. In their chapters, Daniel and McIsaac and Moreira provide examples of how Open Education Resources and online education can offer opportunities to developing countries. They argue that the growth of higher education in the developing world has encountered various constraints. However, Open Education Resources have the potential to address the growing demand for higher education in the developing world. On the other hand, public-private partnerships will play a key role in reaching out to a large numbers of students. Daniels discusses the example of India where private institutions account for more than 75 percent of professional education. However, issues of copyright, quality assurance, and accreditation remain unresolved in several large scale initiatives.

ICT FOR SOCIAL INCLUSION

The second major theme explored here has to do with social inclusion, that is, how ICT for education can promote the inclusion of individuals or communities in society's social and economic wealth. More specifically, social inclusion refers to the extent to which individuals, families, and communities are able to participate fully in society in terms of economic resources, employment, health, education, housing, recreation, culture, and civic activity (Warschauer, 2003). This theme is related to the previous theme of poverty and socioeconomic inequality; however, social inclusion recognizes a broader array of other discriminatory factors such as disability, political views, gender, age, and sexual preference. The authors represented here—particularly Ellis and his colleagues, Power and Sankale, and Ping and Hedberg—suggest that ICT is important to social inclusion yet the role of ICT should not be viewed uncritically. These chapters focus on development issues to be addressed through the effective integration of ICT into education.

Ellis and Ellis explore how the digital divide is manifested in disability and education and show through a moving case study of a college student with a hearing loss that ICT can be successfully used to accommodate the needs of students with disabilities. The authors discuss issues of equity in access of ICT for students with disabilities and analyze the negative implications of educational settings that are not configured to support learning for all students. Ellis and Ellis suggest that ICT can be used to equalize the chances of students with disabilities to be academically successful.

Power and Sankale investigate the relationship between mobile technologies and teacher professional development through an analysis of issues of access and use of mobile communications networks. The case studies they present from South Africa and Kenya identify specific pedagogical practices and structural changes that are needed to capitalize on the mobile revolution as a tool for education and development. Finally, Ping and Hedberg focus on South-East Asia and provide different perspectives on the ICT-related priorities set by countries like Singapore, Thailand, Malaysia, and Indonesia. Their analysis reveals the desire of these countries to develop a culture of thinking and social responsibility, highlighting the advantages gained when local efforts are combined with structural changes. With support at the macro level, it is more likely that the opportunities for productive use of ICT are expanded.

In particular, *e-inclusion* is an idea that can characterize the efforts described in all of the above chapters. This idea is based on affordable access to ICTs as well as the accessibility and usability of ICT tools and services. In addition, the ability and skills of all to use and benefit from ICT is an essential component of e-inclusion. e-Inclusion policies at the macro level aim at reducing gaps and disparities in ICT usage. Such policies promote the use of ICT to overcome social exclusion and improve economic performance, employment opportunities, quality of life, social participation, and social cohesion. Similarly, at the micro level, educational practices such as the ones identified in several of the chapters in this collection highlight the contribution of pedagogies to the realization of e-inclusion. Issues of e-inclusion are evident not only in developing countries but also in developed countries. By ensuring access to ICTs, there are several tangible benefits for all, including improved skills and employability, more access to information that can lead to better health awareness and access to health services. In addition, e-participation can lead to better engagement with public issues and the potential for increased democratic participation.

ICT FOR CULTURAL UNDERSTANDINGS

The last theme that permeates the various contribution to this volume is the role of ICT as a means for enriching cultural understandings. The "cultural embeddedness" of ICT implies that ICT and culture cannot be separated from each other, and thus ICT can be used to promote intercultural education, reconciliation, and peace. Particularly in an era in which ICT has the potential to surpass limits imposed by national borders, ICT can be a powerful tool in the process of facilitating cultural understanding among individuals and communities, including those groups that are in conflict. Once again, a critical view of the role of ICT as a means of enriching cultural understandings highlights the importance of taking into consideration the existing power relations (e.g., among parties engaged in peace and reconciliation). The chapters in this book—particularly those by Brantmeier and Richardson, Bekerman and Horenczyk, Kayler and her colleagues, and Skulnick and O'Connor—suggest that the beneficial use of ICT can be enhanced when pedagogical and structural conditions support efforts to infuse technology into education in ways that it can promote cultural understandings.

Brantmeier and Richardson present a case study in which Cambodians and Tibetans in exile used ICT as a means for social reconstruction. The Tibetan Government in Exile is using ICTs to disseminate information and to work toward peacemaking. Actions of the governments, NGOs, and citizens are propelling the nation of Cambodia and the Tibetan community in exile into informal ICT-supported conflict transformation processes by finding peaceful ways to engage in dialogue, to provide information, to share the realities of their recent conflict ridden pasts, and to build a more secure future.

In their chapter, Bekerman and Horenczyk discuss how CSCIE (Computer-Supported Collaborative Intercultural Education) can serve as a means for the improvement of intergroup relations, particularly in conflict-ridden areas, where psychological—and sometimes real—barriers often prevent face-to-face intergroup contact. The authors describe the Yad2Yad project, aimed at bringing together, through virtual contact, school-age children attending Jewish and Palestinian Arab schools in Israel. Based on the premise that lack of contact is exacerbating the Arab-Jewish conflict in Israel, they show how the design and implementation of Yad2Yad meet the conditions that tend to promote the benefits of intergroup contact.

Kayler and her colleagues examine how online gaming works to strengthen and deepen individual understandings and acceptance of diverse worldviews. Their research shows that time spent together and having access and opportunities to meet virtually and "talk to each other" are crucial components in enhancing players' cultural understandings and creating meaningful friendships. Communication among players and administrators as well as structures and processes shape or hinder individuals' interactions.

Finally, Skulnick and O'Connor focus on a case study of an incident in which the students' use of internet sites such as Facebook might be utilized for issues of multicultural understanding. One important finding of this study is that online forums that are unmonitored do not necessarily function as a safe space for bringing opposing viewpoints together. This is not to say that there are no benefits of the online community, as the authors point out. However, they turn our attention to the challenges of un-moderated online spaces and the negative implications when we attempt to use ICT to address issues of cultural understanding.

CONCLUSION

The interconnected themes of development, social inclusion, and cultural understandings in relation to the role of ICTs create tremendous challenges as well as opportunities for educators. A critical frame of mind toward the possible benefits and pitfalls of ICTs in education is required. The critical use of ICT in education for development and social justice opens opportunities for research, development, and educational practices not previously available to educators and students. ICTs offer access to information for more people, but they have their limitations. A critical education would demand access to ICTs for all, but this access should be accompanied with critical skills and critical sensitivities as well as structural changes that would enable fair and quality access. Although physical access is an important prerequisite to further social inclusion in the educational use of ICT, it is far from sufficient for critical access.

In this book, we emphasize the importance of thinking about ICT in education within a global context, as part of an examination of issues related to development and social justice. ICTs can be useful tools for dealing with poverty, social inclusion, and cultural understandings and their impact on education because ICTs provide an alternative vision and practice. The necessity of dealing with exclusion, injustice, and disadvantage and to forge new solidarities makes this project valuable at this time.

The critical use of ICTs in the contemporary world should attend to the challenges presented by poverty, social exclusion and cultural misunderstandings, and it should empower individuals and groups to analyse and critique the emerging effects of social injustices around the globe. The challenge for the use of ICTs in education today is how to use new technologies to create cultures and societies based on respect for cultural difference with the aim of achieving fuller participation of individuals and groups largely denied social and economic resources. Educators must constantly devise new decolonising strategies, both at the macro and the micro level; ICTs can be one of these strategies for the advancement of a more just and peaceful world.

REFERENCES

Burbules, N. C., & Callister, T. A. (2000). Universities in transition: The promise and the challenge of new technologies. *Teachers College Record, (102)*2, 271–293.

Cochran-Smith, M. (2004). *Walking the road: Race, diversity, and social justice in teacher education.* NY: Teachers College Press.

Cuban, L. (2001). *Oversold and underused: Computers in the classroom.* Cambridge, MA: Harvard University Press.

DEEEP (2008). http://www.deeep.org. Accessed online on May 23, 2008.

Fabos, B., & Young, M. D. (1999). Telecommunications in the classroom: Rhetoric versus reality. *Review of Educational Research, 69,* 217–259.

Feenberg, A. (1995). *Alternative modernity: The technical turn in philosophy and social theory.* Berkeley, CA: University of California Press.

Fraser, N. (1997). *Justice interruptus: Critical reflections on the "postsocialist" condition.* NY: Routledge.

Fraser, N., & Honneth, A. (2003). *Redistribution or recognition? A political-philosophical exchange.* NY: Verso.

Kitalong, K. S., & Kitalong, T. (2000). Complicating the tourist gaze: Literacy and the Internet as catalysts for articulating a postcolonial Palauan identity. In G. E. Hawisher & C. L. Selfe (Eds.), *Global literacies and the World-Wide-Web* (pp. 95–113). London: Routledge.

Lelliott, A., Pendlebury, S., & Enslin, P. (2000) Promises of access and inclusion: Online education in Africa. *Journal of Philosophy of Education, 34,* 41–52

Sen, A. (1999). *Development as freedom.* Oxford, UK: Oxford University Press.

Sloane, S., & Johnstone, J. (2000). Reading sideways, backwards, and across: Scottish and American literacy practices and weaving the web. In G. E. Hawisher & C. L. Selfe (Eds.), *Global literacies and the World-Wide-Web* (pp. 154–185). London: Routledge.

UNESCO (2003). *Poverty eradication through education: Breaking the poverty cycle for children.* Retrieved July 31, 2008 from http://unesdoc.unesco.org/images/0013/001318/131812e.pdf.

UNESCO (2007). *Education for all.* Retrieved April 26, 2008 from http://www.efareport.unesco.org.

UNESCO (2008). *Education for all global monitoring report 2008.* Accessed online on April 22, 2008 from http://www.unesco.org/publishing.

Vrasidas, C., & Glass, G. V (Eds.). (2005). *Preparing teachers to teach with technology.* Charlotte, NC: Information Age.

Warschauer, M. (2003). *Technology and social inclusion: Rethinking the digital divide.* Cambridge, MA: The MIT Press.

Young, I. M. (1990). *Justice and the politics of difference.* Princeton, NJ: Princeton University Press.

Zembylas, M., McIsaac, C., & Vrasidas, C. (2002). Of nomads, polyglots, and global villagers: Globalization, information technologies, and critical education online. In Vrasidas, C. & G. V Glass (Eds.). *Distance education and distributed learning.* Charlotte, NC: Information Age.

CHAPTER 2

ICT FOR EDUCATION, DEVELOPMENT, AND SOCIAL JUSTICE

Some Theoretical Issues

Michalinos Zembylas
CARDET and Open University of Cyprus

The promises and pitfalls of information and communications technology (ICT) constitute a major component of ongoing discussions in the development literature. On the one hand, ICT is presented as a primary means of achieving development goals, especially in developing countries (McMahon & Bruce, 2002; UNDP, 1998). The underlying assumption is that restricted access to ICT is partly responsible for underdevelopment (Schech, 2002). In other words, ICT is regarded as a means for acquiring information and knowledge that leads to modernization; therefore, its lack prevents growth. "Digital divide" is a phrase that is being used increasingly to indicate the inequity in access to ICT between developed and developing communities and nations.

On the other hand, an examination of the threats that ICT allegedly presents for developing countries reveals the different discourses of power and knowledge that exist in development discourses (Schech, 2002). For example, who defines what "development" is? The theorization of ICT as a

ICT for Education, Development, and Social Justice, pages 17–29

force of growth, professionalization, and institutionalization of expertise in the Third World—associated with the expansion of capitalist economy all over the world—is deemed as problematic by some scholars because it normalizes the construction of Western knowledge as "the norm" and the poor and "underdeveloped" as universal subjects (Escobar, 1995). At the same time, there are those who argue that the use of ICT opens up prospects and opportunities for promoting democracy and prosperity in poor parts of the planet; ICT provides tools for disseminating information, participating in decision-making, and for mobilization (Lelliott et al., 2000) of environmental, gender equity, social justice, peace, and health initiatives.

Similar arguments about the strengths and weaknesses of ICT are found in the education literature, especially in relation to the profound implications of ICT for the ways in which sustained learning across the life span may reduce levels of social exclusion (Kellner, 2004; Zembylas & Vrasidas, 2005). The issue of addressing the digital divide—for example, through increasing access to ICT or acquiring the relevant skills necessary to utilize ICT effectively—forces policymakers and educators to address the role of ICT in promoting social inclusion, education, and development. Some argue that ICT integration in education provides a significant opportunity to reduce inequalities and contribute to development; others point out that ICT exacerbates preexisting divisions and inequalities between the haves and have-nots (Selwyn, Gorard, & Williamns, 2001; Wresch, 1996).

This chapter aims at re-visiting and re-visioning the concept of ICT as a means to development, education, and social justice. I argue that ICT cannot be used as an end of development or of education, and therefore focusing on issues of physical access or necessary skills to utilize ICT diverts attention from social and power structures that perpetuate many forms of inequality and social exclusion. Alterative visions and critical practices of ICT for education, development, and social justice cannot be seen as located outside existing power relations (Freenberg, 1995). ICT may indeed lead to new forms of normalization, but ICT can also be transformed in ways that facilitate social inclusion. By presenting the complex interactions among diverse claims about the role of ICT for education, development, and social justice, I seek to promote continued dialogue and reflexivity on the prospects and possibilities of ICT education for social justice and the reduction of inequities.

ICT AS A MEANS OF DEVELOPMENT

There are two dominant "development paradigms" linked to the idea of an information society (Alampay, 2006). According to the first paradigm, ICT plays a part in development and constitutes a potential means of closing the gap among nations (Goldstein & O' Connor, 2000). The second paradigm questions the meaning and type of "development" governments aspire to, given that modernization is a Western concept and thus ICT is not value-neutral but carries particular cultural and political assumptions (see Avgerou & Walsham, 2000; Krishna & Madon, 2003). In the former view, "development" becomes a part of economic discourse while other renditions of its meaning—for instance, cultural development, personal development, spiritual development—are too easily drowned out or marginalized (Selby, 2006). In the latter, "development" aims at being rescued from the capitalist model of expansion that harms people and the environment. "By 'development'", writes Rigby "we mean simply moving forward in time, rather than that the majority world has to convert to the western obsessions with competition and increasing materialism" (cited in Selby, 2006, p. 356).

The first paradigm, which may be called the *modernization development paradigm*, perceives ICT as important in development spreading from the West to the rest of the world. ICT is viewed as crucial in the development agenda because it can be used in public administration, business, education, health, and environment (WSIS, 2003). In particular, it has been argued that ICT assists in poverty reduction and the expansion of opportunities for economic development (World Bank, 2006). The growing use of ICT in the world is linked to economic output, so the argument is that increased access to ICT results in economic growth.

According to the second paradigm, which may be called the *social justice development paradigm*, ICT increases existing inequalities because those who benefit the most are the communities that are already dominant politically and economically (Alampay, 2006; James, 2000). The idea that development results from linking poor nations to ICT, the Internet in particular, is considered a myth (The Economist, 2005). As Hoogvelt (1997) argues, development is dead for those who are already excluded from the global system, thus ICT access becomes irrelevant to them. This uneven development—however one defines the term "development"—can no longer be understood in terms of the First World/Third World dichotomy, but unequal social structures and power relations need to be critically interrogated (Castells, 1998). Therefore, focusing on the effects of ICT on development, considering its limited impact in addressing poverty and inequality in some parts of the world (e.g., India), distracts from efforts to address pressing basic needs that alleviate poverty and injustice (Hoogvelt, 1997).

From a broader perspective, whether ICT is useful for development or not depends on overcoming the same social structures that contribute to inequities and the unjust distribution of wealth. The flow of ICT—just as the flow of commodities and capital—cannot be viewed apart from local and global social and economic conditions. This implies that social and education policy should not only view ICT as tools for progress, but as means of communal and societal participation for a common living that empowers people to tackle their problems and alleviate in particular social exclusion. A critical theory of ICT re-visions the meaning of ICT and development for social reconstruction in the interests of social justice. Such a critical theory contextualizes the use of ICT within social relations and contexts, criticizes deterministic models, and attempts to transform ICT into instruments of social transformation (Kellner, 2004).

Thus, the question is not whether ICT is useful for development. Rather, it is a question of what ICT can and cannot do to help create a more socially just and democratic society. Consequently, the contribution of ICT cannot be seen separately from the macro- and micro-level social forces that contribute to oppression and domination. Understanding the complexity of power relations in the context in which ICT is introduced is critical to addressing the traces that ICT or other social and material forces leave in people's daily lives. In this age of information, argues Boler (2005), creative macro-level processes and micro-level relations that challenge social injustice are needed, such as "digital dissent"—that is, the use of communication technologies to engage in online civic participation that interrupts mainstream narratives.

In other words, we need a more robust theorization of the social conditions of ICT use. Attention to the production and maintenance of these conditions by power structures can reveal the social grounding of ICT for development and social justice. This idea is particularly important in light of the promises of ICT couched in the language of equity, appealing to social justice *and* to efficiency (Lelliott et al., 2000). In many respects, these promises, argue Lelliot and his colleagues, are both false and misleading. They are false because the required investments in ICT cannot be fulfilled by the majority of communities, which struggle for very basic needs. These promises are also misleading because they divert attention from such needs. The point here is that despite the best prospects of ICT, political, institutional, and social powers can constrain opportunities as easily as they expand them, and thus ICT on its own is not sufficient for promoting social transformation. On the other hand, Foucault's (2000) ideas leave space for the productive aspects of power as well; that is, power and knowledge are intertwined, therefore, there is potential for resistance and counter-discourses. The traces of both the constraining and productive aspects of ICT forces can be seen in recent debates about the digital divide.

REDEFINING THE DIGITAL DIVIDE: BEYOND ACCESS

One of the issues that gained attention related to the impact and role of ICT in development and education is the "digital divide" (Alampay, 2006).

The digital divide has been broadly interpreted as the "marked gap in access to or use of ICT devices" (Campbell, 2001, p. 119). On the one hand, there is clear evidence that such a divide exists among and within countries, as it has been shown in various statistical compilations. In particular, the disparities between developing and developed countries in the availability of ICT are increasing; in addition, the divide in the level of access within societies—in relation to race, socioeconomic class, urban and rural location, and gender—is also widening.

On the other hand, there are those who argue that the idea of a digital divide is passé or irrelevant because those who need ICT in the more developed countries already have access, and those who do not have access do not really need it because they have more basic needs (Warschauer, 2004). The issue of the divide, then, is deeply sociopolitical; focusing simply on the dimension of physical access narrowly frames the issue and depoliticizes the problems of poverty and injustice in the world. As Clark and Gorski wrote, "There have been too few questions about the bigger social and cultural implications of the lack of physical access and the history of classism that produces clear messages about who should and should not be given or pursue access" (2001, p. 32). For example, there is evidence that poor communities and socioeconomically disadvantaged people (e.g., people of color) are systematically discouraged from pursuing access to ICT related professions or fields of study (Clark & Gorski, 2001).

In addition, as Bruce (1999) argues, the digital divide is not so much about some groups having less access to ICT while others have more, but that they have a different kind of access and thus the issue is how to bridge these differential types of access. For example, it is deeply problematic, as Clark and Gorski (2001) state, that ICT access for students from low-income backgrounds is limited to drill and practice routines, while students from high-income backgrounds are engaged in more creative activities. Natriello argues that the use of ICT in poor schools and communities is limited to mundane routines; this is in line with Warschauer's position that computer use in schools could actually worsen inequality by failing to address the key issue regarding the way ICT is used. The problem, then, is not resolved by installing computers and providing access to the Internet in low resource schools or in developing countries (Natriello, 2001; Valadez & Duran, 2007; Warschauer, 2004).

Consequently, debates over digital divide entrenched in polarized viewpoints of the haves and the have-nots are not only naïve but also misleading. The role of ICT in overcoming social exclusion has yet to be fully problematized and critically engaged by many education policy analysts—a crucial step toward assessing the role of ICT in development, education, and social justice (Selwyn, et al., 2001). The current conceptualization of digital divide as a binary issue fails to theorize ICT as a means of reducing social exclusion and widening participation. The issue is not about the importance of physical access but the lack of acknowledging first, the existing social and economic inequalities and power differentials that essentially subvert simplistic efforts to increase physical access, and second, the different kind of access between rich and poor communities. In other words, a redefinition of the way that digital divide is theorized is needed in both *sociopolitical* and *pragmatic* terms. A sociopolitical analysis of the digital divide encompasses questions about the extent to which ICT locates the sources of inequity and the traces left in people's lives or perpetuates those. In this manner, the social consequences of the divide are not ignored; instead, social and political conditions are critically considered in the ways ICT may be utilized for furthering the process of social inclusion and wider participation in democratic societies (Warschauer, 2004).

In addition, a pragmatic analysis of the digital divide includes raising questions about the capabilities and "functionings" that ICT permits in practice. This idea is relevant to Sen's (1999) theorization of the Capability Approach, a clearly pragmatic take on the use of ICT to expand the capabilities of individuals and societies. According to Sen, the Capability Approach evaluates social states in terms of creating the conditions in which people have real opportunities for achieving well being; that is, it emphasizes functional capabilities instead of access to resources. In relation to ICT, for example, the emphasis is on how people can use ICT to enhance their capabilities to function in the ways they want, such as eliminating poverty. To return to my earlier discussion on the meaning of "development," the goal of development, according to Sen, is the promotion and expansion of valuable capabilities. This approach contrasts with the predominant view that sees development purely in terms of GNP growth, that is, the modernization development paradigm.

Applying Sen's approach to the theorization of digital divide takes us beyond the notion of resources because it makes distribution—a *fair* distribution—through the expansion of human capabilities, more important than growth. The objective, then, is capability expansion rather than maximizing GNP, an idea that shifts attention from the division between ICT haves and have-nots to the inequalities in ICT, development and education. This broader framework is multidimensional and includes a deeper understanding of the local and global practices and policies that attempt to address complex societal issues with simplistic solutions. Thus access to ICT, just like economic growth, can expand people's capabilities to participate in the potential benefits of the information society (Mann, 2003); however, the focus is on people and how they use ICT, not on access. In this sense I agree with Sen that the fair distribution of opportunities and capabilities is to a certain extent more important than only the fair distribution of goods. In other words, the purpose of a social justice development approach in relation to ICT use is "to ensure that each individual in a community has an equal opportunity, not only to gain access to essential information [e.g., through access to ICT and the Internet], but also receive education in order to benefit from information" (Britz, 2004, p. 199).

It is in this respect that a *critical theory* of ICT in education is needed, that is, a theorization that, on the one hand, develops "criticality" about the uses of ICT as tools of social injustice and domination, and on the other hand, rejects the simplistic assumptions of digital divide. To the "colonizing" potential of ICT, a *decolonising criticality* must be counterposed—a criticality in which oppositional individuals and communities resist colonization to further peace and social justice (Zembylas, & Vrasidas, 2005). This argument highlights the importance of developing a social justice education that promotes criticality in ICT as a strategy of bridging the digital divide. This task is undertaken in the last part of this chapter.

BRIDGING THE DIGITAL DIVIDE THROUGH SOCIAL JUSTICE EDUCATION

"Social justice" remains a hotly contested term in the field of education (North, 2006) and merits a brief discussion before engaging with the theorization of bridging the digital divide through "social justice education." My understanding of social justice is grounded in Fraser's (1997, 2003) proposition that social justice is both redistribution and recognition. This position pays attention to how both "economic disadvantage impedes equal participation in the making of culture, in public spheres and in everyday life" and dominant cultural norms exclude the cultures and identities of marginalized groups from the state and the economy (Fraser, 1997, p. 15). Fraser argues that recognition and redistribution are co-fundamental dimensions of justice; thus both issues and their interrelations are highlighted.

In relation to ICT for development and education, Fraser's analysis may be used to emphasize how a critical theory of ICT exposes the systematic and institutional arrangements that are implicated in ICT use, the practices with which policymakers, educators, parents, and learners create them, and the ways in which critical education may ameliorate their harmful effects. Educators must draw on this reconceptualization of ICT teaching and learning practices and struggle to make them equitable for all students. To do this, they need to ground ICT education in social justice ideas, and not, as is frequently the case, on a technical foundation alone (Clark & Gorski, 2001).

In this chapter, I refer to *social justice education* as those pedagogies and policies that improve the learning and life opportunities of typically underserved students (Cochran-Smith, 2004). In relation to ICT, social justice education highlights three important goals: first, to develop a new way of conceptualizing ICT that begins in social justice education theory and practice; second, to acknowledge and critique the aspects of ICT that have become mainstream and thus shift the emphasis from the polarized issue of access/no access to how ICT can be used in education to expand educators' and learners' capabilities so that they can participate in the benefits of the information society; finally, to modify curriculum and pedagogical practices in ways that promote positive experiences for *all* students. These goals are discussed in the remainder of this chapter.

The first goal of social justice education in efforts to bridge the digital divide is to develop a different conceptualization of ICT, one that is grounded in social justice education theory and practice and does not put technical issues before social justice concerns. Social justice theory is certainly not monolithic, yet it calls for all aspects of education to be constantly interrogated and transformed based on the ideas of equity and social justice (Bigelow et al., 1994, 2001; Kumashiro, 2004; Leonardo, 2004). For example, a socio-politically responsive educational approach to ICT:

> critiques technology-related inequities in the context of larger educational and societal inequities, keeping at the fore of discussion the fact that those groups most disenfranchised by the digital divide are the same groups historically disenfranchised by curricular and pedagogical practices and other aspects of education (and society at large). (Gorski & Clark, 2003, p. 30)

Such a critique is used to create a different theorization of the impact of ICT on education equity or equality of access for all students. Critical educators begin to consider, theoretically or practically, the implications of making ICT a central element of development and education, particularly in relation to institutional aspects such as the equal participation of all citizens in political decision making and the development of every individual's potential (Gewirtz, 1998). Questions about the role of ICT in education, development, and social justice emerge as central. From these perspectives might emerge new conceptualizations to confront educational changes, including the integration of ICT into curriculum and pedagogy.

The influence of ICT on education policies and practices can be seen to have multiple, and conflicting, effects. Not all of these effects can be classified simply as beneficial or not, and some are shaped by tensions and struggles (Burbules & Torres, 2000). A critical theory of ICT, one that is grounded in social justice education, is aware that technologies have unforeseen consequences and that good intentions and seemingly good projects may have undesirable results, such as perpetuating existing inequalities (Kellner, 2004). Critical educators should be prepared then to engage in ongoing interrogation of the attempts to use ICT for education and development. Different parts of the world and various communities will have different needs and problems, and thus any use of ICT should be contextualized.

In light of these concerns, the role of ICT in education, development, and the struggle for social justice should be limned in three directions: the economic impacts, the political impacts, and the cultural impacts. At the economic level, schools need to reconsider their mission in light of social and economic inequalities that are often exacerbated by policies to use ICT in instrumentalist ways. The evidence about the limited opportunities for social and economic mobility (Selwyn et al., 2001) and the relation to present patterns of social exclusion in education and technology require a different theorization of ICT. At the political level, schools have a crucial role to play in addressing the two-tiered educational system, one aimed at the education of the economically privileged with its emphasis on advanced technological skills, and the other designed for the education of the economically disadvantaged with its emphasis on a "drill-and-skill" approach (Clark & Gorski, 2001). Social justice education can interrupt this system, creating school communities that recognize the importance of advanced technological literacy. It is within this context that the notion of using technology for the sake of technology and not for the improvement of teachingand learning and everyday life can be critiqued. Finally, at the cultural level, education policies, practices, and institutions are deeply affected as a result of ICT access and use. From a cultural perspective, the growth of ICT use has encouraged an increased individuation and isolation (i.e., individualism) on the one hand, and on the other hand, a multicultural exchange. The question of "multiculturalism" takes on a special meaning in an ICT context (Zembylas & Vrasidas, 2005). The current debates over multiculturalism and ICT are surprisingly limited both in their theoretical content and their political foresight because they fail to consider ways in which ICT use supports and perpetuates the inequities in education that already exist.

The second goal of social justice education in relation to ICT is to acknowledge and critique those aspects of ICT that have become mainstream. The emphasis then is shifted from the polarized issue access vs no access to how ICT can be used in education in ways that expand educators' and learners' capabilities to participate in the potential benefits of the information society. Such an approach poses two major demands. First, access to ICT should not be seen merely in terms of the duality of haves and have-nots. Beyond the simple issue of access to ICT "come more complex questions of levels of connectivity in terms of the capability and distribution of the access concerned" (Selwyn et al., 2001, p. 271). As discussed previously, the notion of "access" needs to go beyond physical access and include access to support and encouragement to pursue and value technology-related fields and creative pedagogical tasks for *all* students. The danger from focusing simply on the duality of access vs no access is overlooking both the differential access that exists and its sociopolitical implications.

Second, the demand of social justice education is that critical educators examine not only who has access or not, but how ICT is being used by various individuals and communities and by those teaching individuals and communities, insisting that they be used in socially just ways. It has become very clear that integrating ICT in education does not in itself necessarily constitute a progressive or even a new form of education. Although ICT may seem to challenge traditional power relations, it can also reproduce and reinforce hegemonic relations (Kitchin, 1998). While acknowledging, then, the limitations of ICT and its use in education, I agree with Rice and Burbules (1992) that we can educate for critical sensitivities and critical literacy with ICT. Since ICT is transforming education and development, key challenges for critical education involve how to analyse such transformations and how to devise conceptual tools and strategies to make use of ICT that empower traditionally marginalized groups and individuals struggling for justice and equity.

Finally, the last goal of social justice education is to modify curriculum and pedagogical practices in ways that increase positive experiences for *all* students. This includes ICT and covers its content and delivery (Clark & Gorski, 2001). No education can be grounded in social justice if students are denied access to high status knowledge and skills, including the necessary skills and knowledge to succeed in an information society. Curriculum and pedagogy should support students in their mastery of skills in order to give students the equitable level of education each citizen needs to function as a successful member of an information society. This is what Banks (2007) calls "equity pedagogy," that is, the approach that is grounded in facilitating the academic achievement of students from diverse racial, cultural, gender, and social-class groups. Thus, to paraphrase Clark and Gorski (2001), the question for critical educators is not "How can we fit ICT into social justice education?" but "How can we provide the best possible educational experiences for all students? And, in so providing such experiences, do computers and/or the Internet contribute positively to transformative educational ends?" (p. 43).

Curricula with a social justice education focus encourage students to interrogate taken-for-granted ideas and events of life that are, in fact, expressions of oppression (Giroux, 1988; Kincheloe, 2005; McLaren, 2003). When ICT is used in additive and instrumentalist ways it is unlikely that students will be encouraged to question what happens in the world. This is similar to the impact of multicultural education conceptualized as cultural tourism (e.g., fun, food, festivals, fiestas, folklore) (Banks & Banks, 1993). Again, the issue is: Can ICT contribute to encouraging students to be "justice-oriented citizens" (Westheimer & Kahne, 2004)? Various practices designed to support this critical analysis and discussion are seen in the work of practitioners who use ICT to dismantle the socioeconomic divide (see Selwyn et al., 2001; Clark & Gorski, 2001; Zembylas & Vrasidas, 2005).

CONCLUSION

In this chapter, I have argued that educators and policymakers cannot afford to ignore issues of inequality and injustice that ICT may be unable to address. To view the role of ICT as some sort of fix to existing social inequalities is not only shortsighted but also potentially dangerous. ICT may or may not provide opportunities to reduce inequalities and contribute to development; indeed, it may be more likely to exacerbate inequalities. Closing the "digital divide" requires a social activist conceptualization of social justice education. It is in this light that more research is needed to consider how ICT and discourses on the digital divide may inadvertently or purposely recycle the very educational inequalities they claim they want to eradicate.

REFERENCES

Alampay, E. (2006). Beyond access to ICTs: Measuring capabilities in the information society. *International Journal of Education and Development using Information and Communication Technology, 2*(3), 4–22.

Avgerou, C., & Walsham, G. (Eds.). (2000). *Information technology in context: Studies from the perspective of developing countries.* London: Ashgate.

Banks, J. (2007). Approaches to multicultural curriculum reform. In J. Banks & C. M. Banks (Eds.) *Multicultural education: Issues and perspectives, 6th edition.* (pp. 247–269). Hoboken, NJ: Wiley.

Banks, J.A. & Banks, C. M. (1993). *Multicultural education: Issues and perspectives.* Boston, MA: Allyn and Bacon.

Bigelow, B., Christensen, L., Karp, S., Miner, B., & Peterson, B. (Eds.). (1994). *Rethinking our classrooms: Teaching for equity and justice* [Special issue of Rethinking Schools]. Milwaukee, WI: Rethinking Schools.

Bigelow, B., Harvey, B., Karp, S., & Miller, L. (2001). *Rethinking our classrooms: Teaching for equity and justice,* Vol. 2. Milwaukee, WI: Rethinking Schools.

Boler, M. (2005). *Rethinking media in repressive times: Caring about free speech.* Paper presented at the annual meeting of the American Educational Research Association, Montreal, Canada.

Burbules, N., & Torres, C. A. (Eds.). (2000). *Globalization and education: Critical perspectives.* NY: Routledge.

Britz, J. J. (2004). To know or not to know: A moral reflection on information poverty. *Journal of Information Science, 30*(3), 192–204.

Bruce, B. (1999). Speaking the unspeakable about 21st century technologies. In G. E. Hawisher & C. L. Selfe (Eds.), *Passions, pedagogies, and 21st century technolo-*

gies (pp. 221–228). Logan, UT and Urbana, IL: Utah State University Press and NCTE.

Campbell, D. (2001). "Can the digital divide be contained?" The digital divide: Employment and development implications. *International Labor Review, 140*(2), 119–141.

Castells, M. (1996). *The rise of the network society.* Oxford: Blackwell.

Clark, C., & Gorski, P. (2001). Multicultural education and the digital divide: Focus on race, language, socioeconomic class, sex, and disability. *Multicultural Perspectives, 3*(3), 39–44.

Cochran-Smith, M. (2004). *Walking the road: Race, diversity, and social justice in teacher education.* New York City: Teachers College Press.

Escobar, A. (1995). *Encountering development: The making and unmaking of the third world.* Princeton: Princeton University Press.

Feenberg, A. (1995). *Alternative modernity: The technical turn in philosophy and social theory.* Berkeley, CA: University of California Press.

Foucault, M. (2000). *Power: The essential works Vol. 3* (J. D. Faubion, ed.). London: Allen Lane/Pengion.

Fraser, N. (1997). *Justice interruptus: Critical reflections on the "postsocialist" condition.* NY: Routledge.

Fraser, N., & Honneth, A. (2003). *Redistribution or recognition? A political-philosophical exchange.* NY: Verso.

Gewirtz, S. (1998). Conceptualizing social justice in education: Mapping the territory. *Journal of Education Policy, 13*(4), 469–484.

Giroux, H. A. (1988). *Teachers as intellectuals: Toward a critical pedagogy of learning.* Westport, CO: Bergin and Garvey.

Goldsten, A., & O' Connor, D. (2000). *E-commerce for development: Prospects and policy issues* (Technical Papers No. 164). OECD: OECD Development Center.

Gorski, P., & Clark, C. (2003). Turning the tide of the digital divide: Multicultural education and the politics of surfing. *Multicultural Perspectives, 5*(1), 29–32.

Hoogvelt, A. M. (1997). *Globalization and the postcolonial world: The new political economy of development.* Basingstoke, UK: Macmillan.

James, J. (2000). Pro-poor modes of integration into the global economy. *Development and Change, 31*(4), 765–783.

Kellner, D. (2004). Technological transformation, multiple literacies, and the revisioning of education. *E-Learning, 1*, 9–37.

Kincheloe, J. L. (2005). *Critical pedagogy.* NY: Peter Lang.

Kitchin, R. (1998). *Cyberspace: The world in the wires.* NY: John Wiley.

Krishna, S., & Madon, S. (Eds.). *The digital challenge: Information technology in the development context.* London: Ashgate.

Kumashiro, K. (2004). *Against common sense: Teaching and learning toward social justice.* NY: RoutledgeFalmer.

Lelliott, A., Pendlebury, S., & Enslin, P. (2000) Promises of access and inclusion: Online education in Africa. *Journal of Philosophy of Education, 34*, 41–52.

Leonardo, Z. (2004). Critical social theory and transformative knowledge: The functions of criticism in quality education. *Educational Researcher, 33*(6), 11–18.

Mann, C. L. (2003). Information technologies and international development: Concpetual clarity in the search from for commonality and diversity. *Information Technologies and International Development, 1*(2), 67–79.

McLaren, P. (2003). *Life in schools: An introduction to critical pedagogy in the foundations of education, 4th edition.* Boston: Allyn and Bacon.

McMahon, C., & Bruce, C. (2002). Information literacy needs of local stuff in cross-cultural development projects. *Journal of International Development, 14*, 113–127.

Natriello, G. (2001). Bridging the second digital divide: What can sociologists of education contribute? *Sociology of Education, 74*(3), 260–265.

North, C. (2006). More than words? Delving into the substantive meaning(s) of "social justice" in education. *Review of Educational Research, 76*(4), 507–535.

Rice, S., & Burbules, N. (1992). *Communicative virtues and educational relations.* Retrieved August 8, 2008 from http://www.ed.uiuc.edu/pes92_docs/rice_burbules.htm.

Schech, S. (2002). Wired for change: The links between ICTs and development discourses. *Journal of International Development, 14*, 13–23.

Selby, D. (2006). The firm and shaky ground of education for sustainable development. *Journal of Geography in Higher Education, 30*, 2, 351–365.

Selwyn, N., Gorard, S., & Williams, S. (2001). Digital divide or digital community? The role of technology in overcoming social exclusion in US education. *Educational Policy, 15*, 258–277.

Sen, A. (1999). *Development as freedom.* Oxford: Oxford University Press.

The Economist, (2005). The real digital divide. *The Economist*, 12 March, p. 9.

UNDP. (1998). Info21*: Information and communication technologies for development.* New York: UNDP. Retrieved August 8, 2008 from http://www.undp.org/info21/index5.htm.

Valadez, J., & Duran, R. (2007). Redefining the digital divide: Beyond access to computers and the Internet. *The High School Journal, 90*(3), 31–44.

Warschauer, M. (2003). *Technology and social inclusion: Rethinking the digital divide.* Cambridge, MA: The MIT Press.

Westheimer, J. & Kahne, J. (2004). What kind of citizen? The politics of educating for democracy. *American Educational Research Journal, 4*(2), 237–269.

World Bank. (2006). *World development report 2006: Equity and development.* Washington, DC: The International Bank for Reconstruction and Development/The World Bank.

World Summit on the Information Society (WSIS). (2003). *Declaration of principles.* Document WSIS-03/GENEVA/DOC/4-E. Retrieved August 8, 2008 from http://www.itu.int/wsis/docs/geneva/official/dop.html.

Wresch, W. (1996). *Disconnected: Have and have-nots in the information age.* New Brunswick, NJ: Rutgers University Press.

Zembylas, M., & Vrasidas, C. (2005). Globalization, information and communication technologies, and the prospect of a "global village": Promises of inclusion or electronic colonization? *Journal of Curriculum Studies, 37*(1), 65–84.

PART 2

ICT FOR DEVELOPMENT

CHAPTER 3

E-HOPES AND PUBLIC EDUCATION IN LATIN AMERICA

Gustavo E. Fischman
Arizona State University

José Luis Ramírez Romero
University of Sonora

INTRODUCTION

> During the 1990s, echoing developments in the U.S., the U.K., Canada, and Australia, most school reform programs in Latin America emphasized Neoliberal political-pedagogical discourses in which the concepts of choice, accountability, efficiency, and decentralization figured prominently. The Neoliberal rationale presented to societies and educational communities as legitimization of these reform programs had the appeal of an apparently simple message: less ideological posturing, more technical efficiency. (Fischman, Ball, & Gvirtz, 2003)

After several decades of criticisms and protests about stifling state control, bureaucratically-managed changes, financial irresponsibility, authoritarian systems, blatantly ideological curriculums, and poor results, those in charge of implementing the reform found fertile ground for their ideas. In

ICT for Education, Development, and Social Justice, pages 33–51

country after country, the reforms were preached as gospel, promising societies to deliver a new era for education in Latin America by implementing a few simple changes: reduction of the state interventionism in the administration of schools, coupled with expanded schools' institutional autonomy to "liberate" the entrepreneurial energies at schools and produce better teaching and learning. It is important to emphasize that the gospel of education reform and transformation in the region was also accompanied by a vigorous discourse advocating massive incorporation of ICTs into schools. Before looking specifically at ICTs in schools, we consider it relevant to summarize briefly the general situation of ICT infrastructure in Latin America, emphasizing the cases of Argentina, Costa Rica, Ecuador, and Mexico.

ICT GENERAL INFRASTRUCTURE IN LATIN AMERICA

Since the middle of the 1990s, most countries in Latin America have increased the number of telephones and telephone connections, internet access, the number of computers in homes and schools, and the number of cyber cafés. However, the levels of ICT development have been weaker than in other parts of the world. Development has not been homogeneous across countries, regional areas, or social class, and the lack of trustworthy studies is a major gap in knowledge, complicating any analysis in this area. Moreover, as Hilbert and Katz (2003), authors of an influential ECLAC report on these issues, noted, "the lack of information about the development of an Information Society in Latin America and the Caribbean is a major obstacle in itself" (p. 289).[1] Tables 3.1 and 3.2 show the huge disparities among countries and

TABLE 3.1 ICT Infrastructure for Selected Countries

HDI rank[a]	Country[a]	Internet users (per 100 people)[b] 2002	PCs per (100 people)[b] 2002	Telephone lines (per 1000 people)[a] 1990	Telephone lines (per 1000 people)[a] 1999	Mobile phones (per 1000 people)[a] 1990	Mobile phones (per 1000 people)[a] 1999	Internet hosts (per 1000 people)[a] 1995	Internet hosts (per 1000 people)[a] 2000
1	Norway	30.72	52.83	503	712	46	617	20.1	193.6
6	USA	50.10	62.44	545	682	21	312	21.1	179.1
34	Argentina	10.93	8	93	201	0	121	0.2	8.7
41	Costa Rica	20.29	20.32	101	204	0	35	0.6	4.1
51	Mexico	10.69	8.30	65	112	1	79	0.2	9.2
84	Ecuador	4.14	3.10	48	91	0	31	0.1	0.3

Sources: Human Development Report 2001
[a] http://hdr.undp.org/reports/global/2001/en/pdf/techindex.pdf
[b] International Telecommunication Union / http://www.itu.int/ITUD/ict/statistics/at_glance/Internet02.pdf

TABLE 3.2 ICT Infrastructure for Middle Income and High Income Regions

Region	Telephone lines (per 1000 people)		Mobile phones (per 1000 people)		Internet hosts (per 1000 people)	
	1990	1999	1990	1999	1995	2000
Middle income countries	22	69		34	0.1	1.0
High income countries	473	594	13	371	11.0	96.9

TABLE 3.3 Digital Opportunity Index Selected Countries 2005/2006

Country	Opportunity	Infrastructure	Utilization	Digital Opportunity Index	World Rank
Argentina	0.97	0.36	0.21	0.51	54
Costa Rica	0.89	0.27	0.23	0.46	74
Ecuador	0.89	0.21	0.08	0.40	97
Mexico	0.94	0.24	0.25	0.47	66
USA	0.98	0.59	0.41	0.66	20
S. Korea	0.99	0.74	0.67	0.80	1

Source: Networked Readiness Index 2002–2003, 2003–2004, 2004–2005. http://www.itu.int/osg/spu/publications/worldinformationsociety/2007/WISR07_full-free.pdf

regions in ICT infrastructure, and also the differences in the rate and speed of incorporation of personal computers, telephone lines, and internet hosts, all deemed crucial components for bridging the digital divide.

Another relevant measure in relation to technological development is provided by the *Networked Readiness Index Ranking* (NRIR) (See Table 3.4). The Networked Readiness Index (NRI) is defined as a nation's or community's degree of preparation to participate in and benefit from ICT developments. The NRI is a composite of three components: the environment for ICT offered by a given country or community, the readiness of the community's key stakeholders (individuals, businesses, and governments) to use ICT, and finally, the usage of ICT among these stakeholders (Dutta & Jain, 2004, p. 3–4).

Table 3.4 shows that in the *Networked Readiness Index (NRI)* of 2005, Argentina dropped in the ranking from position 45 to 76; Mexico from 47 to 60; Costa Rica from 49 to 61; and Ecuador from 75 to 95. It is also interesting to note that the NRI rankings among the four countries varied from 2003 to 2005: Argentina went from first place in 2002–2003 to third place in the next two periods (2003–2004 and 2004–2005); Costa Rica went from third place in 2003–2004 to second in the last two periods; Mexico went

TABLE 3.4 Networked Readiness Index (NRI) for Latin American Countries 2002–2005

Country	2002–2003	2003–2004	2004–2005
Brazil	29	39	46
Chile	35	32	35
Argentina	45	50	76
México	47	44	60
Costa Rica	49	49	61
Uruguay	55	54	64
Republic Dom.	57	57	78
Trinidad & Tobago	58	52	59
Colombia	59	60	66
Jamaica	60	53	49
Panama	61	58	69
El Salvador	63	62	70
Venezuela	66	72	84
Peru	67	70	90
Guatemala	73	86	88
Ecuador	75	89	95
Paraguay	76	91	98
Bolivia	78	90	99
Nicaragua	79	94	103
Honduras	81	98	97
Haiti	82	100	

Source: Networked Readiness Index 2002–2003, 2003–2004, and 2004–2005.

from second place in 2002–2003 to first place in the following periods; and Ecuador has always been in fourth place.

It is well-known that the levels of urbanization of a society coupled with dynamics associated with class, race, and ethnicity are key influences on access and use of technology. For example, in Argentina, the country in Latin America with the highest degree of urbanization, people from upper-middle classes and wealthy families represent only 17% of the total population, and own 60% of the country's PCs (Castiglioni, 2000). In Costa Rica, while 29.3% of urban homes have a computer and 13.42% have access to the Internet, only 10.59% of rural homes have a computer and only 3.13% are able to access the Internet (Monge & Hewitt, 2004, pp. 13–14). Monge and Hewitt also report that 53.63% of rich households have computers, while only 3.18% of homes in poor neighborhoods have PCs. Internet access follows the same pattern. According to a report from the United Nations Development Program (2001, p. 54), most Ecuadorians are unable to buy computers or have Internet access at home, given the fact that most people earn very low wages in Ecuador (between $180 and $200), and a computer costs about $1000.

The digital divide in society at large is in turn reproduced in schools. In a study for the Latin American Institute of Educational Communication (ILCE), Monge and Hewitt (2004) concluded that schools from rural or marginalized urban areas attended by children living in poverty are neglected in the distribution of ICTs, increasing the marginalization of those children. These authors noted "there is a clear lack of proportion in internet access between schools located in communities with greater family income and those with the lowest income. Thus, while 48.9% of students from schools located in communities with less than 20% of poor homes has internet access, only 8.6% of students from poor communities has the same type of access" (Monge & Hewitt, 2004, p. 23). Similarly poor levels of distribution are reported for Mexico, where 66% of the schools that have ICTs are located in the urban areas, while only 12% of those in rural areas have access to such technologies (ILCE, 2003e).

E-HOPES FOR ICT IN SCHOOLS IN ARGENTINA, COSTA RICA, ECUADOR, AND MEXICO

The previous discussion about the state of ICT infrastructure in Latin America may suggest a very pessimistic scenario, and yet, in both the specialized literature and our survey of key educational actors, a different perspective emerges (FOD, 2007; UNDP, 2001). First, in Latin America, there is a growing and dizzying tendency to incorporate ICTs in education, but in most cases, without a comprehensive strategy or without well-grounded projects (Brunner, 2000). A study conducted by UNESCO (2004) observed that, "Several countries in South America have initiated projects for the development and the integration of ICTs in education, but it is well-known there is a lack of a national policy that regulates its use" (UNESCO: 2004, p. 62). Along the same lines, Robert Hawkins from the World Bank, wrote, "one of the bottlenecks that the project World Links has found is the lack of a clear policy about the use of computers in education by the ministries" (Hawkins, 2002, p. 41).

Most commentators conclude that ICT projects emerge every day with multiple, and sometimes even contradictory, goals. ICT initiatives are, in a sense, very popular, and are implemented by a vast array of public and private agents aiming to solve different problems, ranging from national plans to equip each teacher and student with a laptop computer, to the creation of education portals, networks, and websites.

During the period 1990–2005, ICT initiatives by educational levels were focused on three sectors:

1. The basic education level (K–12). These efforts concentrated on providing computers for schools; creating and running education portals, networks and websites, teacher training and programs for students; designing educational materials and software, games and tools that were ICT-based; and in some cases, providing personal computers for teachers or students or helping them acquire one.[2]
2. Higher education institutions also focused on infrastructure, access, connectivity, and acquisition issues. However, most of them, though in varying degrees, are beginning to pay greater attention to the creation of education portals, networks, and websites; to offer teacher training or programs for students; to design educational materials and software, games and tools; to provide ICT-based support for regular courses; and to create distance or virtual education programs. A few of them are also supporting basic education through various activities, such as training teachers, creating educational software, and managing ICT projects for elementary and secondary schools.[3]
3. In the non-formal education sector, the main efforts also focused on providing access for marginalized groups, such as children with long-term illness, people from rural or extremely poor areas, women, senior citizens, immigrants, or indigenous groups. In spite of the great variety and good intentions of most of these initiatives, the number of projects serving marginalized populations is quite limited.[4]

The variety of types and range of coverage of programs and projects for all ages, and for all educational levels, suggest a fertile, dynamic, and innovative incorporation of ICTs into schools. Similarly, our review of relevant literature (Anfossi, 2007; FOD, 2007; Zúñiga, 2003) coupled with the analysis of interviews with key education scholars, practitioners and administrators, indicates that there are very high expectations for the presumed key benefits of introducing ICTs into schools. MZ, a leader in the Omar Dengo Foundation's Research Department (Costa Rica) with more than 10 years' experience working in this area, offers a good example of the strong support and belief in the transformative potential ascribed to ICTs.

We have been able to observe improvements in students' self-concept as learners. The teachers also mention an improvement in teachers and students' self-esteem, motivation and attitudes.... In the community we have been able to observe the creation of a positive attitude of parents towards technology and towards the value of technology in education, and due to that attitude they have revalued education and the relevance of school. (MZ Costa Rica).

MZ's strong backing and related high expectations for ICTs were typical among our respondents. ICT's support is wide-ranging throughout the region, and it appears to be especially strong among faculty and school administrators. Some of the positive beliefs we gathered in our interviews were:

> ICTs are a real tool for the transformation of education. We should use them! (IT, Argentina)
> We are betting on ICT to improve cognitive development. (AM, Ecuador)
> The potential is enormous, we cannot miss it! (LM, Mexico)
> It is transforming the way parents see schools. (MM, Costa Rica)
> It is improving teaching and learning. (BB, Argentina)

A complementary and equally strong theme emerged from our interviews with regard to ICTs. Scholars and practitioners alike noted that the implementation of technologies was accomplished without the support of well-grounded empirical studies or as part of well-planned education policies. The next two testimonies help with understanding some of these issues. In the first case, MP, a researcher working for the Latin American School of Social Science (FLACSO-Argentina) and former consultant on ICT for the Ministry of Education of Argentina, notes specifically the problems associated with the lack of policy evaluation:

> There is no policy evaluation. There is not even data that allow us to start an investigation.... [I]n Argentina educational policies are not documented.... [T]here are not numbers, no one knows how many schools or what schools were covered. No one knows if those schools were located in rich or poor areas. There are no quantitative indicators. Therefore, the policies cannot be evaluated, simply because there is no information.... [I]t is a culture of administrative disorder. (MP Argentina)

In the second case, AG, a noted researcher from Costa Rica, with several publications on the topic of ICT in education, also commented on the lack of studies, but as it also happened with the other interviewees, this deficit is not translated into an openly negative or skeptical perspective.

> I have no doubts about the importance of the National Program on Technology, but I would like to know what transformation has generated in the schools, in the students, and in the teachers of urban and rural areas. (AG Costa Rica)

Our analysis indicates that high expectations and positive opinions about ICTs are not affected by the lack of well-defined implementation policies, independent evaluations, or follow-up studies assessing the results and impact of the programs developed. After more than 15 years of "ICT-friendly reforms," the general consensus expressed among our respondents about the positive effects of ICTs is a bit remarkable, yet, it should not be misperceived as a lack of critical perspectives. In our analysis, we have identified several areas of critical concern among the respondents that for the purposes of this chapter we have grouped in two categories: a) infrastructure and policy implementation; and b) pedagogical concerns. In the next section, we summarize these concerns expressed by our respondents and return to the question of the high expectations about ICTs in the concluding section.

E-CONCERNS ABOUT ICTS

As mentioned above, topics related to technical infrastructure were the most pressing concerns for each person interviewed. More specifically, the top items in this category were: insufficient basic services (such as electricity and communication lines), poor communications, outdated equipment, and lack of connectivity. The testimonies of NS, a member of the team in charge of designing the education portal of Ecuador for the Department of Education, and MP, a researcher from Argentina, offer a good summary of the most frequently-mentioned infrastructure challenges:

> 25% of the schools do not have electricity and even fewer have any kind of electronic or digital communication or anything that allows us to connect with them. An ideal scene would be first to guarantee that all schools had the basic services, including telephone or some type of communication device, or to look for a way to lower the costs to connect them or to improve the infrastructure of communications. (NS Ecuador)

> The levels of connectivity of the system make anyone laugh. Even in Buenos Aires, there are absolutely precarious conditions of connectivity. Even in the better-equipped schools, the teacher must shout, "Guys, pass me the cable," then one has to disconnect the secretaries or go over something, connect the cable, make the telephone connection and make the boys wait for thirty or more minutes to download an Internet page... and I am speaking about Buenos Aires! (MP Argentina)

There is no doubt that among the respondents in these four countries the most pressing concerns in the area of technical infrastructure are financial, such as the high costs associated with providing and maintaining adequate equipment to every school and university. However, they also noted the importance of cultural and political influences. Cultural dissonance, bureaucratic barriers, and fears associated with poor or inappropriate use of software were identified as relevant problems, but the key and somewhat surprising element in connection with infrastructural issues was at the policy level. The testimony of DE, a director in an NGO from Costa Rica promoting the use of ICTs, reflects the cultural concerns:

> There are important barriers as far as equipment and infrastructure that make things go very slow, for example the limited number of hours to access the Internet and the number of computers available. But also administrators in schools are afraid that the computers might get broken, and the people get blamed, ... [T]hen all these things are obstacles that hinder the access to computers for all. (DE Costa Rica)

As noted above and related to technical and infrastructure problems, the lack of national policies or at least adequate levels of policy coordination emerged as the key area of concern for the majority of the respondents. For example, MB, an important administrator for the Department of Education of Ecuador, coordinating a national program providing computers and training to public school teachers, and FU, a well-known researcher from Mexico, pointed out that:

> We have a variety of important programs, but there is not coordination between them. We need a policy to orient all the programs that are being developed. Another great challenge is to guarantee the program continuity because the changes of government do not always assure continuity. (MB Ecuador).

> There is no coordination. The different programs are overlapped. It is very peculiar. We have everything: we have school networks, community plazas and digital community centers. Then we have independent digital community centers, digital community centers that are school networks, digital community centers that are community plazas, community plazas that work with school networks, and community plazas that are school networks. We have everything, but every one coordinates his or her own. I wish we could have coordination of efforts in this country. (FU, coordinator of projects at the Latin American Institute of Technology (ILCE) Mexico)

We want to emphasize that for many of our respondents, reflecting on ICTs generates some degree of ambivalence. On the one hand, it is clear that the countries are poor, and therefore, the finances set important limits; on the other, it is the "the lack of coordination" that creates problems. This ambivalence is present in the testimonies of MR and GF, who explicitly acknowledged having "important programs" and "everything" to have an impact in schools, but it is the lack of coordination that prevents their systems from accomplishing their educational goals:

> If by national policy you understand a strategy that takes into account the country integration problems and the complexity of the country, then I can confirm that there are no national policies. We never had them. There were some initiatives, but there is no frame, there is not a diagnostic that helps us organize things, at least in a sense that goes beyond the circumstantial swings of politics. It is an issue that is labeled as important, but most initiatives belong to a particular political party, so when the party falls from power, their initiatives also collapse. There are policies created by the state, but I do not see them as policies but as mere initiatives. There are no policies in the sense of strategic decisions that pursue strategic objectives. (TL, ICT consultant to the Department of Education of Argentina)

> The country has entered the field of ICTs, but this incursion has been limited by the lack of clear policies, by the lack of decisiveness of the authorities, by the lack of planning. (PV, ICT researcher from Costa Rica)

The lack of policy coordination at the institutional level was also identified as a significant barrier by several of the academics we interviewed. Even in the field of higher education, institutional strategic planning appears to be missing. In a few cases, the scholars noted initiatives promoted by schools or faculties, or by groups or individuals usually around buying equipment or solving technical issues, but stressing the need for improving the planning and coordination tools.

There is not institutional strategic planning in any school or department at the university. There is no plan where one can find what we are going to do in one, two or five years. We do not have programs. We do not have that type of mentality or discipline (TM Argentina author of several books and articles about ICT in education).

When our respondents were asked to explain the lack of clearly defined national or institutional ICT policies, another quite surprising dynamic emerged. As noted above, such "coordination deficit" was almost unanimously presented as a key descriptor of national, local, or institutional problems; and yet it was explained by most of the interviewees to be a result of influences that apparently cannot be controlled "internally." Our interviewees offered explanations that touched on the following: the financial pressures related to the programs of structural adjustment; the general demands of globalization and internationalized economies; the "need" to send the signal to investors that the country was on the right track toward becoming "modern" and serious, and even in a few cases, the results of fortuitous events. A few examples illustrate these different positions:

> The international context is not only setting the standard for the national agenda in ICT-related matters, but it is also overflowing it. It is impossible to leave this wave, this technological avalanche, because the World Bank and the Inter-American Development Bank are those that are investing in this educa-

> tive reform and they are the ones that have given the government millions of dollars to buy materials, to buy computers...The government bought the computers because it had to fulfill the Inter-American Development Bank conditions. Then the government bought the computers but without at least verifying that they were working properly, to such degree that the equipment arrived at the country without operating systems. (PV studies ICT and education in Costa Rica)

> The higher education system is following the international guidelines set by UNESCO, including those related to the incorporation of ICTs. In my university, I believe that we are responding to a process of national development. I believe that the Latin American fashion is to follow the international trend to computerize everything to endorse the teaching processes. (MB University Professor, researches on ICT issues, Mexico)

> As frequently happens in our countries, these activities were not planned. We are forced by the international scenario, but without enough preparation or coordination. (SE Director of Research in a major public university from Ecuador)

> In a visit of President Fox to the United States, he met Bill Gates, and Bill Gates decided to support the Mexican people. I would not say that it was a negotiation, but an agreement. The national project e-Mexico and some other interests of the Mexican government had some things in common with the objectives of the Gates Foundation. (FU coordinates projects for the Latin American Institute of Technology (ILCE) in Mexico)

Lack of coordination, chance, luck, and the need to convince outsiders are all elements that appear to give the impression that for our informants ICTs were incorporated almost without the control or intervention of the traditional "internal" actors in education policies. This sense of "lack of control" and externality was confirmed when our respondents highlighted their specific pedagogical concerns about ICTs. Most of the respondents from Argentina, Ecuador, and Mexico emphasized the absence of pedagogical visions to sustain the projects.

> We know that the pedagogical component is at the center of everything, but there is a lack of it because the people designing these ICT programs were outsiders, engineers, software experts, technicians, but nobody from education. (FF Ecuador)

> I can tell you that we have incorporated ICTs and . . . pretty soon it was clear that we were going to have to develop a pedagogical program to figure out what to do with them. (PM, Argentina)

The exception to this realization of the need to have a conceptually strong perspective was evident in the remarks of a few colleagues from Costa Rica, who indicated that the main pedagogical problem was not the lack of vision or the lack of theoretical approaches, but the imposition of a single model that was "alien" and did not emerge from the national authorities or education systems:

> The Omar Dengo Foundation has a vision about ICT in education, which is... a vision external to the school system, it is a... vision, and I want more openings about ICTs in schools and a shared reflection, but for them (Omar Dengo Foundation), they have an attitude of dominating and not having a dialogue with us. (GB, Costa Rica)

In all cases, it was stressed that the programs presented are mostly technically inclined or technically oriented and the language used was "strange," not familiar to teachers and administrators. The use of a technical language in the presentation of programs was also highlighted as challenging, given the lack of collaboration and the communication difficulties between, on the one hand, those in charge of software development and technical issues, and on the other, education experts and teachers.

Another typical answer that reinforces our interpretation about the "external" character of ICTs was the broadly-shared opinion about the absence of curricular contents related to the "internal reality" of the country. As JJ, a researcher with ten years' experience working with teachers from Mexico, noted:

> Those who have interest in ICTs bring content that completely ignores the perceptions or necessities of the students. In many cases, the computers are used essentially to teach the students how to use them, mainly to learn commercial software or programming languages that also serve commercial interests. (JJ Mexico)

Despite the geographic differences, distinctive levels of access to ICTs and educational realities described by the participants of our study, it appears that in general, there are broad coincidences and similar concerns about the incorporation of ICTs in schools and universities in Argentina, Costa Rica, Ecuador, and Mexico. First, ICTs generate a good deal of pedagogical hope, related to a not-yet-demonstrated exceptional potential for solving educational and social problems. Second, based on that potential, ICT infrastructure and technical issues should be national and institutional priorities. Third, currently ICT infrastructure and technical issues are identified as the key challenges associated with lack of financial resources, but even more importantly, to the lack of national policies. Fourth, the recent incorporation of ICTs appears to be connected to or dependent on "outside" or unpredictable factors. Fifth, a better incorporation of ICTs would require long-term systematic planning and should be addressed in a coordinated manner, particularly by developing national policies.

Taken all together, these five points constitute what can be labeled, for lack of a better term, "E-hopes." Among the most important E-hopes are the following: to help students improve their academic performance, learning, attendance, motivation, attitudes, self-image, creativity, social and cognitive skills; to help teachers' training, professional development, attitudes towards technology, knowledge, self esteem, and to enrich their teaching practices; to improve educational infrastructure, curriculum enrichment of schools, development of a digital culture, reduction of marginalization of rural and urban areas, greater participation of parents and communities in educational issues, better use of technological infrastructure to generate opportunities for the community, and improvement of life conditions in the communities where they are introduced; poverty reduction and increasing each country's competitiveness.

In short, it seems that any initiative implemented in relationship to ICTs in education was and will be positive, and that more of them will, perhaps almost magically, solve the region's severe educational challenges. Undoubtedly, ICTs have entered and altered the pedagogical arena in Latin America and perhaps, more importantly, the pedagogical imagination in the region. We will discuss these changes in our final reflections.

FINAL REFLECTIONS

In a region accustomed to widespread and constant criticism of its schools and universities and a long history of failed education reforms, it was a bit surprising to find the broad consensus on what we have labeled "E-hopes." These pedagogical hopes, expressed as a high regard among our respondents for almost every single ICT initiative, stand out in view of the lack of any substantive study supporting the notion that the financial resources dedicated to ICTs in education have been effectively spent. Moreover, in the last few years, many scholars and analysts noted that an uncritical incorporation is resulting or might result in at least the following: the replication of patterns of social exclusion similar to the historical experiences of adopting industrial technologies or R&D models within economically dependent and politically unequal frameworks (Arunachalam, 2003; Wallerstein, 1975, 1999); a greater digital divide among countries and among social classes (Tedesco, 2006; Monge & Hewitt, 2004); unfulfilled expectations and promises associated with their use, such as the improvement of students' learning, academic performance, motivation and attitudes, and of life conditions in the communities (Castiglioni et al., 2000; Johnson & Barrer, 2002; Marchesi & Marin, 2003; Ramírez, 2001, 2003; Salinas et al., 2004; Tedesco, 2006); greater gaps between promises of the potential of ICTs and the real changes produced in the schools (Mcmillan, Honey, & Mandinach,

2003); and additional economic and labor burdens to the academic and knowledge production sectors (Everett, 1998).

In short, the lack of general positive education results in the four countries studied and the lack of any substantive study sustaining the high regard that ICTs have generated over the last two decades, coupled with the traditional attitude of resistance of professional educators in Latin America to most programs of school reform, generates a quite intriguing pedagogical situation.

As expected, most of our respondents noted the important deficits in terms of technical infrastructure affecting the pedagogical performance of schools and universities. Poor equipment, lack of connectivity, and financial problems are important but not as determinant as the lack of overarching coordination of ICT policies. Furthermore, it seems that the lack of coordination is related to the fact that the wide-spread incorporation of ICTs was the consequence of "external," "non-pedagogical" forces or agents, but this "externality" is not seen as threatening as other reforms, perhaps, because the ICT incorporation was done in such an extended, varied, and unsystematic way.

If the quasi-magical educational virtues of ICTs have emerged from their "external" and technical makeup, and they are considered beyond the control of any individual actor, emerging continuously, without clear definition or standards, or following a precise plan, it is possible to speculate that the "E-hopes" are also expressing shifts in the pedagogical imagination in the region.

What we want to call attention to is the fact that understanding the role and potential of ICTs in the region cannot be accomplished without incorporating into the analysis the impact of the Neoliberal inspired education reforms. These reforms were proposed as technical, and not ideological. Some sort of "ideology without ideology" was set over and against the "failures" and inability of the more socially and welfare-oriented systems in meeting the needs of all citizens. In Latin America, Neoliberalism gathered discursive strength and political influence from both its promises of a new kind of non-ideological freedom and a telling critique of democratic failures. It represented, in its own terms, a move beyond politics and back to a state of nature, back to the "natural" impulses of individualism and competition, that in a unique way, takes away pedagogical power from educational institutions and gives it back individual actors.

It is important to emphasize that our criticisms of Neoliberalism in schools are not based on a nostalgic longing for a golden era, where supposedly a truly democratic public school system existed, but in the assessment that after more than twenty years of implementing Neoliberal-inspired reforms, the results are far from delivering good education results (Fischman, Ball, & Givrtz, 2003; Hursh, 2006). Even if the measures of education achievement do not reveal the expected good results, it is undeniable that Neoliberalism as an educational discourse has been very influential not only in changing school practices, but also in defining the educational common sense, what can be thought or imagined about schools.

Recognizing the complexity and contradictory features of these processes does not imply, however, that one should overlook the influence and power of those discourses, which naturalize ICTs and advocate them as new gospel. We are not attempting to minimize the impact, undoubtedly enormous, of the extensive use of ICT in the transformation of everyday life; however, we wish to avoid considering cyberspace and ICT as the new redeeming tool. As Wertheim (1997) noted,

> Today's proselytizers of cyberspace proffer their domain as an ideal "above" and "beyond" the problems of the material world. While early Christians promulgated heaven as a realm in which the human soul would be freed from the frailties and failings of the flesh, so today's champions of cyberspace hail it as a place where the self will be freed from the limitations of physical embodiment. (p. 296, cited in Bauman, 1998, p. 19)

We conclude by stressing that it is quite stimulating to find hopes about the possibilities of educational improvement for the schools and universities in Latin America. Indeed, we are not critical of our respondents' E-hopes, but we read them within the political and pedagogical frame of Neoliberalism and its political and pedagogical limitations. Men and women have always envisioned and attempted to create innovative technologies, sometimes in the form of magical devices, silver bullets, and redemptive spells to solve once and for all humanity's social problems. Religion, ideologies and science have been fertile fields providing innovative technologies that when applied, produced enormous damage to those who were deemed not worthy or unable to understand the miraculous nature of the innovation. As Foucault called to our attention

It is impossible to think that it [technologies] would have been developed and adapted had there not been in the play and strategy of human relations something, which tended in that direction. What is interesting is always interconnection, not the primacy of this over that, which never has any meaning (Foucault, 1993, p. 169).

In other words, E-hopes, technology-related educational wishes, and high expectations about the presumed effects that the current and future implementation of ICTs will have on schools and universities are not "a problem" that needs to be fixed, but a good starting point for further reflection and an important expression of the interconnection between educational actors, educational needs, and the possibilities of educational transformation.

REFERENCES

Anfossi, A. (2007) The integration of computers in primary schools of Costa Rica—experiences of the last 20 years. Available in: http://www.fod.ac.cr/publicaciones/

Arunachalam, S. (2003). Information for research in developing countries: Information technology, a friend or foe? *International Information & Library Review, 35,* 133–147.

Aviram, R. & Tami, D. (2004). *The impact of ICT on education: The three opposed paradigms, the lacking discourse.* The Center for Futurism in Education, Ben Gurion University of the Negev, Israel. Available at http://www.elearningeuropa.info/extras/pdf/ict_impact.pdf

Bauman, Z. (1998). *Globalization: The human consequences.* New York: Columbia University Press.

Brunner, J. J. (2000). Educación: Escenarios de Futuro. Nuevas tecnologías y Sociedad de la Información. Working paper. Programa de la Promoción para la Reforma Educativa en América Latina (PREAL). Santiago de Chile., PREAL

Castiglioni, A., Clucellas, M., & Sánchez, G. (2000). Educación y Nuevas Tecnologías: ¿Moda o cambio estructural? Buenos Aires: Veredit.

Cuban, L. (2001) *Oversold and underused.* Boston, Massachusetts: Harvard University Press.

Demo, P. (2005). Inclusão digital: Cada vez mais no centro da inclusão social. *Inclusão Social, 1*(1), 36–38.

Dutta, S. y Jain, Amit (2004) The *networked readiness of nations.* INSEAD. Available in: http://www.weforum.org/pdf/Gcr/GITR_2003_2004/Framework_Chapter.pdf

Everett, M. (1998). Latin America on-line: The Internet, development, and democratization. *Human Organization, 57*(4), 385.

Fischman, G. E., Ball, S., & Gvirtz, S. (2003). Towards a Neo-liberal education? Tension and change in Latin-America. In *Education, Crisis and Hope: Tension and Change in Latin-America* (pp. 1–19). New York: Routledge-Falmer.

FOD (2007) Programa nacional de informatica educativa. Costa Rica. http://www.fod.ac.cr/contenidos/pronie/logros.htm

Foucault, M. (1993). "Space, Power and Knowledge." *The Cultural Studies Reader. S.* During. London, Routledge.

Hursh, D. (2006). The crisis in urban education: resisting Neoliberal policies and forging democratic possibilities. *Educational Researcher, 35*(4), 19–25.

ILCE (2003a) Disponibilidad y uso de la tecnología en educación básica. Resumen Analítico. México: ILCE.

ILCE (2003b) Disponibilidad y uso de la tecnología en educación básica. Resumen Ejecutivo. México: ILCE.

ILCE (2003c) Disponibilidad y uso de la tecnología en educación básica. Encuesta Nacional. México: ILCE.

ILCE (2003d) Disponibilidad y uso de la tecnología en educación básica. Estudios de Caso México: ILCE.

ILCE (2003e) Disponibilidad y uso de la tecnología en educación básica. Censo de Recursos Tecnológicos. México: ILCE.

ILCE (2003f) Disponibilidad y uso de la tecnología en educación básica. Contexto Institucional. México: ILCE.

Hawkins, R. (2002) Ten Lessons for ICT and Education in the Developing World, en: *The Global Information Technology Report 2001–2002: Readiness for the Networked World.* Oxford University Press. Available in: http://www.cid.harvard.edu/cr/pdf/gitrr2002_ch04.pdf

Hilbert, M., & Katz, J. (2003) *Building and Information Society: A Latin American and Caribbean Perspective.* Santiago de Chile, ECLAC.

Johnston, J., & Barrer, T. (2002). *Assessing the impact of technology in teaching and learning: A sourcebook for evaluators.* Institute for Social Research. University of Michigan. Available in: http://rcgd.isr.umich.edu/tlt/TechSbk.pdf

Marchesi, A. & Martín E. (2003) Tecnología y aprendizaje; Investigación sobre el impacto del ordenador en el aula. Madrid, Instituto IDEA.

Mcmillan, C. K., Honey, M., & Mandinach, E. (2003) *A retrospective on twenty years of education technology policy.* U.S. Department of Education, Office of Educational Technology.

Monge, R., & Hewitt, J. (2004) *Tecnologías de la Información y las Comunicaciones (TIC) y el futuro desarrollo de Costa Rica: el desafío de la exclusión.* Comisión Asesora de Alta Tecnología de Costa Rica (CAATEC). Serie Costa Rica Digital. N.3. Disponible en: http://www.pln.or.cr/docs/crd3.pdf

Ramírez, J. L. (2001). Educación y computadoras: una aproximación al estado actual de su investigación en México. *Revista Mexicana de Investigación Educativa.* Vol. VI, num. 11, enero-abril, 2001. pp. 119–138.

Ramírez, J. L. (2003). Las tecnologías de la información y de la comunicación en la educación en cuatro países latinoamericanos. *Revista Mexicana de Investigación Educativa.* Vol. 11, num. 28 enero-abril, 2006. pp. 61–90.

Salinas, B., Porras, L., Santos, A., & Ramos, J. (2004) Tecnologías de Información, Educación y Pobreza en América Latina. México: Plaza y Valdés.

Tedesco, J. C. (2006). "Las TICs y la desigualdad educativa en América Latina". *Revista electrónica: Magazine de Horizonte, Informática Educativa, Año VII, No. 75.* Buenos Aires, Argentina. Available in: http://www.enlaces.cl/archivos/doc/200511281906400.TICs_Desigualdad(3).pdf

UNESCO (2004). *Las Tecnologías de la Información y la Comunicación en la Formación Docente.* Montevideo, Uruguay: UNESCO, División de Educación Superior.

United Nations Development Programme (2001) *Human Development Report 2001 Making new technologies work for human development* Available in: http://hdr.undp.org/reports/global/2001/en/United Nations Development Programme (2006) *Human Development Report 2006 Beyond Scarcity: Power, Poverty and the global water crisis.* Available in: *http://hdr.undp.org/hdr2006/statistics/indices/default.cfm*

Wallerstein, I. (Ed.) (1975). *World inequality: Origins and perspectives on the world system.* Montreal: Black Rose Books.

Wallerstein, I. (1999). *The end of the world as we know it: Social science for the twenty-first Century.* Minneapolis, London: University of Minnesota Press.

Zúñiga, M. (2003) Aprendizaje mediado por tecnologías digitales la experiencia de Costa Rica, En: *Educación y Nuevas Tecnologías. Experiencias en América Latina.* IIPE—UNESCO—Sede Regional Buenos Aires, 2003 (pp. 99–114). Available in: http://www.fod.ac.cr/publicaciones/

NOTES

1. A few of our respondents indicated that when independent evaluations were conducted, they were either not published or not available for public inspection, which makes it extremely difficult to assess such results and impact. One of the few exceptions to this is the study of availability and use of technology in Mexico conducted by ILCE (2003) that was published and widely distributed. We also would like to express our gratitude to official personnel from Ecuador for the generosity they showed in sharing documents and unpublished studies with us.
2. Some examples of these efforts are: in Ecuador, the *Comision Nacional de Interconectividad (*National Commission for Connectivity), *Maestr@s.com, Educar Ecuador,* and several web portals. In Costa Rica, we found the projects run by the Omar Dengo Foundation (FOD) and the Ministry of Education, such as the *Programa Nacional de Informática Educativa (*National Program for Educational Informatics*)*, the *Red Telemática Educativa (*Educational Network*)*, the project *Pequeñas redes de computadoras en las aulas* (Small Networks for the Classrooms), the *Proyecto Alianza, Innova,* and *Intel Educar para el Futuro (*Intel education for the future*)*. In Argentina, the most important ones are the *Campaña Nacional de Alfabetización Digital (National Campaign for Digital Literacy), Educar, Experimentar, REPORTE,* other educational portals run by the provinces (states), and currently under discussion, the possible implementation of the "One laptop per child" initiative. In Mexico, we detected the portal *E-Mexico* run by the Mexican government; some of the projects run by the Department of Education (SEP) and the Latin American Institute of Educational Communication (ILCE) such as *Red Escolar (School Network)* and *Red Edusat,* as well as others run by the department of Education. such as *ENCICLOMEDIA, PRONAP en línea,* and *RED NORMALISTA*. For a more detailed description of these programs, see: Ramírez (2006).
3. Some of the leading projects at this level are: in Ecuador, the Red de Información Científica y Tecnológica del Ecuador (REICYT) (Ecuadoran Scientific and Technological Information Network) run by the Fundación para la Ciencia y la Tecnología (Foundation for Science and Technology) (FUNDACYT); the Red Latinoamericana de Educación *(RELATED*) (Latin American Education Network); *Cyber-ESPE* of the Escuela Politécnica del Ejército (ESPE) (Army School of Technology); the project "virtual classrooms" run by the Universidad Técnica Particular de Loja (UTPL) (Loja Private School of Technology); the project *Innovación de la Educación Pública Primaria en la Península de Santa Elena (*Innovation in public schools in the Santa Elena Peninsula) run by the Escuela Superior Politécnica del Litoral (Politechnical School of the Litoral); and the computer applications for the teaching of middle school basic subjects developed by the Escuela Politécnica Nacional (EPN) (Nacional School of Technology). In Costa Rica, some of the more important projects are the distance education program of the Distance University of Costa Rica; the projects run by the Technical Institute of Costa Rica; and other projects on innovation and materials, and on-line courses developed by the faculty of the University of Costa Rica. In Argentina, the those most frequently men-

tioned are the projects *RUEDA,* the *virtual campus* of Quilmes University, and the University of Buenos Aires project *UBA XXI.* Even though most Mexican universities engage in important activities related to the use of ICTs, especially in the area of distance education and support for regular courses through institutional websites, those that have higher visibility in this area are run by the Autonomous National University of Mexico (UNAM), the National Polytechnic Institute (IPN), the University of Guadalajara(UG), the System of Technical Institutions from the Department of Education, and the Technological Institute of Higher Education of Monterrey (ITESM). For a more detailed description of these programs, see: Ramírez (2006).

4. Some of the main projects in this area are the following: for people with special needs, the Mexican portal *Discapa@cinet* and a project of the University of Matanza (Argentina); for children with long-term illness,the *Red Nacional Acercándote @l Mundo (*National Network Getting Close to the World), part of the project *Chicos.net* from Argentina; for people from rural or extreme poverty areas, the *Fondo para el desarrollo de telecomunicación en áreas rurales y urbano marginales* (National Fund for the Development of Telecommunications in Rural and Marginalized Urban Areas), and *Redes Amigas (*Friends Network) in Ecuador; in Costa Rica, the project *Lincos Segunda Generación (*Lincos Second Generation) run by the Fundación Costa Rica para el Desarrollo Sostenible (Costa Rica Foundation for Sustainable Development); *Aventuras para vos* (Adventures for you) part of the project *Chicos.net* from Argentina; the *Community Plazas* supported by the *Consejo Nacional de Educación para la Vida y el Trabajo* (National Foundation for Education for Life and Work), and the *Centros Comunitarios de aprendizaje (*Community Learning Centers*)* supported by the Technological Institute of Higher Education of Monterrey (ITESM) from Mexico; for traditionally segregated groups such as women, senior citizens, immigrants, or ethnic groups, the *Programa para Ciudadanos de Oro* (Golden Citizens Program) from Costa Rica; the program A*dultos en Red* (Networked Adults) from Argentina; and the portals *e-Migrantes* (e-migrants), *e-Indígenas* (e-indians), and *e-Mujer* (e-woman) from Mexico. For a more detailed description of these programs, see Ramírez (2006).

CHAPTER 4

THE EXPANSION OF HIGHER EDUCATION IN THE DEVELOPING WORLD

The Contribution of Distance Education

Sir John Daniel
Commonwealth of Learning

INTRODUCTION

A higher education system in which students, parents, employers, and governments can have confidence is an important public good for all countries. Globalisation presents new challenges to providing such a public good because it is accelerating the expansion of higher education and driving it to greater diversity of provision. This chapter explores the processes of expansion and diversification of higher education in the developing world with a special focus on India, the world's largest democracy. We have argued elsewhere (Daniel, Kanwar, and Uvalić-Trumbić, 2006) that the growth of higher education in the developing world is a tectonic shift that will break up the old order. In a decade or two, most university and college students

ICT for Education, Development, and Social Justice, pages 53–63

will be in the developing world and this will redefine the norms in higher education globally.

GROWING DEMAND

There is no doubt about the demand. For two decades worldwide enrolment growth has exceeded the most optimistic forecasts. A milestone of 100 million enrolments was passed some years ago, and an earlier forecast of 120 million students by 2020 looks likely to be reached by 2010. Indeed, if part-time students are counted, numbers have already passed 130 million. Growth is, if anything, accelerating as more governments see the rapid expansion of higher education as key to their transition to developed country status.

Thus, in China enrolments doubled between 2000 and 2003. By 2005, with 16 million students, China had overtaken the US as the world's largest higher education system. Malaysia also illustrates the trend. It plans to increase enrolments in higher education by 166 percent in the next four years, from 600,000 to 1.6 million, in order to achieve developed-nation participation rates. Mauritius has recently passed legislation to create a third university for its 1.2 million people, having added a second only five years ago.

Growth has been rapid in other developing countries as well—but usually from a very low base. Across the world there is a massive disparity in the higher education participation rates of people between 18 and 23 years old (known as Age Participation Rates, or APRs). APRs of around 50 percent are now the norm in developed countries, whereas in numerous countries in South Asia and Sub-Saharan Africa they languish below 10 percent.

To date the growth of higher education in the developing world has been constrained by various obstacles, notably cost. But today, spreading connectivity, allied with the massive creation of open educational resources based on open-source technology, could create the radical reduction in costs necessary for higher education to serve the four billion people at the bottom of the world's economic pyramid. Were that to happen, it would generate over a hundred million more students.

MEETING THE DEMAND

How can developing nations respond to the massive demand for higher education that they will face? Will the patterns of provision that have worked for industrialized countries suffice, or are new approaches needed? Since developing countries will soon account for the majority of enrolments in higher education worldwide, their answers to this question will effectively define the global profile of higher education in the 21st century. The profile seems likely to change in three ways.

First, it will include a much greater role for private, for-profit institutions. Seeing a massive market opening up, first-world for-profit institutions will expand their cross-border provision of educational services. No doubt they will soon by joined by large for-profits from the developing world that will take advantage of their lower costs to beat the rich countries at their own game. In India, for example, privately managed institutions, mostly locally owned, already account for over 75 percent of professional education. How will both the public and the private sector provide higher education to the millions of new students in the developing nations? Much of it will likely follow traditional patterns of classroom teaching on locally owned campuses, but distance learning, offered both locally and across borders (COL/UNESCO, 2006), will have an increasing and prominent profile.

DISTANCE LEARNING

Open and distance education is a good way of reaching out to large numbers. The example of India, which accounts for a quarter of the population of the developing world and already has the world's third largest higher education system, illustrates this. Today India's higher education system provides access to less than 10% of the 18–23 age cohort despite massive growth in distance education. Note that in India increasing the age participation rate by just one percentage point means adding one million more students. Therefore, moving from a 10% to, say, a 35% APR will add 25 million more students. It is against this background that India's Knowledge Commission, alongside various recommendations for a systematic reform of higher education, has called for the number of Indian universities to grow from 350 today to 1500 by 2015—and that is only to cope with a doubling of the current participation rate from 7% to 14%.

Distance learning is already a significant component of Indian higher education. Today 24 percent of all enrolments—well over two million students—are in distance education—specifically in 13 national and state open universities and 106 institutions, mostly public, which teach both on campus and by correspondence. The government's target is that by 2010, 40 percent of all higher education participation will occur through distance education.

The Indira Gandhi National Open University now has 1.5 million students and India's state open universities are growing rapidly. For example, the Netaji Subhas Open University in West Bengal had fewer than ten thousand students in 2000 but is set to achieve 100,000 students—and mega-university status—in 2007. The Tamil Nadu Open University was only created in 2003 and already has 60,000 students.

Professor Rajan Velukar is Vice-Chancellor of the Yashwantrao Chavan Maharashtra Open University, which has 200,000 students. He aims to increase that to 400,000 by around 2010. Some of the other state open universities, such as Rajasthan's Vardhaman Mahaveer Open University, Kota, and the open universities in the large states of Bihar and Uttar Pradesh have not yet grown to serious numbers, but the potential is there for them to do so as pressure of demand continues to increase.

Such numbers put the contribution of cross-border provision of distance education into perspective. In developing countries its role is still negligible (Daniel, Kanwar & Uvalić-Trumbić, 2005). Cross-border providers of all types focus on countries at a relatively high level of development as measured by the UNDP's Human Development Index.

The most active cross-border providers in developing countries are, not unnaturally, from other developing countries. The Indira Gandhi National Open University, the world's largest unitary university, is already active in 26 other countries. The University of South Africa (UNISA), a distance-teaching university created back in the 1940s that now has a quarter of a million students, has long had students throughout Africa. Nelson Mandela and Robert Mugabe are both graduates, having studied in prison. Today, as well as recruiting students individually, it is setting up institutional agreements to augment provision in countries like Ethiopia.

All these are public institutions. Although distance education began in the commercial sector as correspondence education, public institutions, particularly those called open universities, have made the running in the last thirty years. They converted correspondence education into multi-media distance education and implemented effective student support systems to complement the learning materials. More recently they have introduced ICTs on a large scale.

Will the private sector re-enter the field in a big way? Profit margins per student are lower for distance learning than for face-to-face provision, but the volumes could be enormous. C. K. Prahalad's book, *The Fortune at the Bottom of the Pyramid,* (Prahalad, 2004) suggests that by making radical innovations in technology and business models and creating highly distributed, small-scale operations married to world-scale capabilities, educational enterprises might serve this huge market profitably.

Private cross-border provision might be part of the answer, but it is only in its infancy even in face-to-face provision. The number of cross-border providers in India increased from 27 in 2000 to 114 in 2004. But in light of India's potential student numbers, their role is negligible. Moreover, their quality is problematic: a third of the institutions are not recognized or accredited in their country of origin, and an equal proportion of their Indian collaborators are not part of the formal higher education system either.

Even when the foreign providers are universities, they are not in the premier league and have mediocre reputations in their own countries. Neither branch campuses nor franchise agreements have had much success, with the exceptions of 61 twinning and articulation arrangements that allow students to go to the source country in the final year and stay on for employment purposes. But an additional market of tens of millions of students should be tempting for major and serious providers of distance education. But will students want what they have to offer? To make distance learning attractive they must address the five A's of affordability, accessibility, appropriateness, accreditation, and acceptability.

AFFORDABILITY, ACCESSIBILITY, APPROPRIATENESS AND ACCREDITATION

Affordability is a major challenge. India, like many developing countries, is trying to transform higher education from an elite to a mass system aimed at the needs of a vibrant democracy. To succeed, providers of distance learning must devise a business model that can take them beyond the elite to reach out to the masses, in order to realize the cost efficiencies associated with large numbers of students and to address the nation's education goals. A series of developments in the ways that technology is used could stimulate the dramatic reduction in educational costs that is required for a radical widening of access.

New methods of education have always attracted private providers. Even before Britain introduced the penny post in 1840, Isaac Pitman had begun offering a correspondence course in shorthand, and private providers subsequently dominated the correspondence education industry. The next wave of distance education, led by the large multi-media open universities, was dominated by the public sector. In addition to widening access dramatically in some countries, these institutions also showed that distance learning can be of higher quality, as well as less expensive, than conventional higher education because it has to be developed and delivered in a much more systematic way.

The current wave of distance learning, often called eLearning because of its extensive online components, seems once again to have a special appeal to the private sector. It has a cost structure in which a higher upfront investment is rewarded by lower marginal costs when volume is achieved. The for-profit institutions' access to capital markets allows them to make those investments. Moreover, providers wishing to use eLearning now have available a rapidly growing body of open educational resources; freely available learning materials that can be adapted to particular local needs. I shall return to this crucial development. The combination of expanding connectivity and the swelling reservoir of open educational resources is potentially revolutionary, not least for its capacity to cut costs.

Accessibility is not just a matter of cost. Higher education also requires access to the technology and allied infrastructure through which education is delivered. Internet connectivity is particularly important, yet the proportion of people online is only 4% in India, 1% in Africa (half of them in South Africa) and 0.1% in Bangladesh. But in contemplating the limited use of the Internet in sub-Saharan Africa and South Asia, remember that twenty years ago the online technology that now permeates the West hardly existed. Communication links are already beginning to alter the way that poor villages in the developing world function. As bandwidth costs go down, increased Internet connectivity will accelerate that trend.

Cross-border providers often fail the test of *appropriateness*. Their subject offerings are limited, and liberal education often loses out to more market-driven programs such as business and information technology. Students from a variety of cultures and linguistic backgrounds have to follow the curriculum of the country of origin, baseball or cricket analogies and all, with no recognition of social, cultural, and ethnic differences. Cross-border provision will become fully relevant only when it responds to country priorities, which is best done through strong partnerships between the overseas provider and local institutions to develop curricula and methods of delivery and student support.

The next “A” is *accreditation*. In reality students' requirements go beyond formal accreditation to a more informal notion, the fifth “A” of *acceptability*. Students like the convenience and flexibility of distance learning. Furthermore, those students who thought that they might miss the human contact associated with face-to-face instruction often find that when distance learning has an effective student support system, contact is both more personal and more effective than in conventional systems.

Students want the academic titles that they earn to be not only recognized, but also endowed with a good reputation. However, the respect that the public accords to institutions changes slowly. It takes time to build up an institutional reputation and, barring egregious mistakes, it also takes time to lose one. Although the UK Open University acquired high esteem within the academic community very soon after its establishment, it took twenty years before employers began to say that if faced with two job applicants of similar merit they would prefer the Open University graduate. This development had nothing to do with formal accreditation but rather with the accumulation of experience of Open University students and graduates by employers that led to wide acceptability.

Even the oldest of India's open universities is barely twenty years old; so they have barely had time to acquire a reputation for quality, even where they might deserve it. Furthermore, the open universities have had to contend with the poor reputation created for distance education by the correspondence courses offered by India's conventional universities. These longstanding operations, which enrol hundreds of thousands of students were, and mostly still are, poor quality operations with shoddy learning materials and minimal student support. The universities use them as cash cows to subsidise their campus operations.

Ironically, although many of the courses are of poor quality, they have the advantage of being associated with prestigious universities such as the University of Delhi and the University of Madras. So students looking for distance learning have a choice between low quality courses, with no student support, that carry the name of a well-known university, and better courses from an open university that has yet to acquire its reputation.

India's Distance Education Council, the DEC, had the task of creating a quality assurance system that would make the correspondence systems of the conventional universities improve their offerings. In practice this has not yet happened for two reasons. First, until recently the DEC was embedded in the Indira Gandhi National Open University, creating a conflict of interest. Second, the conventional universities fight any move to improve quality that would reduce revenues from their correspondence courses, the profits from which outweigh any financial incentives to improve quality that the DEC can offer.

THE VIRTUAL UNIVERSITY FOR SMALL STATES OF THE COMMONWEALTH

Having sketched the case of India let us look briefly to the challenges facing small countries in expanding higher education. The Commonwealth of Learning (COL) serves the 53 countries of the Commonwealth, two thirds of which are small countries, mostly with populations of one million or fewer. Their challenge is to expand higher education whilst keeping under control the foreign exchange costs of sending students abroad or importing programmes.

As a partial solution their ministers of education have created the Virtual University for Small States of the Commonwealth. Its title is somewhat misleading. It is a collaborative consortium rather than a new institution and, although courses are being developed virtually, they will mostly be delivered by a variety of distance and face-to-face methods depending on the infrastructure available. The Commonwealth of Learning is helping with its implementation. At the moment groups of countries are collaborating virtually to create open educational resources for various courses on Wiki-Educator, a Wiki launched by COL. These can then be adapted and used by participating countries – and indeed by anyone else since they are open educational resources.

This work has thrown up some interesting questions. The first is "How open is open content?" There is open content and then there is open content. For the OERs created by collaboration within the Virtual University for Small States of the Commonwealth COL is using a Creative Commons licence qualified only by two restrictions: BY, meaning that if you use the material you must acknowledge the source; and SA (Share Alike) which requires that if you adapt the material you must put your adaptation back into the pool under the same licence.

Another challenge is how to organise quality assurance and accreditation. COL's approach is to use systematic quality processes in designing the OERs but not to attempt any kind of quality kite-marking, partly because the whole point of OERs is to generate multiple versions and assessing them all would be a nightmare. Our hypothesis is that kite marking occurs indirectly through accreditation when an OER becomes a taught course through an institution. This is not straightforward either, because most of our Commonwealth small states do not have their own universities so we need some wider transnational arrangements for recognition and credit transfer. COL and its partner countries are working with the South African Qualifications Authority on this issue.

QUALITY ASSURANCE

Within two decades the global tertiary education enterprise could have more than doubled in size, be predominantly based in what today we call developing countries, and present a greater diversity of both providers and provision. How will the world ensure the quality of such a vast enterprise? Specifically, how are governments to protect their citizens from fraudulent providers and bogus qualifications, especially when they emanate from another country? eLearning is attractive to unscrupulous operators because they can close down a website even faster than a post-office box. Cross-border tertiary education makes students particularly vulnerable to scams. Some for-profit providers only seek commercial benefit, ignoring developmental objectives and intellectual advancement. How can we create an international ethic of integrity and quality assurance?

As tertiary education expands, governments' role will increasingly be to monitor and regulate it, rather than to provide it. Many developing countries currently lack quality-assurance mechanisms, and where they do exist, as in India, they are not always properly equipped to cope with diversifying types of provision. However, countries realize that the GATS— the World Trade Organisation's General Agreement on Trade in Services—has created an inexorable trend towards increasing cross-border education supply. Governments will best respond to this trend by building strong frameworks for regulation, quality assurance, and accreditation that cover all tertiary education provision within their borders. The task for UNESCO, the Commonwealth of Learning and other intergovernmental organizations is to support national and regional developments effectively.

The tertiary education market already has plenty of dubious providers and bodies offering accreditation—some of the latter even claiming a phoney affiliation with UNESCO! Clipping the wings of such operations is in the public interest, but how can it be done? Empowering students, parents, and employers to make informed decisions is the best bulwark against deception and fraud. There are no easy solutions but here are five of the tools that already exist or are emerging:

1. UNESCO has published Study Abroad, its international guide to tertiary education institutions and scholarships, for nearly 60 years (UNESCO, 2006). It covers more than 150 countries. Recent editions include more on open/distance learning and have a section "Tools for Students." This is based in part on the excellent work of South Africa's Council on Higher Education on promoting quality literacy about tertiary education among secondary students (Naidoo, 2005).
2. UNESCO and the OECD, in an alliance covering both exporting and importing countries, have developed Guidelines for Quality Provision in Cross-Border Higher Education. They address all six stakeholder groups: governments, institutions and their staff, quality assurance agencies, student associations, professional groups, and qualification-recognition bodies (UNESCO/OECD, 2006)
3. Since the World Trade Organisation's General Agreement on Trade in Services, the GATS, is still making waves in international education, the Commonwealth of Learning and UNESCO have published a simple guide to what GATS is and is not (COL/UNESCO, 2006).
4. In 2006 UNESCO launched the pilot of a portal on recognised tertiary institutions in order to explore the feasibility of maintaining such a facility at the world level. The project follows on naturally from the Guidelines for Quality Provision in CBHE and shares their objective of protecting students from low-quality offerings and empowering them to make informed decisions based on transparent information on the quality of higher education provision.

   The basic concept is that UNESCO hosts the portal, with the competent national authorities of participating countries providing reliable information on the recognized, registered and/or accredited institutions in their country and keeping this information up to date. This obligation will stimulate some countries to rethink the issue of how they define institutions of quality and how they create the capacity to assess them.

5. The various stakeholders concerned with the quality of international education now meet under the aegis of the Global Forum on International Quality Assurance, Accreditation and the Recognition of Qualifications. It convened for the third time in Tanzania in 2007 under the theme, Learners and New Higher Education Spaces.

CONCLUSION

Starting with the objective of a significantly lower price point and using technology and good management to achieve it with a quality programme is still a revolutionary concept in education. Most for-profit institutions are still content to be "cream skimmers" operating just a little more cost effectively than their rivals. Most public institutions assume a direct correlation between cost and quality and resist attempts to achieve lower price points.

However, the millions who still thirst for tertiary education must hope that some providers, both public and for-profit, will espouse this revolutionary concept successfully. The combination of better connectivity and open educational resources could enable them to do so. If they can rise to the challenge these providers will create a tectonic shift that will bring the benefits of learning and knowledge to millions.

ACKNOWLEDGEMENTS

I acknowledge my debt to my colleagues Professor Asha Kanwar (COL) and Stamenka Uvalić-Trumbić (UNESCO) who have contributed to the data and ideas contained in this chapter.

REFERENCES

COL/UNESCO (2006) *Higher education crossing borders: A guide to the implications of the general agreement on trade in service (GATs) for cross-border education* http://www.col.org/colweb/site/pid/4059.

Daniel, J. S., Kanwar, A., & Uvalić-Trumbić, S. (2005) *Who's afraid of cross-border higher education? A developing world perspective.* Presented at the Final Plenary Session: Quality Assurance in Transnational Issues, (INQAAHE), Annual Conference

2005–Wellington, New Zealand (1 April 2005) http://www.col.org/colweb/site/pid/3617.

Daniel, J. S., Kanwar, A., & Uvalić-Trumbić, S. (2006) A tectonic shift in higher education? *Change Magazine,* July/August, *38*(4), 16–23.

Naidoo, P. (2005) *Student quality literacy and empowerment,* Council on Higher Education, South Africa.

Prahalad, C. K., (2004) *The fortune at the bottom of the pyramid: Eradicating poverty through profit.* Wharton School Publishing.

UNESCO (2006) *Study abroad,* UNESCO Publishing, http://publishing.unesco.org/details.aspx?Code_Livre=4431.

UNESCO/OECD (2006) *Guidelines for quality provision in cross-border higher education* http://portal.unesco.org/education/en/ev.php-URL_ID=41508&URL_DO=DO_TOPIC&URL_SECTION=201.html.

CHAPTER 5

THE ROLE OF ICT IN BRIDGING THE DIGITAL DIVIDE IN A HIGH-POVERTY SCHOOL DISTRICT

Amy S. C. Leh
California State University San Bernardino

Lee Grafton
Palm Spring Unified School District

Sylvester Robertson
California State University San Bernardino

INTRODUCTION

Over the last fifty years, since the initiation of the "great society" movement by President Johnson and the "War on Poverty," the federal government tracked the number of poor children in pubic schools and the breakdown of students by race to determine the effectiveness of funding. Based on the number of low-income families in a school or school district, low- or high-poverty schools were defined. In most situations, such schools also had a

ICT for Education, Development, and Social Justice, pages 65–83

high minority population reflecting the general population in the school's attendance area. Funding fluctuated depending on the political climate in the United States Congress. The achievement gap between Whites and Blacks that was identified during the initial period persists today. However, the racial and ethnic composition of enrollment in U.S. public schools has changed. In 1972, 22 percent of the students were minorities. By 2003, this number had increased to 40 percent (U.S. Department of Education, 2005), largely due to growth in the number of Hispanic students. In 2003, Hispanic students represented 19 percent of public school enrollment, up from 6 percent in 1972. The proportion of public school students who were Black or members of other minority groups increased less over this period than the proportion of students who were Hispanic (U.S. Department of Education, 2005). This shift in ethic groups compounded the achievement gap with which schools have struggled over the years. When computers were introduced into public schools, many believed they would be the innovation that would close the gap particularly in schools of high poverty and high minority enrollment.

Have computers or technology closed the gap? Unfortunately there has not been consistent evidence to support the assertion that computers have closed or even narrowed the achievement gap (Barton, 2001; Cuban, 2001; Healy, 1998; Wenglinsky, 1998; Wilson, 1999). Instead, a new problem, the digital divide, arose when computers were introduced to schools. "Digital divide" refers to the divide between people with access to new technologies (computers and the Internet) and those without (Irving, 1998). The divide arose not only in U.S. households but also in public schools. In public schools, several factors contributed to the divide and to the achievement gap, such as a low number of minorities entering and remaining in the teaching profession, high poverty schools more often having inexperienced teachers, and teachers in high poverty schools not being provided with adequate technology and not using available technology as frequently as teachers in low poverty schools.

First, low number of minorities entered and remained in the teaching profession. In 2000, only seven percent of Blacks received bachelors degrees in education (Hoffman & Uagas, 2003). Among minority teachers in K–12 schools, U.S. Department of Education (2003) reports indicated that the number of minorities, especially Blacks, who will be leaving the teaching profession (retiring) soon will outnumber teachers who recently entered the profession.

Second, schools with high minority, high poverty enrollments employed more inexperience teachers than schools with low poverty, low minority rates. National education data (U.S. Department of Education, 2003) suggested that the percentage of new teachers (three to five years experience) was higher in high poverty, high minority enrollments than in low poverty, low minority schools. Compared with White teachers, a greater proportion of Black and Hispanic teachers in public schools were beginning teachers. Similarly, public schools with the highest percentages of minority students and those with the highest percentages of limited-English proficient (LEP) students were more likely to employ beginning teachers than schools with the lowest percentages of minority students and those with the lowest percentages of LEP students.

Third, teachers in high minority, high poverty schools were generally less likely than teachers in low minority low poverty schools to use computers or the Internet for a wide range of activities (gathering information, creating instructional materials, communicating with colleagues, and instructing students). Smerdon, Cronen, Lanahan, Anderson, Lannotti, and Angeles (2000) noted that teachers in schools with lower (less than 6 percent) minority enrollments were more likely than teachers in schools with the highest (50 percent or more) minority enrollments to use technology to gather information for lesson plans (61 percent vs. 46 percent), to create instructional materials (81 percent vs. 71 percent), to conduct Internet search (53 percent vs. 41 percent) and to prepare multimedia presentations (40 percent vs. 29 percent). In addition, teachers "with more computers or computers connected to the Internet in their classrooms generally used these technologies more often than teachers with fewer computers or Internet connections" (Smerdon et al., p. 18).

Differences in the use of technology in instruction between teachers in low poverty schools and high poverty schools impacted the use of technology by students in learning. According to Hoffman and Uagas's study (2003) on Blacks in education, Black students were less likely to use computers at school than Whites. When it came to using computers at home for schoolwork, the gap was wide (36 percentage points) between Whites and Blacks and the gap continued to grow.

To bridge the digital divide between high minority, high poverty schools and low minority low, poverty schools, a great deal of the responsibility inevitably falls on school administrators and teachers. The most critical element in technology use was the preparedness and skill level of those who employed it (Wilson, 2002). Hart, Allensworth, Lauen, and Gladden (2002) suggested that once administrators provided students and teachers with sufficient and reliable technology, essential support was needed to propel its use forward. It was imperative that these educators be fully supported in this regard through adequate pre-service preparation and ongoing in-service activities (Noeth & Volkov, 2004). In return, teachers must be held accountable for the effectiveness of their uses of technology to support an enhanced learning environment.

CASE STUDY

A case is presented below that demonstrates the use of ICT to bridge the digital divide in the Palm Springs (CA) Unified School District (PSUSD), a high minority, high poverty school district. The project was supported by an Education Through Technology Competitive grant (EETT-C). The section starts with an overview of the grant and the background of the school district. We then describe the student program and faculty development, followed by the project evaluation.

Background

The EETT-C grant supported the project "Step Up to Math Mastery Integrating Technology" (SUMMIT) of PSUSD. The primary goal of the grant was to improve access to technology and to provide technology integration training to teachers and students in grades four through eight to enhance teaching and to further learning of the state academic content standards. Eligibility is limited to high-need districts. A high-need district is a district that:

> Is among those in the state with the highest numbers or percentages of children from families with incomes below the poverty line and; Serves one or more schools identified as Program Improvement (PI) schools or; Has a substantial need for assistance in acquiring and using technology, defined as having an average of 10:1 student-to-multimedia computer ratio or greater in schools serving fourth through eighth grades in the district or an average of less than 50 percent of classrooms connected to the Internet in schools serving fourth through eighth grades in the district as determined by the California School Technology Survey for the year prior to the grant award. (California Department of Education, 2007)

PSUSD, located in southern California is one of the high-need districts with the characteristics stated above. Educational Demographics 2006–2007 at California Department of Education indicated that only 21% of the students at the district were White/non-Hispanic. Hispanic or Latino students were 70% of the student population while the rest of students were Asians, African Americans etc. The district received an EETT-C grant during 2005–2006 to train 30 math teachers at two schools. The district continued to secure the EETT-C grant during 2006–2008 to train additional 30 teachers at another two schools.

The intent of the EETT-C program SUMMIT at PSUSD was to improve student achievement of California sixth to eighth grade math content standards and support the delivery of the district's state-adopted math curriculum through the use of ICT, and to permit schools to acquire the appropriate modern technology.

EETT-C Student Program

The student program was delivered with ICT that facilitated the implementation of research-based instructional strategies. These strategies, identified by Marzano et al. (2001) and Schmoker (1999), included, but were not limited to, data-based decision making, cues, timely feedback, visual and contextualized learning, synthesis of learning for deeper understanding and retention, accessibility to instructional support, and parental involvement.

Data-Based Decision Making

The school district used data generated from various electronic assessment tools to guide data-driven decision making to improve student math achievement. The tools were used to analyze each student's a) level of proficiency measured by the California Math Content Standards and district benchmarks, b) learning styles and c) level of technology proficiency. All math teachers at the school district belonged to a Site Data Team based on the grade level they taught. For example, all sixth-grade math teachers had their Site Data Team while all seventh-grade teachers had their own team. Working with teachers who taught the same grade, teachers analyzed the student data in Site Data Teams and collaborated to design instructional strategies that a) differentiated instruction, b) met individual student academic needs, and c) encouraged students to reflect on teaching and learning strategies to adjust for improvement.

Cues

Wireless InterWrite SchoolPads drew students' attention. Students were visually cued to conceptual content as engaging and reproducible curricular resources were projected through a classroom projection station—an LCD projector and an Internet-connected multimedia computer with audio system. Attention was focused with the use of electronic highlighters and drawing tools as students and teachers used Bluetooth-compatible, wireless SchoolPads to extend the capability of the classroom projection system. The SchoolPads enabled the user (teacher or student) to access, highlight, and draw on the screen from remote locations throughout the room to prompt students to attend to important material.

Timely Feedback

Qwizdom, an interactive student response system, allowed students and teachers to receive instant feedback. Students took mini-quizzes using Qwizdom. Using a Bluetooth remote device, each student selected a multiple-choice or true-false answer to solve a series of problems, for example, two-step equations. Each student's response was immediately recorded and accessible to both the student and teacher, providing instant feedback. Each student who had trouble with the concept could be immediately identified and retaught "on the spot." Immediate feedback kept student learning on target.

Visual and Contextualized Learning

Visual media were used to extend student knowledge and facilitate recall. Digital video clips from Discovery's education streaming[1] were used to motivate and engage students by providing visual representations of the concepts to be learned with contextual examples. The lessons were accessible to all students through the classroom projection station.

Synthesis of Learning for Deeper Understanding and Retention

ICT was used to enable students to access information and construct multimedia projects that demonstrated a synthesis of knowledge. At the end of curricular strands, each student worked on an individual or group project. The purpose of the project was to demonstrate and explain a mathematical concept using a "real world" example. The student accessed information and resources through Internet resources, on-line experts, and on-line communities. The student selected appropriate software applications such as *Inspiration* to organize their presentations and *Microsoft Office* products to create and display their work. Each project was evaluated by the student's teacher according to a rubric developed with the Site Data Teams. Each project included a learning reflection.

Accessibility to Instructional Support

The SchoolPad enabled the teacher to access data files and resources and provide whole class instruction from anywhere in the room. This mobility was used to encourage students to stay on task, monitor student learning, and facilitate instructional support.

Parent Involvement

ICT was used to facilitate communication with parents and students and to provide access to resources to support each student's work beyond the classroom. Attendance records, homework assignments, and grades were accessible to parents and students through Parent Connection, an on-line portal to the District, accessible from school, home, city library or neighborhood center with Internet access. Students, parents, teachers and site administrators communicated via e-mail to enable each student to accomplish learning goals.

EETT-C Faculty Development

According to research (Cradler, 2002; NCREL 2000), professional development for technology integration is most effective when the focus is on teaching and learning, rather than on technology itself. Faculty development strategies were designed to provide the teachers with the skills and aptitudes necessary to deliver the program for students. Strategies used in the program are described below.

Coaching and Mentoring to Develop Teacher Expertise

Research (Cradler, 2002) indicates that when teachers participate in coaching and mentoring programs, the teachers a) practice the new strategies more frequently, b) develop greater skills, c) use the strategies more appropriately, d) retain the basic tenets over time, and e) are more likely to discuss the new strategies with their students so the students understand what learning goals are expected. Coaching and mentoring have also been found to be an integral element in a constant improvement cycle focused on student achievement (Neufeld & Roper, 2003).

Therefore, each PSUSD EETT-C funded school had two math Coaches who attended a Coaching Academy, a partnership between California Technology Assistance Project (CTAP), the state's regional development agency, and the district. The Coaching Academy prepared the Coaches to use peer coaching methods to guide teachers in the effective use of technology to deliver the district's state-adopted math curriculum. The Coaches were trained in classroom observation skills to monitor, assess and record each targeted teacher's progress and to provide meaningful feedback to facilitate improvement. The Coaching program was on-going and Coaches met regularly with the district program manager to provide feedback to improve the program and to receive support as needed.

To ensure the Coaching Academy clearly supported the state and district standards, CTAP and the district collaborated with the CA Beginning Teacher Support and Assessment (BTSA) program, a state program that was designed to support and to increase the retention rate of beginning teachers. The collaboration ensured that the Coaching Academy and district training were consistent with and led to the attainment of the state's BTSA's Program Standards. In addition, CTAP, Coaches, and the district program manager all attended AB 466 training, a program receiving its name from an assembly bill that was created to provide specified professional development for teachers of reading and math in the public schools, to ensure the faculty development program was consistent with and clearly supported the district's state-adopted curriculum materials.

Assessment of Instructional Activities Related to Student Achievement

Research (Carter, 2000; Schmoker, 1999) shows that when teachers periodically assess instructional activities to improve instruction to increase student achievement, student academic performance improves. Therefore, each teacher, including the Coaches, developed Individual Learning Plans (ILP). With the support and instructional guidance of CTAP and the district program manager, the Coaches collaborated with the teachers to support the development of their individual plans. The ILP described the steps that teachers would take to improve their qualifications to use technology to improve student achievement and meet the goals of the program. Each teacher, including the Coaches, kept artifacts and records to document progress in meeting the goals of the ILP.

All teachers also collaborated routinely in the analysis of student performance data in Site Data Teams to target the academic learning needs of each student and reflect on the effectiveness of their teaching strategies.

Access to Differentiated Professional Development Opportunities

The program was multifaceted with a) training directly related to the teacher's content area and instructional goals, b) opportunities appropriate to teachers' varying levels of knowledge and skills, c) training in instructional and classroom management strategies to facilitate effective technology integration into the delivery of curriculum, d) training planned with input from teaching peers, e) training over multiple sessions, f) just-in-time training and support, g) training to enable teachers to assist students in the use of computers to learn higher-order concepts, h) time to rethink instructional approaches, and i) opportunities to meaningfully engage with colleagues and materials.

A variety of opportunities was available to enable the teachers to customize the training to fit their individual needs. Summer one-week training, weekly Data Team meetings, online, and other face-to-face and hands-on opportunities were offered from the district, Coaches, and CTAP. All activities were: a) focused on improving each student's grade-level proficiency in mastering the CA Math Content Standards; b) planned with input from teaching peers; c) delivered and supported over time, as appropriate; d) based on learner's needs as determined by the Coaches and through a Technology Integration Proficiency Survey. Just-in-time support was provided by the Coaches, district program manager, district help desk technicians, and through on-line training opportunities.

Time and the structure to rethink instructional strategies were facilitated with the development and sharing of the ILPs and collaborative planning opportunities. Collaboration with colleagues was available through the District's network, website, e-mail, and structured professional learning communities. Time for collaboration was paid through grant funds and was important for grant development. The teachers developed and shared standards-based lessons and curricular resources through these media.

Access to High Quality Curricular Resources

When professional development programs include teacher access to high quality curricular resources that use technology to improve student achievement, teacher use of technology for teaching and learning increases (ISTE, 2001). Teachers referred to the district website for lessons and resources that were directly related to the curriculum materials and the CA math standards, such as resources compiled by the CTAP Region IV Middle School Math Project. Teachers also collaborated to share lessons and resources on the district network.

PROGRAM EVALUATION

Classroom is the core of K–12 education in our society and is also the place where content, professional development, and educational theories are intertwined and presented (Cohen & Ball, 1999; Lampert, 2001). Thus, the program evaluation mainly relied on data collected from classroom observations and interviews. An external evaluator, a university professor in Instructional Technology, conducted the program evaluation. We report here on evaluation conducted during 2005–2006.

Data Collection and Analysis

The external evaluator conducted two classroom observations: one at the end of January 2006 and the other at the end of May 2006. For each classroom observation, she randomly selected ten teachers from the grant participating teachers, five teachers from each school. To ensure that the evaluations were conducted at all grade levels (grade six, seven, and eight) and at classrooms of both male and female teachers, the professor randomly re-selected teachers when necessary. The teachers were informed ahead of time about the classroom observations and interviews. The classroom observation of each teacher lasted 40–50 minutes, depending on the length of the class period.

The evaluation was conducted using mixed methods, combining quantitative and qualitative components. The evaluator used a classroom observation method and instrument that were developed by the American Institutes for Research and modified by the evaluator. During the classroom observation, the evaluator kept a narrative log documenting classroom activities with the clock time at each shift of activity. For example, when the teacher moved from one activity (teacher presenting information) to another activity (teacher walking around and guiding student work), the time was recorded. After the observation, she analyzed the data by sorting the narrative data according to eight categories and later converting it into numerical data. During the analysis process, only major activities were categorized. For example, the activity of the teacher checking student attendance was not considered to be significant and was not categorized. The eight categories were: Activity Organization, Teacher Activities, Student Focus, Student Behavior, Student Engagement, Technology Use by Teachers, Teacher's Familiarity with Technology, and Technology Use by Students. Technology in the categories referred to technology covered in the EETT-C professional development activities. Within each category were subheadings (see Table 5.1).

The evaluator conducted interviews after classroom observations. She asked the teachers to clarify information relevant to the classroom observations and to answer questions about their professional development. During the interviews in January, each interviewee described the impact of the professional development on their personal productivity and instruction. They also provided details on their most beneficial training and offered suggestions on making the EETT-C professional development better. During the interviews in May, each interviewee explained how the professional development impacted a) his/her teaching, specifically on course preparation and instruction, b) his/her students' learning, specifically on how students learned, classroom behavior, and performance, and c) his/her communication, specifically with his/her colleagues, students, and parents. In addition, the interviewees provided advice to teachers participating in the following year's grant activities and gave suggestions on improving the professional development.

RESULTS

The results gathered from the classroom observation during January indicated that the teachers either frequently used the technology, which was introduced through EETT-C program, or rarely used it. Seventy-three percent of the activities contained instruction in which teachers spent 76% to 100% of class time on using the technology (see Table 5.2). These technologies were all new to the teachers, but through the training, the majority of the teachers became familiar with their use. Students showed high levels of engagement and low levels of class disruption (see Tables 5.3 and 5.4). The results revealed the success of the professional development strategies during the first stage of program implementation.

TABLE 5.1 Classroom Observation Coding Sheet

Activity Organization	
AO1	Teacher-led whole class
AO2	Student-led whole class
AO3	Small group or pair cooperative
AO4	Independent activity
Teacher Activities	
TA1	Presenting information
TA2	Leading student work
TA3	Supporting student work
TA4	Providing feedback for students
TA5	Evaluating progress
Student Focus	
SF1	Whole class led by instructor
SF2	Whole class interactive
SF3	Student or group presentation
SF4	Individual reading or work
SF5	Pair work
SF6	Interactive group work on a project
Student Behavior	
SB1	No significant classroom disruptions
SB2	Small disruptions from multiple sources
SB3	Small number persistently disruptive
SB4	Large number disruptive throughout
Student Engagement	
SE1	0–25% exhibiting on on-task behavior
SE2	26–50% exhibiting on on-task behavior
SE3	51–75% exhibiting on on-task behavior
SE4	76–100% exhibiting on on-task behavior
Technology Use by Teachers	
TT1	0–25% teacher's time using technology
TT2	26–50% teacher's time using technology
TT3	51–75% teacher's time using technology
TT4	76–100% teacher's time using technology
Teacher's Familiarity with Technology	
TFT1	0–25% familiarity
TFT2	26–50% familiarity
TFT3	51–75% familiarity
TFT4	76–100% familiarity
Technology Use by Students	
TS1	0–25% student's time using technology
TS1	26–50% student's time using technology
TS1	51–75% student's time using technology
TS1	76–100% student's time using technology

TABLE 5.2 Technology Use by Teachers

	January
0–25% teacher's time using technology	27%
26–50% teacher's time using technology	0%
51–75% teacher's time using technology	0%
76–100% teacher's time using technology	73%

TABLE 5.3 Student Engagement

	January
0–25% exhibiting on on-task behavior	0%
26–50% exhibiting on on-task behavior	0%
51–75% exhibiting on on-task behavior	14%
76–100% exhibiting on on-task behavior	86%

TABLE 5.4 Student Behavior

	January
No significant disruptions	86%
Small disruptions from multiple Sources	0%
Small number persistently disruptive	5%
Large number disruptive throughout	9%

When the results of the January evaluation were presented to the Coaches and program manager, many classroom activities were marked as "Whole class passive," ("Whole class led by Instructors" in the coding sheet). Some Coaches wondered why the whole class was considered to be passive while student engagement level was high and while teachers frequently used technology. The evaluator explained that during the observations a common practice appeared repeatedly: a teacher presented multiple-choice questions using the SchoolPad and students chose a response—1, 2, 3, or 4. Although students were engaged, they were passively responding to teachers' questions. This practice was also noted by a couple of Coaches during their observations. They found that instructional strategies that were previously used seemed to be significantly decreased or disappear from classroom. After an extensive discussion, the grant leadership team decided to bring the professional development to a higher level by emphasizing appropriate use of technology and its connection with other instructional strategies.

This modification later contributed to a greater number of instructional activities in the classroom. Instructional activities increased from 22 in January to 36 in May (see Table 5.5). The variety of classroom activities also noticeably increased in May. For example, in January only one teacher had four major instructional activities while in May five teachers had four or more major instructional activities. The practice, common in January, of a teacher only presenting multiple-choice questions using the technology and students choosing an answer, had significantly decreased by May. Instead, the professor observed a variety of classroom activities, such as students teaching each other, constructing questions for other students, and presenting their work. This change resulted in a shift of students' role from passive to active in learning (see Table 5.6): from 68% to 31% in the subheading of "whole class led by instructors" ("whole class passive").

The results gathered from the classroom observations indicated that a) the teachers frequently used the technology introduced in the professional development (see Table 5.7), b) students showed high level of engagement (see Table 5.8) and low level of class disruption (see Tables 5.9), c) student use of technology increased noticeably (see Table 5.10), and d) all of the teachers who utilized the technology were familiar with the use of such technology (see Table 5.11). The results indicated the success of the program.

TABLE 5.5 Instructional Activities and Technology Use

	January	May
# of activities	22 # of Activities: 1 2 3 4 # of Teachers: 1 4 3 1	36 # of Activities: 1 2 3 4 5 # of Teachers: 1 0 4 2 3
Interwrite	89%	90%
Qwizdom	22%	50%
Video	0%	20%

TABLE 5.6 Student Focus

	January	May
Whole class led by Instructors	68%	31%
Whole class interactive	14%	36%
Student presentation	0%	6%
Individual work	14%	19%
Pair work	0%	8%

TABLE 5.7 Technology Use by Teachers

	January	May
0–25% teacher's time using technology	27%	22%
26–50% teacher's time using technology	0%	0%
51–75% teacher's time using technology	0%	0%
76–100% teacher's time using technology	73%	78%

TABLE 5.8 Student Engagement

	January	May
0–25% exhibiting on on-task behavior	0%	0%
26–50% exhibiting on on-task behavior	0%	3%
51–75% exhibiting on on-task behavior	14%	11%
76–100% exhibiting on on-task behavior	86%	86%

TABLE 5.9 Student Behavior

	January	May
No significant disruptions	86%	86%
Small disruptions from multiple Sources	0%	6%
Small number persistently disruptive	5%	6%
Large number disruptive throughout	9%	2%

TABLE 5.10 Technology Use by Students

	January	May
0–25% student's time using technology	86%	53%
26–50% student's time using technology	0%	8%
51–75% student's time using technology	0%	11%
76–100% student's time using technology	14%	28%

TABLE 5.11 Teacher's Familiarity with Technology

	January	May
51–75% familiarity with technology	12%	0%
76–100% familiarity with technology	88%	100%

During the interviews, all teachers in one form or another addressed the usefulness of the district EETT-C program. They reported that the professional development increased their personal productivity, enhanced their instruction, and impacted their students' learning and behavior. To them, the students were more "motivated," "engaged," "involved," "focused," "active," and "excited." The teachers interviewed stated it was difficult to say if the professional development made an impact on student academic performance; nevertheless, the teachers believed that the program will make an impact on student academic performance in the near future. Furthermore, the project fostered a rich professional learning community in which teachers frequently communicated with each other, exchanged their instructional material, and shared instructional resources via district network.

DISCUSSIONS

Data from the U.S. Department of Education (2003) indicated that a low number of minorities entered and remained in the teaching profession. PSUSD presented a different picture. Data in California Department of Education showed that, during 2001–2002, 89% of the teachers at the district were White/non-Hispanic, 6% of the teachers were Hispanic or Latino, and 6% teachers were Asians, African Americans etc. During 2006–2007, 84% of the teachers at the district were White/non-Hispanic, 10% of the teachers were Hispanic or Latino, and 6% teachers were Asians, African Americans or other racial or ethnic groups. The data revealed that the number of minority teachers at the district slightly increased from 12% to 16% during the past five years. This indicated that the district has been working to increase number of minority teachers at the district.

Although the number of minority teachers at the district increased, the racial composition of the student body was not reflected in the racial composition of the teacher body. Educational Demographics 2006–2007 at California Department of Education indicated that 21% of the students at the district were White/non-Hispanic, 70% of the students were Hispanic or Latino, and 10% students were Asians, African Americans or other racial or ethnic groups. During the same year, 84% of the teachers at the district were White/non-Hispanic, 10% of the teachers were Hispanic or Latino, and 6% teachers were Asians, African Americans or other racial or ethnic groups. In other words, the 80% of all students were minorities, while only 16% of all teachers belonged to a minority. This discrepancy is not district specific, but is a known national phenomenon.

Teachers in high minority, high poverty schools were generally unlikely to use computers or the Internet for a wide range of activities (gathering information, creating instructional materials, communicating with colleagues, and instructing students) at schools (Smerdon et. al., 2000). This phenomenon was apparent at the two schools that were added to the 2006–2008 EETT-C program. There the external evaluator observed classes before the start of the EETT-C program and noticed that only technology available in the classrooms consisted of overhead projectors and a couple of old computers sitting in the corners. With those types of technology, it was difficulty, nearly impossible, for the teachers to create instructional materials and instruct students in the same way as teachers who were equipped with the 21st century ICT.

Hart, Allensworth, Lauen, and Gladden (2002) suggested that administrators should provide students and teachers with sufficient and reliable technology. Administrators of PSUSD worked hard and successfully secured the million-dollar EETT-C grant to provide math teachers of middle schools at the district with modern ICT. The technologies, such as mobile carts, InterWrite SchoolPad, the student response system (Qwizdom, unitedstreaming etc.) allowed the teachers to use computers and the Internet for a wide range of activities.

Noeth and Volkov (2004) emphasized the importance of professional development. After putting technology into teachers' hands, PSUSD administrators further fully supported the teachers through ongoing in-service activities and technology training, for instance, summer training, weekly Data Team meetings, and just-in-time mentoring.

The evaluation results indicated that the use of ICT positively impacted the EETT-C teachers. Noeth and Volkov (2004) noted that, in return, teachers must be held accountable for the effectiveness of their use of technology to support an enhanced learning environment. Teachers of the PSUSD EETT-C program were held accountable for the effectiveness of their use of technology. At Data Team meetings, teachers brainstormed ways of using technology for effectively teaching mathematics and shared their instructional materials via the district computer network. In addition to supporting the district learning environments, some teachers further shared their projects at regional and national conventions to benefit educators beyond the district.

The PSUSD EETT-C 2005–2006 program has ended and its 2006–2008 program is in its second year of implementation. The program has successfully transformed the math departments of the four EETT-C schools with state-of-the-art technologies and with better-trained teachers. The grant project has also served as an impetus for organizational change. More departments, e.g., special education, of the four EETT-C schools have started searching for funds to support them in conducting similar activities for their teachers. The changes at the four EETT-C schools are impacting other schools as well; for instance, other schools are also seeking funds to purchase hardware and /software used in the EETT-C program.

While district administrators experienced the successes of the EETT-C program, they also encountered challenges. One of the challenges was student access to technology at schools. EETT-C purchased mobile carts with laptops and sets of Qwizdom for student use in class. Since the number of carts and sets was insufficient, teachers had to take turns using the devices and consequently had to plan their instruction around the availability of the technology. Scheduling their instruction around availability of equipment has not been a good approach to technology integration. As to be expected, several teachers voiced the need for their own sets of Qwizdom and laptops.

In addition, student access to technology at home was another challenge. Since the majority of the students came from low-income families and did not have computers or Internet access at home, it was difficult or nearly impossible for students to work on assignments that depended on access to computers or the Internet. Consequently, for them learning with technology, e.g., conducting research using the Internet, has been limited at home.

This challenge also occurred when teachers tried to communicate with parents electronically. Many teachers expressed that EETT-C program greatly enhanced communication between them and other teachers, e.g., teachers sharing instructional resources via district network. However, communicating with parents electronically was a challenge. A teacher explained that she experimented with sending parents information via email instead of through regular mail. Later, she switched back to paper-based communication due to parents' lack of access to technology.

Fulfilling the public's expectations for student performance was another challenge. The public is inclined to measure success of a project like EETT-C by student achievement test results. If student achievement scores do not increase, they question the effectiveness of such a program. Expecting student performance to increase in one or two years is not realistic for a project that has technology as an integral part. As professionals know, it takes time to train teachers in the use of technology and in integrating technology effectively into instruction, and only then can the teacher training impact student learning, which will be reflected in student performance only over time.

CONCLUSION

The achievement gap has existed in the U.S. public schools for decades. It was hoped that the introduction of computers to schools would bridge the gap. Unfortunately, results have been mixed in this one example, and the disparities between schools continued with the rise of the digital divide as computers were introduced to schools. To bridge the digital divide, PSUSD secured a million-dollar EETT-C grant and delivered a student program and faculty development program. Instructional strategies used to deliver the student program included, but were not limited to, data-based decision making, cues, timely feedback, visual and contextualized learning, synthesis of learning for deeper understanding and retention, accessibility to instructional support, and parental involvement. Faculty development consisted of coaching and mentoring to develop teacher expertise, assessment of instructional activities related to student achievement, access to differentiated professional development opportunities, and access to high quality curricular resources. Classroom observations and interviews revealed that the program was successful. The program not only made a positive impact on the participating teachers and students but also could serve as a professional development model for the district, especially for high minority, high poverty school districts, as well as for other communities.

REFERENCES

Barton, P. E. (2001) *Facing the hard facts in education reform.* Princeton, NJ: Educational Testing Service.

California Department of Education. (2007). *Enhancing education through technology (EETT).* Sacramento, CA: California Department of Education.

Carter, S. C. (2000). *No excuses: Lessons from 21 high-performing, high-poverty schools.* Washington, DC: The Heritage Foundation.

Cohen, D., & Ball, D. L. (2001). Making change: Instruction and its improvement. *Phi Delta Kappan,* 73–77.

Cradler, J. (2002). Research implications for preparing teachers to use technology. *Learning & Leading with Technology, 30*(1) 50–54.

Cuban, L. (2001). *Oversold and underused: Computers in the classroom.* Cambridge, MA: Harvard University Press.

Hart, H. M., Allensworth, E., Lauen, D. L., & Gladden, R. M. (2002). *Educational technology: Availability and use in Chicago's public schools.* Chicago: Consortium on Chicago School Research. [http://www.consortium-chicago.org/publications/pdfs/p56.pdf]

Healy, J. M. (1998). *Failure to connect: How computers affect our children's minds—for better and worse.* New York: Simon & Schuster.

Hoffman, K., & Uagas, C. (2003). *Status and trends in the education of blacks, NCES 2003-034.* Washington, DC: U.S. Department of Education, National Center for Education Statistics.

Irving, L. (1998). *Falling through the net: Defining the digital divide.* Washington DC: U.S. Department of Commerce, National Telecommunications and Information Administration.

ISTE. (2001). *National educational standards for teachers.* Eugene, OR: ISTE NETS Project.

Lampert, M. (2001). *Teaching with problems and the problems of teaching.* New Haven: Yale University Press.

Marzano, R. J., Pickering, D. J., & Pollock, J. E. (2001). *Classroom instruction that works: Research-based strategies for increasing student achievement.* Alexandria, VA: ASCD.

McArthur, D. (1987). Developing computer tools to support learning and performing complex cognitive tasks. In D. Berger and C. Pedzek (Eds.), *Applications of cognitive psychology: Computing and education* (pp. 281–307). New Jersey: Lawrence Erlbaum Associates.

NCREL, (2000). *Critical issue: Providing professional development for effective technology use.* Retrieved January 18, 2005, from NCREL Web Site: http://www.ncrel.org/sdrs/areas/issues/methods/technlgy/te1000.htm.

Neufeld, B., & Roper, D. (2003). *Coaching: A strategy for developing instructional capacity.* Washington, DC: Annenberg Institute for School Reform.

Noeth, R. J., & Volkov, B. B. (2004). *Evaluating the effectiveness of technology in our schools: ACT policy report.* Iowa City, IA: American College Testing ACT Inc.

Schmoker, M. (1999). Results: The key to continuous school improvement (2nd ed.). Alexandria, VA: ASCD

Smerdon, B., Cronen, S., Lanahan, L., Anderson, J., Lannotti N., & Angeles, J. (2000). *Teachers' tools for the 21st century: A report on teachers' use of technology.* Washington, DC: U.S. Department of Education, National Center for Education Statistics.

U.S. Department of Education. (2003). *The Condition of education 2003. NCES 2003-067.* Washington, DC: U.S. Department of Education, National Center for Education Statistics.

U.S. Department of Education. (2005). *The Condition of education 2005, NCES 2005-094.* Washington, DC: U.S. Department of Education, National Center for Education Statistics.

Wenglinsky, H. (1998). *Does it compute? The relationship between educational technology and student achievement in mathematics.* Princeton, NJ: Educational Testing Service.

Wilson, J. I. (2002). A visit to the Springdale school system in 2012. In *Visions 2020: Transforming education and training through advanced technologies.* Washington, DC: U.S. Department of Commerce. [http://www.technology.gov/reports/TechPolicy/2020Visions.pdf.]

Wilson, T. (1999). Unequal computer access and the achievement gap. *Computer Equity @ School, Equity Coalition,* 5, 26–31.

NOTE

1. http://streaming.discoveryeducation.com/index.cfm

CHAPTER 6

IS THERE A ROLE FOR INFORMATION AND COMMUNICATIONS TECHNOLOGIES IN THE EDUCATION AND DEVELOPMENT OF DISADVANTAGED RURAL COMMUNITIES?

Tom Power
The Open University, UK

Kimberley Porteus, Brian Ramadiro, Nomakholwa Tshume
Nelson Mandela Institute, South Africa

Shumi Makalema
DEEP

Rhodri Thomas
The Open University, UK

ICT for Education, Development, and Social Justice, pages 85–102

INTRODUCTION

In this chapter we explore the intersection of development, education, and Information Communication Technologies (ICTs), in the contexts of schools serving disadvantaged rural or peri-urban communities in the Eastern Cape, the poorest province of South Africa. We draw primarily upon the experiences of research and development collaboration carried out between 2001 and 2006 by two teams, one from the Nelson Mandela Institute for Education and Rural Development (NMI) in South Africa, and the other from the UK Open University (OU). Both teams brought experiences and insights into the educational experiences of rural communities (Nelson Mandela Foundation, 2005) and the possibilities of new mobile technologies for teacher education and practice in such communities (Leach, Ahmet, Makalima, & Power, 2006). These teams worked together to explore and evaluate the impacts of ICT interventions in schools serving disadvantaged rural communities in the Eastern Cape, some of the findings of which are presented here.

Possibly more significant than the evaluation findings themselves, the process of working together, talking and thinking through the issues of the messy intersection of rurality, education, and ICT, caused the two teams to grapple with difficult and diverse conceptual understandings and perspectives. Despite deep mutual respect, personal affinity, and common goals between the teams, this struggle for shared understanding proved profoundly difficult. Nonetheless the teams decided to push through, to try and jointly conceptualize an understanding that gave room and voice to the lived experiences of the rural poor, of their hopes and struggles with educational challenges, of the promise and the pain that ICT offered them, and of the deeper tides that turned the waters we were wading through.

At the forefront of this effort, was our late friend and colleague, Professor Jenny Leach. This chapter draws heavily on internal documents shared between NMI and OU teams, many authored by Professor Leach, and responded to by Kim Porteous, the director of NMI, though they are all the product of team discussions. This chapter is a first attempt to set out publicly some of the ideas and issues we grappled with. It is incomplete and partial, drawing on fragments and starting points. It does not seek to provide answers, nor even questions, but it seeks to bring to the surface some of the slippery concepts and challenges that we have struggled to grasp and to name. It is a beginning.

First, we will set the scene by considering some of the issues around rurality, education, and development in the global south. We will then consider some of the discourse and rhetoric around the role of ICT for education and development. We will then describe the methodology and rationale for our evaluation of an ICT intervention in rural schools in the Eastern

Cape (EC), before presenting the findings. In our discussion, we seek to understand how the discourse, concepts, and practices are playing out in the experiences of those in rural schools, and what the implications are for future roles of ICT in rural education and development

EDUCATION, DEVELOPMENT, AND RURALITY

There can be little doubt that education is a core component of any meaningful vision of international development, having an impact on a broad range of development indicators:

> macroeconomists have emphasized the impact . . . on economic growth . . . microeconomists . . . estimate both private and social rates of return . . . are high . . .
>
> [Education plays] a crucial role in the adoption of new agricultural technologies . . .
>
> Education is also seen as a means to improve health and reduce fertility . . .
>
> [Education] is seen as an intrinsic good in itself . . .
> (Glewe & Kremer 2005, p. 1)

The Department for International Development (2006) reports that in low-income countries:

- With each additional year of education, average earnings rise 11%.
- With each additional year of a girl's education, her eventual wages rise 10–20%.
- With each additional year of a girl's education, the death rate of her children under 5 years falls by 8%.

Increasingly, education is being seen as "the" core component of international development (UNICEF 2005, Moon, 2007); indeed Gordon Brown recently identified education as "the key to the ultimate development goal: the empowerment of the poor, and of the world's poorest countries" (Brown & Benn 2006).

But there are multiple and complex challenges in providing free, high quality education to all the world's children; in most developing nations, there are issues of grade repetition, low leaving age, teacher absenteeism, teacher shortages, building shortages, double shifts and large class sizes (Glewe & Kramer, 2005, p. 2), as well as a predominance of under-trained or untrained teachers (UNESCO, 2000, 2005). These challenges are often most acutely experienced in rural areas (Mulkeen, 2005), where 70% of the world's poor live (FAO & UNESCO, 2003, p. 27). Of the seventy-two million children in the world who have no access to even the most rudimentary education (UNESCO, 2007, p. 1), recent estimates suggest that over 80% of these live in rural areas (UN 2006, p. 7).

Nor is it just children who experience greater educational difficulties with the situation in rural schools and communities; teachers too face substantial challenges beyond those met by their urban colleagues. Mattson (2006) points to the isolation experienced by rural teachers, the lack of access to reference and other teaching materials, and poor management and support. Indeed, for many, the prospect of teaching in rural communities is sufficiently difficult and daunting that trained teachers try to avoid rural placements "... people are going to kick against posting to the very places where their services are needed" or relocate to towns and cities and soon as they are able (Hedges, 2002).

Such circumstances did not just "come to be," we must also take into account how such social systems have been constructed, to consider the historical placement of power and justice (Kincheloe & McLaren, 2002) within the previously colonized south (Ngũgĩwa Thiongo, 1986). In the particular circumstances of South Africa, by the end of the apartheid period, only 14% of the land belonged to the black majority, with most of this under communal tenure, with many African people concentrated in re-tribalised homelands (Nelson Mandela Foundation, 2005, p. 133); the 1954 Bantu Education Act removed the bulk of African schools to such rural areas, with separate curricula and colleges of teacher training. The teachers, mostly women, were unable to access housing subsidies in the villages, as land was owned communally or was under the control of the village chief. Teachers were therefore drawn to live in townships and towns rather than in the rural communities where they taught. This legacy is one factor that contributes to the current situation, where many teachers commute to rural schools, living separate lives in towns (where their own children are often educated), and experiencing tensions with the local community of the school (NMF, 2005, p. 134). It is within these contexts that our evaluation took place.

Emerging voices celebrated the educational achievements of ten years of democracy in South Africa, with reforms in administration, budgeting, curriculum, school infrastructure, school nutrition programs and the establishment of democratic structures for local school governance. But at the same time, it was acutely aware of how differently these reforms were experienced between urban and rural communities.

> Rural education, in particular, lags behind educational development in other parts of the country. This is despite the fact that the vast majority of school going children in South Africa live in rural areas. The poverty of education in rural areas is integrally linked to inadequate employment, infrastructure, nutrition and health, rest, exercise and entertainment of the rural poor... (NMF, 2005, p. 132)

So we see that although education is widely recognized to be at the heart of international development, there are particular challenges to achieving educational quality in the rural areas where the majority of the world's poor live. If educational development goals are to be meaningfully achieved, it will be necessary to better understand and take account of issues of rurality.

IS THERE A ROLE FOR ICT?

The majority of ICT projects in low income countries are located in urban contexts, even when the projects explicitly aim to be working towards the Millennium Development Goals (InfoDev, World Bank, 2003, p. 83). There is sparse empirical research on the particular experiences of rural and impoverished communities in the use of ICT for teaching and learning, and the voices and experiences of those living in such communities are rarely heard.

In the discourse of global capitalism, ICT tools and networks are seen as the glue that binds together the global community, through communication, education and economic activity. In such a discourse, disadvantaged rural communities are "black holes" (Castells, 1998). The implication from this is that on passing the "event horizon" one leaves the networked world, and can no longer interact. Such communities are effectively invisible to and excluded from the wider world. In such a discourse, where isolation from the digitally networked world is the definition of the problem, connection to the digitally networked world is the only definitive solution. This is the essence of the narrative of the digital divide.

Within such a narrative, ICTs have come to symbolically represent the bridge between impoverished and wealthy spaces; the between "bad" and "good" education; offering the possibility of inclusion and participation. We shall see later just how pervasive this symbolic imagination has become. If one accepts such a narrative, then the "need" for ICT in rural communities is inevitable. This discourse deals with the WHY and WHAT issues of rural ICT: if the WHY is to achieve development (economic, educational, political, social)—then the WHAT, is inevitably to provide ICTs. A second layer of discourse may be seen as addressing the WHO, WHERE, HOW issues. Here there is a competition between the relatively powerful "technical" discourse and a weaker "educational" discourse.

The "technical discourse" is largely defined by technology experts, focusing on questions of capacity, infrastructure, form and function, to specify large scale ICT-and-educational investments. Pimienta (2007) argues that many of the "ICT for development" projects fail to achieve any significant impact "in the field" (sic), because the investment has been focused predominantly on technical matters, such as the provision of equipment, connectivity and security: what Pimienta calls the "Infrastructure." In our experience, many donor driven ICT interventions in rural communities tend to focus their funding and effort almost exclusively on such infrastructure.

This is in tension with the educational discourse, that argues such investments can only succeed if seen exclusively through the lens of educational perspectives.

> The digital divide is nothing other than the reflection of the social divide in the digital world...Offering an access to ICT does not necessarily imply that the people who benefit from the technologies can thus access opportunities for human development...education...plays an essential part in the process...
>
> As long as decision makers...are not ready to consider these issues, and keep on favoring a mere technological vision, we will suffer... (Pimienta, 2007, p. 1)

We argue that one of the most important contestations around ICT for rural education and development is to strengthen the voice and power of educators and their communities over the discourse of technicians and global capital. Along with a growing discourse among African intellectuals (Nabudere, 2003) we focus on the "unheard" voices, and the context in which these voices and experiences are derived.

This requires a nuanced approach. It becomes important both to listen to and to separate out the "promise" of ICT (what it has come to represent) and the "lived experience" of ICT(what effect, good or bad, it has had), for rural schools and their communities. This is exemplified in the following story, told by colleagues in the NMI, of a visit to a school that had received a new, high quality ICT suite from a donor:

> This was a very rural school, by the time you arrived, you hoped it wasn't going to rain because it would be a difficult drive back. I sat down with the entire staff team and asked them to tell me about the school. They began to tell me everything that they did wrong. They spoke softly, emanating a sense of failure. I asked them about what was going well at the school—a small thing that made them proud. They looked down. The principal said she could not think of anything.
>
> I started asking about the computer lab. They said they had received the donation (12 months ago). They said they were extremely grateful. They said that they knew that computers made a good school. They said that the community had started to send their children to this school in more numbers, seeing now that the school would be "high quality." They had received a small amount of training in a nearby town. There was a generator that could light a small city that they feared to turn on. We went to the computer lab, and all the computers were still wrapped in plastic. We went to the generator and

showed them how to turn it on. We then turned on all the computers, and the software seemed to be loaded properly.

Finally opening up, they talked about the heaviness of what they carried. They said that the relationship between the community and the school had reached a low. Parents blamed teachers for having "everything that is needed" to provide a high quality education, and still they were "failing." As we were pulling out, the teachers asked us if we could please turn off the computers. They were convinced that they may break them if they turned them off themselves.

AN EVALUATION OF ICT INTERVENTIONS IN RURAL SCHOOLS

Rationale

In 2002, a consortium of partners came together to create "ICT centres of excellence" in fifteen schools associated with the NMF in the Eastern Cape, aiming to "put ICT into schools as tools for educators to use primarily to deepen the process of teaching and learning." A technical specification was derived to equip schools with suites of new desktop computers, internet access and the latest software. In 2004 the NMI started to take a lead role in this initiative. They found that most of the designated schools had not yet received ICT equipment, the experience of those that had reported as "disempowering—at times in the extreme." The NMI carried out a monitoring exercise amongst those schools still expecting to receive equipment, finding them far from ready. They were able to slow the process a little and implement a range of thoughtful strategies and tools to involve the communities in making this an educational intervention, including:

- Creating an assessment team to visit each site;
- School based planning workshops;
- School by school negotiations with a range of stake-holders;
- Formulating school ICT development plans;
- Agreements of honour outlining the roles of stake-holders.

Photo 6.1 School governing body meeting.

Ultimately 16 schools were involved in the project, with a further eight schools which had received ICT suites prior to this project. The funders hoped to create these schools into "centres of excellence" through this investment in technology. A team of young people, with the technical skills to install computer networks, retrofit classrooms with wiring and security measures, and the resilience to live and work as a team was recruited, to spend a week at a time living with each rural community, installing the equipment and training the teachers and community members. Most of the schools also participated in a subsequent one week ICT and curriculum training program, delivered through SchoolNet South Africa.

The URSD's internal NMF (2005b) report drew on comprehensive documentation to summarize the work undertaken. Two key messages came out of this document: first, that rurality presented distinctive challenges and opportunities; second, the complexity involved:

> Understand the complexity... Interventions, including ICT, are mediated transactions (do not talk to them or for them, talk with them), try to get a shared understanding....
>
> [there are] other dimensions that go beyond "just ICT." In certain instances one needs to get a bigger picture of events/relations, than just narrower focus on ICT. (Nelson Mandela Foundation, 2005b)

One of the report's main recommendations was that a further evaluation of participants' experiences be carried out that might contribute to developing an ICT concept document, exploring how ICTs can contribute toward quality education and community development. This is the work reported here.

Methodology

A joint Open University and URSD research team collaborated to design a small scale evaluation, drawing on a range of data sources, including a qualitative survey in schools, observations, interviews, questionnaires, artifact collection, numerical aggregates of equipment and demographic characteristics as well as visual images, both photographic and those drawn by teachers. We judged that such an approach would allow us to gain the deepest insights in the brief time available.

During a one week period in October 2005, the researchers worked in two teams, each having one OU and one URSD team member, supported by one ICT specialist. The teams visited nine (38%) of the twenty-four rural schools that participated in the intervention, interviewing school principals and representatives of the school governing bodies; observing learners using the computers; assessing technical issues; forty-five teachers were interviewed and thirty-five teacher questionnaires administered. Of the forty-five teachers, 71% were male; ten specialized in science, ten in literacy and eight in numeracy, with a range of other subjects being represented in small numbers.

The main limitation of the research activity was time; the data could only provide a snapshot of issues and experiences. It was also hoped that observations of learners using computers would provide an opportunity to discuss their uses and views of ICT. In the event, teachers needed time to talk about their experiences, as well as to raise issues with the technical specialists. In some cases learners had left for home by the time we arrived at the school. It was possible, nevertheless, to observe many learners using the computers and explore computer hard drives to get a picture of the kind of products commonly being made, together with the software applications in common use.

Findings

First and foremost, it is important to say that the ICT interventions succeeded in their aims, in that in all nine schools visited:

- School governing bodies and school staff had been involved in school based planning workshops and had drawn up school ICT development plans;
- A classroom had been retrofitted as a computer suite, with computers, servers and software all installed, powered, networked and working;
- Several members of the school staff (and often some members of the community) had participated in week-long school-based training using the schools new computers;
- There were two or more teachers who felt confident in turning the computers on and off, rudimentary uses of office software, and "first line" trouble shooting of minor technical problems.

Furthermore, over 90% of all the teachers rated the training they had received as having "some" to "significant" impact. Over a third of the teachers completing the questionnaires reported using the new computers for school based work for between one to two hours a week; seven of the teachers also had computers at home, which they reportedly used for preparation. So, in achieving the goals of many ICT for development projects, these rural school interventions had been remarkably successful. Not only was equipment installed and working in every rural school, but teachers had been trained in ICT skills, in school, on the equipment they were to use;

furthermore, the local community and school had prepared ICT development plans together. Below are some representative teacher comments:

> After I have attended the training I have attained some growth professionally.
>
> The computers save a lot of time, for example, when planning for classroom work.
>
> Some learners are very keen and they spend extra time often [after] school.

So on a technical level, this seemed to be a very successful set of interventions, particularly given the rural nature of all the schools. But what impact had the interventions had on the teachers, pupils and schools?

Sixteen teachers said training had "some" to "high" impact on their ability to use computers with learners. Although three quarters of the teachers were subject specialists in literacy, numeracy or science, none of these teachers were able to give any examples of how they had used computers to support work with the learners in their subject. On examining the computers, the research teams were unable to find any curriculum related artifacts (such as teacher resources or pupil work). The teams came across no evidence of any kind that the computers were making any contribution to the practice of teaching or learning in any of the schools, except for the "subject" of ICT. One of the teachers stated in the interview: "We are experiencing a shortage of programmes for my subject—history. Computers must be included in our curriculum."

Only four of the teachers were subject specialists in computer literacy, yet twenty-three (more than half) of those interviewed now found themselves responsible for teaching ICT as a subject to learners, since showing some aptitude with the computers during the training. The teachers we spoke to knew why they were not able to use the computers to transform teaching

Photo 6.2 Teacher working in computer suite after school.

and learning in their classrooms. They didn't have any curriculum related training or resources that might have supported their use of the computers for literacy, numeracy, science or other subjects. In addition, the location of computers in a single room meant they were not available for the teacher and her pupils in their own classroom, where and when they needed them. Often times, school principles would lock the computer room for security, and not even allow teachers in to practice the skills they learned during training, let alone allow pupil access outside lessons. Furthermore, many teachers commuted to and from school, so they were teaching their subject all day, then had to get into the taxi [communal mini bus] as soon as school finished. They had no opportunity to explore the computers at school and the teachers didn't know anyone who could help them develop their computer skills and they were isolated from professional support networks.

For the most part, teachers felt powerless to change any of this. Yet despite these practical frustrations, teachers still called upon the symbolism of the computer to bring positive change. Below are examples of their statements during the interviews:

> It is of much importance to use computers because we can link with other people and organizations globally.
>
> It is very good for the rural learners to have access to this modern technology so that they do not migrate to the cities leaving their grannies behind.

In almost every school visited, we observed a small group of (between two and four) ICT enthusiasts who had developed a close relationship with the "ICT teacher." Such groups effectively established "ownership" of the computer lab, and were observed to be very much at home with ICT use and engaged in collaborative professional activities, including carrying out

Photo 6.3 ICT enthusiasts working after the school day.

whole school and management tasks (e.g., timetabling, school principals' letters).

It could be argued that there is merit in the pupils being exposed to computers and learning basic ICT skills which are a commodity in themselves, and that this, at least on a technical level, represents a successful outcome. But the ICT tools and skills seemed largely unconnected to any wider activities that might count as success from educational or development perspectives.

DISCUSSION

The most compelling argument for wading in the water of ICT in rural schooling is woven into our emerging understanding of the nature of the global ICT revolution, the magnitude and impact of which may be comparable to earlier social/technological revolutions, such as the invention of the printing press or the industrial revolution. This argument, put forcibly by Castells (1998), suggests that access to the language, skills and tools of this revolution is so critical for contemporary inclusion (social, political and economic), as to be construed as a basic human right, almost to be conflated with basic education. In this discourse, the "computer" has a symbolic representation as the bridge between two kinds of space: rich and poor, isolated and connected, quality education and failing education, economic participation and economic deprivation.

Many of the teachers we spoke to, despite working or living in often quite remote rural communities, showed that this kind of symbolism was powerfully present in their imagination, and central to their desire to have computers in their schools, and to be seen as competent to use them. A teacher stated:

> In model C schools [former apartheid white schools] we have seen more progress in every subject. That's why learners are having good marks. We thought if we could have this [computers] the pass rate will improve.

Yet from the evidence collected, even though all these schools now have computers and teachers trained in computer skills, there is little that would lead one to expect the pass-rate of any subject to improve, as the computers are not having any impact either on the teachers professional knowledge (about their subject or how it might be taught), or upon their classroom practice. We identify four barriers to educational ICT interventions in rural schools succeeding.

Poor intervention design: oriented by the technical or global capital discourse, emphasizing technical rather than educational or social capacity, leaving teachers unequipped to use the technology to benefit teaching and learning.

Costs: most donor interventions "hit and run," providing equipment (sometimes training) and then leaving schools to go it alone. Power (2006) has used a Total Cost of Ownership model to demonstrate that the costs of using and maintaining a "free" suite of desktop computers are greatly beyond the means of most rural schools, often resulting in unused or unusable computers, or increased fees.

Social conditions: much of the empirical evidence of the "promise" of ICTs has been largely gained in well resources urban schools and communities (InfoDev, 2003). Larger scale policy visions seek to extend such models to impoverished contexts with little focused attention on creating the enabling conditions for success, and with insufficient research to identify what, in the context of rural schools and communities, those enabling conditions might be.

Disempowering educators: there is danger in the perception that technology is the determining factor in producing educational quality. In other words, it is computers that make good education, not the knowledge, values and practices of the teacher and the school community. Such a view may further erode the agency of rural educators, by locating "quality" further away from their locus of control.

Setting Up the Fall

Going beyond the notion that successfully introducing ICT in rural educational settings "may be difficult," we suggest that without due care, we may be implicitly setting up rural and impoverished schools for failure. In the case of South Africa, the intention of the apartheid education system was not to create a system that empowered rural learners and their communities to achieve social, economic and intellectual autonomy or empowerment; the system was scaffolded to produce low quality educational outcomes. Yet at the level of "public awareness," the "failure" of rural schooling is becoming increasingly dissociated from its historic roots and increasingly associated with the "failure" of education departments and "useless" rural teachers and principals. Rural educators are often demoralized and have far too few experiences of "victory," absorbing patterns of failure into a self-consciousness of defeat (NMF, 2005).

The public (urban and rural, teachers and the communities they serve) is increasingly buying into a discourse that places a direct link between ICT and educational quality. This link was made time and time again by teachers we spoke to. Yet there is little evidence that "computers" of themselves make any difference to educational quality. When rural schools have computers, and teachers trained in ICT skills, yet experience no change in the quality of practices or outcomes educationally, there are essentially two responses: to reject the symbolism of computers as mediators of educational quality, and seek to develop a more nuanced understanding of the role of ICTs, or to blame the school and it's teachers for failing to mediate the promise of the ICTs effectively.

In our experience, the dominant discourses are so powerful, that it is far easier to take the second response; it is the teachers who have let us down. This is exemplified by the following story, recounted by colleagues from the NMF, of their visits to a rural school:

> He was a principal of a secondary school. A company had made a donation of several top quality computers to his school but no one had any training. He kept the keys, and would not allow anyone to use the facilities. After training was provided, he still kept the keys. The teachers said that simply put, the computer centre was not used. In the next meeting he described how terrible the relationship was between the school and the community. He said that the only solution was to get more computers. He said that the community loved computers, and if there were more in the school it would make him look like a good principal.

Opening up the Possibilities

Of course, such a scenario is not inevitable. Pimienta (2007) defines three categories against which ICT interventions may be costed: the infrastructure (computers, networks and retrofitting), the infostructure (information resources, databases, social networks) and infoculture (the knowledge, practices and processes that people develop and appropriate to use ICTs for their own purposes). Applying that framework to this evaluation, we see that the rural schools were provided with infrastructure, but insufficient infostructure for supporting their professional subject knowledge or classroom practice. The initial one week school-based training was oriented largely around basic 'office' ICT practices, rather than an educational infoculture.

Most schools also participated in a further weeks training in educational uses of ICT, delivered by SchoolNet SA (www.school.za), one of a number of large scale programmes at work within South Africa, which focus upon developing infostructure and infoculture, including , Microsoft Partners for Learning and Intel Teach to the Future. In each of these, there are well thought out programs of teacher professional development supported by a rich variety of learning resources. However, in many cases, these are still oriented around the practices of well-resourced urban schools, for example presuming fast internet access for whole class project research, or teachers having computers on their lap or desk, for direct entering of attendance or marks ("Expert Witness" interview, 2005)

The authors made some first steps towards developing a new infoculture of rural education (Leach et al., 2006, Power & Thomas, 2007) through working with teachers in rural communities over an extended period (2001–2007) to explore the kinds of ICT tools and practices that most effectively support their teaching and learning. Together with the work of the NMI, in raising awareness about the complexities of ICT we have tried to articulate here, this has contributed to a move within the Eastern Cape towards a much more exploratory approach to ICT for rural education and development. The provinces response to the national governments white paper on e-Education (Department of Education, 2004) was notable for including an extended period of exploring different models of ICT equipment and use.

CONCLUSIONS

Our writing emerges from the messy exchange between "wading in the water" of working with ICTs in rural schools, and the longing to think more critically about what this represents, and how it can be harnessed within the larger political goals of human emancipation. It is an attempt to publicly set out some of the ideas and issues that we believe have not yet been fully considered, that lie just under the surface of our ways of thinking and doing, in relation to "ICT" and schooling in historically impoverished contexts. It is incomplete and partial; not providing answers, nor even questions, but bringing to the surface slippery concepts and challenges that we have tried to grasp and to name.

ICTs must not be seen as a goal in themselves, as the symbolic representation of quality in education or development, but as a means of supporting best practices in education and development (OECD 2005), with the emphasis and evaluation being upon educational or development goals, processes and outcomes. We must move beyond thinking of "ICTs" as being only desktop or laptop computers, taking account of the specific circumstances of rural communities, of the nature of appropriate ICTs and practices in such communities, and the enabling conditions that are needed to support such practices.

We cannot afford to ignore the possibilities of new technologies for disadvantaged rural schools and communities; indeed, as we show in another chapter in this book, the 'mobile revolution' is bringing new communications technologies and networks into the hands of the rural poor on an unprecedented scale, with fundamental implications for the nature of rurality. At the same time, we must not look away from the pain and re-colonizing potential of ICT interventions which, *under current circumstances*, can lead to the poor ultimately being blamed if such interventions fail to mediate the perceived promise.

To identify the role of ICT in rural education and development will require donors, policy makers and educators to walk much more softly with rural communities, using participatory and ethnographic approaches to develop new practices and make new meanings together, and to allow the voices of such communities to rise above the discourse of global capital and its technicians: "[unqualified]..Africans are denied respect and opportunities for development; they could not sing out, articulate and develop the unique patterns of African civilization" (Vilakazi, 2002, quoted in Nabudere, 2003).

REFERENCES

Brown, G. & Benn, H. (2005). Foreword to Department for International Development: *Keeping our promises: Delivering education for all.* London: U.K.: DFID http://www.dfid.gov.uk/Pubs/files/education-delivering-promises.pdf

Castells, M. (1998). *The information age: Economy, society and culture. Volume 3: end of millennium.* Malden, MA: Blackwell

Department for International Development (2006). *Keeping our promises: Delivering education for all,* London, U.K.: DFID http://www.dfid.gov.uk/Pubs/files/education-delivering-promises.pdf.

Expert Witness Interview (2005) [unpublished]: Janet Thompson, director of 'SchoolNet South Africa', interviewed by Power, T. and Porteus, K.

Food and Agriculture Organisation of the United Nations & United Nations Educational, Scientific and Cultural Organisation (2003), *Education for rural development. Towards new policy responses.* Rome, Italy: Food and Agriculture Organisation of the United Nations. http://www.fao.org/sd/2003/KN12033_en.htm.

Glewwe, P., & Kremer, M. (2005). *Schools, teachers and education. Outcomes in developing countries.* (CID Working Paper No. 122. September 2005). Cambridge, MA, U.S.: Centre for International Development at Harvard University http://www.cid.harvard.edu/cidwp/pdf/122.pdf.

Hedges, J. (2002). The importance of posting and interaction with the education bureaucracy in becoming a teacher in Ghana. *International Journal of Education Development, 22*(3–4), 353–366.

InfoDev (2003) *ICT for development. Contributing to the millennium development goals. Lessons learned from seventeen InfoDev projects.* (Information for Development Program)., Washington, USA: World Bank http://www.infodev.org/en/Publication.19.html.

Kincheloe, J. L., & McClaren, P. (2002) Rethinking critical theory and qualitative research. In Y. Zou & E. Trueba (Eds.). *Ethnography and schools: Qualitative approaches to the study of education* (pp. 87–138). Lanham, MD: Rowman & Littlefield.

Leach, J., Ahmed, A., Makalima, S., & Power, T. (2006) *DEEP IMPACT: an investigation of the use of information and communication technologies for teacher education in the global south. Researching the issues.* (DFID Research Series No. 58) London, U.K.: DFID http://www.dfid.gov.uk/pubs/files/ict-teacher-education-no58.asp.

Mattson, E (2006). *Field-based models of primary teacher training. Case studies of student support systems from Sub-Saharan Africa.* Researching the Issues 63; London, UK: DFID Research Series. http://www.dfid.gov.uk/pubs/files/field-based-models-teacher-training-63.pdf.

Moon, B. (2007). *The global teacher crisis—meeting the challenge through new technologies and new modes of teaching and learning.* 12th Cambridge International Conference on Open and Distance Learning. Cambridge, UK. September 28, 2007. http://www2.open.ac.uk/r06/conference/BobMoonKeynoteCambridge2007.pdf.

Mulkeen, A. (2005). *Teachers for rural schools: A challenge for Africa* (Ministerial Seminar on Education for Rural Peoples in Africa: Policy Lessons, Options and Priorities) Addis Ababa, Ethiopia. September 7–9, 2005.

Nabudere, D (2003). Towards the establishment of a Pan-African University: A strategic concept paper. *African Journal of Political Science, 8*(1). http://archive.lib.msu.edu/DMC/African%20Journals/pdfs/political%20science/volume8n1/ajps008001002.pdf.

Nelson Mandela Foundation (2005). *Emerging voices. A report on education in South African rural communities.* Cape Town, South Africa: HSRC Press. http://www.hsrcpress.ac.za/product.php?productid=1957

Nelson Mandela Foundation (2005b). *ICT consolidation report* (Unpublished internal project document,). East London, South Africa: Nelson Mandela Foundation.

Ngũgĩwa Thiongo (1986). *Decolonising the mind: The politics of language in African literature* (Studies in African Literature Series). Heinemann, ISBN 0435080164.

Organisation of Economic Co-operation and Development, (2005). Good practice paper on ICTs for economic growth and poverty reduction. *The DAC Journal 2005, 6*(3), 1–69. http://www.oecd.org/dataoecd/2/46/35284979.pdf.

Pimienta, D. (2007). *Digital divide, social divide, paradigmatic divide,* Santo Domingo, Domincan Republic: Funredes. http://funredes.org/mistica/english/cyberlibrary/thematic/Paradigmatic_Divide.pdf

Power, T. (2006). *Using suites of "free" refurbished computers may cost over four times more than buying and using "state of the art" learning technologies* BERA, Warwick, U.K. 6–9 September 2006 http://www.open.ac.uk/deep/Public/web/publications/pdfs/TPower2006-BERA.pdf.

Power, T., & Thomas, R. (2007). 'The classroom in your pocket?' *The Curriculum Journal, 18*(3), 373–388. http://dx.doi.org/10.1080/09585170701590031

Soloway, E (2002). *Palm-sized devices are the personal computers of choice,* (Colloquium series; November 12, 2002) Massachusetts, USA: MIT Media Lab http://www.media.mit.edu/events/movies/video.php?id=soloway-2002-11-12.

United Nations (2006). *The millennium development goals report.* New York: United Nations. http://mdgs.un.org/unsd/mdg/Resources/Static/Products/Progress2006/MDGReport2006.pdf

United Nations Children's Fund–UNICEF (2005). *Annual report 2005.* New York: UNICEF http://www.unicef.org/publications/index_34144.html

United Nations Educational, Scientific and Cultural Organisation (2000). *Education for all 2000 assessment,* (Statistical Document) Paris: UNESCO.

United Nations Educational, Scientific and Cultural Organisation (2005). *EFA global monitoring report: Regional overview (Sub Saharan Africa).* Paris: UNESCO http://portal.unesco.org/education/en/file_download.php/73a941d1b5f931d7beee73443402fed4sub_saharan_africa_ENG.pdf.

United Nations Educational, Scientific and Cultural Organisation (2007). *The EFA global monitoring report 2008. Education for all by 2015. Will we make it?* Paris, France: UNESCO http://portal.unesco.org/education/en/ev.php-URL_ID=49591&URL_DO=DO_TOPIC&URL_SECTION=201.html.

CHAPTER 7

OPEN RESOURCES FOR SUSTAINABLE EDUCATION

Marina Stock McIsaac
Arizona State University and CARDET

António Moreira
University of Aveiro, Portugal

OPEN EDUCATION RESOURCES AND OPENCOURSEWARE

Open Education Resources (OER) and OpenCourseWare (OCW) can be catalysts for social change to promote inquiry, problem solving, and knowledge building in an emerging information society (Hewlett Foundation, 2007). The concept of free and readily available educational materials has caught the imagination of educators who have programs, courses, and materials already developed and in place. One goal of the movement is to provide online educational materials and courses to anyone at little or no cost. This has the potential to promote the international advancement of equality and justice through equitable and sustainable development of educational opportunities for all. The use of Information and Communication Technologies (ICTs) to disseminate educational materials may contribute

ICT for Education, Development, and Social Justice, pages 103–120

to improved cultural understanding through the production and sharing of locally owned content in support of cooperative educational efforts to sustainably meet a country's development goals (United Nations Development Programme, 2001).

ICTs, and particularly Web 2.0 applications, embody a set of principles and practices that tie together various activities and web services. They support the goals of OER and OCW by incorporating user-generated content to promote exchange of ideas. Web 2.0 is marked by the introduction and use of social software that promotes collaboration by setting up virtual worlds where one can meet like-minded colleagues, discuss issues, work together on projects and share ideas The combination of open course materials and open resources, combined with Web 2.0 social software offer powerful tools for educators.

Our work in professional development and teacher training has taken us to many countries. We have chosen two examples of countries we have worked with in Africa to highlight the potential benefits that OER and OCW can bring to those countries seeking to develop sustainable resources for building an educated society. We are using case studies of situations in which educational interventions have the characteristics or potential to solve identified pedagogical problems. These case studies seek to answer the question, "Can freely available educational materials help promote equitable access to learning and improved quality of education, through the sustainable use of appropriate technologies, in countries like Cape Verde and Nigeria?" As rapid developments in web-based communication appear, can social networks encourage collaboration and spread user-generated knowledge among citizens of many cultures? In countries with underdeveloped ICT infrastructure, complex political scenarios, and limited resources, is there the opportunity to build an information society that meets the targets of WSIS and the Millenium Development Goals for the year 2015?

OpenCourseWare

One of the most innovative and promising movem ents in collaborative online learning is the OCW movement and its corollary, OpenLearn at the British Open University. These projects are tied to OER in that collaborative efforts are openly shared and modified by constituents of the network community. This revolutionary concept was pioneered in 2001 by Massachusetts Institute of Technology (MIT) through its OCW Initiative in an effort to make all the materials used in their courses freely available via the internet for any non-commercial research use. In effect, it put digital books on the library shelves, available for free. MIT was an early adopter of OCW through their MERLOT (Multimedia Educational Resource for Learning and Online Teaching) portal. Their goal was to put the information for all of their courses online over the next few years.

OCW as developed by MIT is "... a free and open educational resource (OER) for educators, students, and self-learners around the world. It is true to MIT's values of excellence, innovation, and leadership" (MIT OpenCourseWare, 2007). Another early provider of freely available courses is the World Lecture Hall (WLH). WLH is hosted by the University of Texas as an "entry point to free online course materials from around the world" (World Lecture Hall, 2006). As early as 1994, the WLH won accolades as "best resource on the Internet" by educators. Users are encouraged to browse for courses, search for areas of interest and conduct searches of the site content. WLH links users to pages and content created by faculty around the world who use the Web to deliver their course material.

In October 2006, The British Open University launched its new program, OpenLearn, aimed at broadening access to education by making educational resources freely available on the internet. The OpenLearn website makes materials available with state of the art learning support and collaboration tools to connect learners and educators. Visitors to the OpenLearn website are able to access free open educational resources made available under an Attribution-Non Commercial-ShareAlike Creative Commons license. Visitors are able to copy, distribute, amend and re-use the learning materials on the condition that they acknowledge the original source of material. Users cannot use the resources for commercial purposes and if they alter, transform or build upon the material, the resulting work must be distributed only under an identical license. Because of the open concept, there are concerns about issues of quality assurance and issues of copyright.

There are currently more than a half million people in 160 countries using the free materials available online through the Open University's (OU) portal, (OpenLearn, 2006). This philosophy of sharing knowledge is promoting the formation of communities of learning around the world with teachers and learners taking materials from the site, repurposing them, and adding to the knowledge base. Course materials from MIT, World Lecture Hall (WLH), and OU have all been developed around the philosophy of open education resources.

Open Education Resources

In July of 2002, UNESCO reported in its Education News section, a new initiative designed to bring together sixteen universities from both developing and developed countries to meet with six international organizations to help develop a plan to make universal education resources available to all people. The movement was to be called Open Education Resources (OER), and its definition was "technology-enabled, open provision of educational resources for consultation, use and adaptation by a community of users for non-commercial purposes" (UNESCO, 2002a). These resources were to be used mainly in higher education by teachers and students, and distributed primarily through the Web. They include course materials, lectures, bibliographies, scientific demonstrations and other educational resources. A number of institutions joined the project. MIT presented MERLOT as a portal for their OCW materials. The initiative to provide free and universally available digital information for education came about as a solution to the problem of inaccessibility of educational materials for much of the world's population.

UNESCO recognized the potential of OER and subsequently received generous support from the William and Flora Hewlett Foundation to further develop this concept of freely available materials. OER refers to digitized materials offered freely and openly for educators, students, and self-learners to use and re-use for teaching, learning, and research (Hewlett Foundation, 2007).

The hope of the William and Flora Hewlett Foundation that funds this initiative is that this concept of open resource will mobilize the entire worldwide community of educators. The OER Initiative seeks to use information technology to help equalize access to knowledge and educational opportunities. The initiative targets educators, students and self- learners worldwide. At the heart of the movement toward OER is the simple and powerful idea that the world's knowledge is a public good and that technology in general, and the World Wide Web in particular, provides an extraordinary opportunity for everyone to share, use, and reuse knowledge.

The movements of OCW and OER have caught the imagination of educators in countries with a paucity of educational materials and lack of financial resources to meet the educational needs of growing populations. Developing countries in particular have the opportunity to benefit from the work of developed countries willing to share their knowledge to promote education for all. Despite the altruistic goals of the Hewlett Foundation and other educators, a critical perspective would encourage us to ask the questions:

- Whose knowledge is being distributed?
- Whose reality is being described?
- Whose perspective is shown?
- Whose contributions are being made?

It is clear that materials are developed from the culture and point of view of their creators. It is especially important that materials exported to non-Western countries reflect sensitivity to cultural differences, divergent points of view, and alternative worldviews. When cultural relevance is taken into account, networked educational resources can be valuable tools in helping to provide a rich variety of educational opportunities for all. When we talk about open educational resources, and courses available freely on digital networks, we must pay particular attention to avoid "Westernizing" education, and we must examine issues of sustainability.

MILLENIUM DEVELOPMENT GOALS AND SUSTAINABILITY

The term "sustainability" became popular following the Brundtland Report (World Commission on Environment and Development, 1987). In that report the authors wrote, "Sustainable development requires meeting the basic needs of all and extending to all the opportunity to satisfy their aspirations for a better life." When applied to education, sustainable educational materials are those that are affordable and consistently available to all without changes in access and without increased costs. (Ibid, 1987) Open education provides free and inexpensive resources for sustainable education. OERs extend to all the opportunity for affordable and accessible education.

In 2000, the United Nations Development Programme supported the development of the Millenium Development Goals (MDG) adopted by all the world's governments as a blueprint for building a better world in the 21st century. The eight MDGs for the year 2015 included, among other items, promoting the reduction of poverty, promoting equality for women and minorities, and increasing educational opportunities for all by achieving universal primary education. Goals 1 and 2 specifically target education (see Figure 7.1).

The 2006 MDG progress report indicated clear signs of hope. The report suggested that providing every child with a primary school education is within reach and that women are gaining in political participation and representation. At the same time, the gap is widening between the richest and the poorest. The report noted that much can be done by developed countries to help developing countries use their own resources for sustainable development (Millenium Development Goals Report, 2006).

Critics of the MDG caution that progress toward meeting the goals is drawn from national statistics provided by the governments and reported by statistical agencies, and then adjusted for comparison purposes (Global Information Society Watch, 2007). When governments do not generate the appropriate data, statistical agencies estimate comparison figures based on data from neighboring countries. This lack of reported data from some developing countries has led to initiatives to develop local statistical capacity building. Despite the shortcomings of the MDG report, the goals are

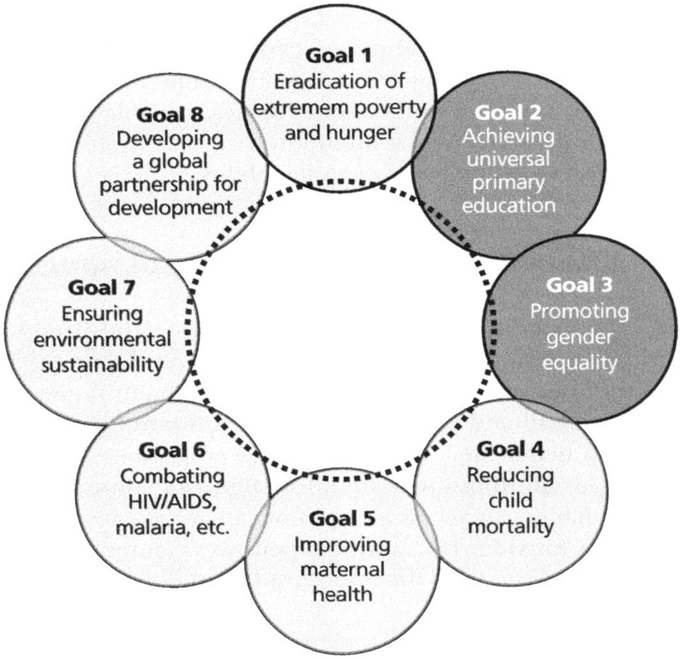

Figure 7.1 Millenium development goals (UNESCO).

slowly showing that there is improvement in most areas. One of the greatest concerns with attaining these goals is the issue of sustainability. Previous initiatives that have provided technology or expertise to developing countries have often not been sustainable, and the benefits of intervention have disappeared quickly. Sustainability, conservation, and quality of life are issues that are attracting the attention of scientists, economists, business people, and educators around the world.

Much has been written about how ICTs can produce economically sustainable environments in the workplace, making the workplace more environment friendly and creating a better society (Millenium Development Goals Report, 2006). Some examples of ways that ICTs can generate alternatives to the destruction of non-renewable resources in the workplace are the reduction of waste, the use of online activities to reduce transportation costs, and the reduction of energy consumption. Activities include telecommuting, teleworking between sites, using online financial services, online shopping, online entertainment and online learning. The sustainability of online learning environments is particularly valuable to countries looking to find high quality educational materials that they can repurpose using their own cultural materials. Sustainability was a topic on the agenda of the World Summit on Information Society in 2003.

WORLD SUMMIT ON INFORMATION SOCIETY AND DIGITAL OPPORTUNITY

In an effort to support digital networking and access to information for all people, the United Nations, working with the International Telecommunications Union (ITU), organized a World Summit on the Information Society (WSIS) in Geneva (2003) and Tunis, (2005). Its goals were to bridge the "digital divide" and achieve an information society that was available to all and relied on shared knowledge. The plan of action, among other things, included the goal of providing online capability for 50% of the world's population, and developing a global public infrastructure to support the EFA and MDG goals for 2015.

In 2003, the WSIS identified common goals; to direct the use and development of ICTs, and to build a people-centered, inclusive and development-oriented society, one where everyone can create, access, utilize and share information and knowledge, enabling sustainable development and improving the quality of people's lives. In 2005, at the follow-up World Summit in Tunisia, the representatives reaffirmed that desire, and resolved to promote ICTs as effective tools to promote peace, security and stability, and to enhance democracy, social cohesion, good governance, and the rule of law. They also emphasized their desire to build ICT networks and develop applications, in partnership with the private sector, based on open or interoperable standards that are affordable and accessible to all, available anywhere and anytime, to anyone and on any device, leading to a ubiquitous network. They reiterated the need to encourage and foster collaborative development, interoperative platforms and free and open-source software (WSIS, 2005).

Although many issues within WSIS have been contentious, especially over the Internet governance process, some progress has been made. There is greater inclusion of civil society groups who are addressing issues of human rights, freedom of expression, and publishing on the Internet. There is also increased investment in telecommunications infrastructure in developing countries where the need is greatest. The World Information Society Report (Peña-López, 2007) monitors policies and progress in implementing goals of WSIS in meeting the needs of developing countries. This report charts progress toward building the Information Society in light of the WSIS targets and MDGs. It evaluates access to telecommunications and digital opportunity in 180 economies worldwide through the Digital Opportunity Index (DOI), as called for in the WSIS Geneva Plan of Action.

The report combines statistical analysis of the latest ICT trends with insights into the impact of ICTs. It uses the DOI to monitor different aspects of the Information Society, particularly the growth of mobile telephony that is of primary importance to developing countries.

The report ranks both developed and developing countries in terms of their digital opportunities. The index (DOI) for each country is combined with the country's opportunity, infrastructure, and utilization ratings to give it a world ranking. Although the index is widely used to measure digital opportunity, it has also been criticized. There are those who believe that the index lacks an analytical foundation and suffers from a number of cumulative problems such as the addition of scores from dissimilar categories. James (2007) argued that "these and other problems all suggest that one should be cautious in drawing policy conclusions from the DOI" (p. 46).

Nevertheless, the index is useful for looking at relative digital opportunities among countries. When we examine opportunities in Africa, Cape Verde is ranked 13th and Nigeria is ranked 29th on the Digital Opportunity Index (DOI) for the development of communication technology, particularly mobile telephony that is making such strides in many developing countries. For example, the increase of mobile licenses in Nigeria alone in 2007 has led to a "phenomenal growth of telephony" (http://www.ncc.gov.ng/).

Western Africa: Cape Verde and Nigeria

Africa is a large continent made up of countries with many different problems, priorities and populations. Nevertheless, there are a number of issues that these countries share in common. Political unrest, civil wars, and other disturbances combined with lack of sufficient funds to develop sound educational programs for all people have resulted in huge differences in education across countries. In a global effort to provide equal educational opportunities to all children and adults, UNESCO launched its Education for All initiative in 1990 with the goal of providing universal primary education to all and to significantly reduce illiteracy by the year 2000. The initiative also promotes the eight MDGs, particularly the second goal related to primary education, and the third goal related to gender equality in education by the year 2015. (UNESCO, 2002 b.)

Cape Verde is one of the smallest countries in Africa, whereas Nigeria is the largest in terms of population. Both countries share a need for a well-educated populace. Cape Verde is a small country with few natural resources and a small population situated in an archepelago of islands off the West Coast of Africa. Nigeria is a large country of 140 million people with rich resources but with internal and political problems that create barriers to providing full equality of education to all its citizens. Both countries need sustainable, economically feasable opportunities to provide education for all. They share a goal to empower citizens to become well-informed, productive workers in a global information society. The sharing of resources could help to overcome inequality and promote knowledge building through access to economically affordable information networks using sustainable development principles. For countries like these, education should not be simply a privilege. Ensuring the right of education for all should be a matter of morality, justice and economic sense (UNICEF, 1999). There are opportunities for learning from others and for repurposing previously developed educational materials. There are opportunities to collaborate, to promote knowledge based decision-making and democratic principles essential to maintaining a civil society.

With the current capability of social networking, and the Web 2.0 platforms, the Web provides powerful tools for collaboration between geographically dispersed populations. The joint creation of knowledge allows people to develop their own social networks and to promote social justice movements that speak directly to the people. Thus, ICTs can offer serious challenges to traditional forms of communication managed by political organizations and traditional media. In a truly international setting, traditional notions of democracy give way to ideas of a "global civil society" (Mueller et al. 2007). Collaborative networks are economically viable, democratic, and sustainable. The availability of resources, training materials and networks for collaborative knowledge-building could change the picture of education in both countries.

Cape Verde

The archipelago of Cape Verde was completely unpopulated before it was discovered by the Portuguese in 1456 and African slaves were brought into the islands to work on plantations owned by Portuguese settlers. Because of the inter-racial contact of these slaves with Portuguese, Spanish, and Italian sailors who were given possession of land in this colony, most people from Cape Verde are mestiços (Portuguese for "mixed people"). The rest of the population descend from several other European settlers (Netherlands, England, France), which entitles Cape Verde to be labeled as the most European of African countries. Settlers also arrived from other parts of Africa, Asia, and America. The island of Santiago is the most populated, with half the total population of the archipelago.

The country has very few natural resources and this is the main reason why people try to find better conditions abroad. It is calculated that of the total population from Cape Verde scattered around the world, only one third actually lives in the archipelago. With a population of nearly 500,000 people, all teenagers age 15 and older can read and write, making 76.6% of the total population literate.

In 2005, in an effort to help the people of Cape Verde train teachers, The University of Aveiro, Portugal, began offering teacher training programs. Since Portuguese is a common language of the country, it was a cost effective way for the University of Aveiro to develop a program tailored to the needs of the Cape Verde teachers. The materials, however, remain the property of the University of Aveiro and are not available to Cape Verde institutions for their own use. A distance learning videoconference system was used to supplement regular visits to the archipelago by university faculty. The teacher training course was organized around a set of thematic modules: Theories of Education, Sociology of Education, School Organization and Management, Curriculum Development and Didactics.

These modules were preceded by a face-to-face session, with two teachers from the University of Aveiro, so as to explain procedures (technical and curricular) and establish a first bond between teachers and trainees. At the end of the course, a final face-to-face session was offered for revision and consolidation of acquired knowledge and closure of the course activities. Conditions were difficult, given the regular power outages and high cost of electrical service. In Cape Verde, money is short and bureaucracy makes it difficult for institutions to keep pace with regular payment of bills. On the other hand, and given that computer resources were centralised in the Higher Education Institute in Praia, the capital of Cape Verde, trainees from other islands expended a great deal of money and time traveling from their islands to Praia, to be able to follow the course.

Some open access resources were made available, and materials other than books purchased in Portugal and taken to Cape Verde were also produced for the course. These were made available to the trainees and to other students who may need them. All but one of the trainees completed the course.

ICT is a high priority in Cape Verde. Educators understand the importance of communication networks in providing collaborative learning environments. OERs are of great importance for Cape Verde given that internal production is next to non-existent and buying power in the country is reduced. Whatever funds exist, are diverted to other more immediate priorities, like the country's infrastructure. Cape Verde is a country composed of several islands, where traveling is both expensive and not regularly done. Open Education Resources, distributed over the Internet, can be an important asset for all of education and for teacher education in particular.

Nevertheless, the problems to be overcome include constant and prolonged power cuts, and the associated difficulty of maintaining Internet service though available providers. It is common for internet service providers to suddenly cut off access to the Internet, due to delayed payments.

Financial support to establish ICT infrastructure is available through international educational programs, but government policies must indicate that education is a top priority

In Cape Verde, Portuguese and French are the preferred foreign languages amongst most people. However materials in English such as specific modules of courses or programs already developed by the Open Courseware Consortium or the British Open University, can benefit Cape Verde's teacher training efforts. These materials are slowly becoming available for the Cape Verde's teacher training courses. The high quality and variety of available OER materials makes it worthwhile to adapt them to the specific reality and educational contexts of the archipelago, reducing the financial effort of locally developing materials from scratch.

The further development of OER in Cape Verde would be of great financial benefit to the country. As an example, a teacher distance education course offered by the University of Aveiro specifically directed to teachers who lacked professional qualifications, involved 19 students and five teachers, for a span of nine months (5 modules of 70 hours each) with only two face-to-face sessions (beginning and end of course). The budget was 25,000 euros, of which only 10% was spent on the acquisition of books for the library of the Cape Verde institution where students gathered to follow the course online. The remainder of the budget covered institutional overhead, travel and accommodation expenses of teachers involved, and tutoring fees. Such a budget would have been put to better use by directing it towards the adaptation of existing OER materials, redesigned to be culturally relevant to the Cape Verde context. Costs for translating and localizing OER materials for Cape Verde could be absorbed into such a budget. At present, materials used for this specific course, are still the property of the University of Aveiro. Royalty fees and reusability agreements have not been determined.

OER and OCW can help meet UNESCO's "Education for All" initiative particularly if there were a stronger commitment on the part of Internet Service Providers to come up with affordable prices for institutions and individuals in underdeveloped countries. This would ease distribution and access to these materials. A change in policy to provide affordable internet service to established Higher Education Institutions would also be of paramount importance. Although gathering used books to be offered to these countries might be useful, the fact is that OER and OCW offer quality courses and resources much more in line with a more modern commitment to education for all. Electronic distribution is an added means of improving the ICT literacy of the peoples in these countries. Given the access and infrastructure problems faced by these countries, electronic distribution becomes a realistic solution when governments and institutions make electronic access to information a high priority for education.

Nigeria

Nigeria has a long and distinguished history of education. Nigeria's university education has suffered since the 1960s when education was well supported. In the early days, postcolonial Africa had few institutions as venerable and fully developed as Nigeria's universities. The University of Ibadan in southwest Nigeria, the intellectual home of the Nobel Prize-winning writer Wole Soyinka, was regarded in 1960 as one of the best universities in the British Commonwealth.

Nigerian institutions have educated a revolutionary generation of nation builders and statesmen, doctors and engineers, writers and intellectuals. Now, however, tertiary institutions throughout Africa are collapsing. Since autonomous rule, many countries find themselves in financial difficulties. In addition, international development policies have favored basic education over higher learning even as a population explosion propels more young people than ever toward the already strained institutions. These developments resulted from a number of events. Corruption and mismanagement of funds in postcolonial Africa led to unrest in universities. In addition, World Bank and International Monetary Fund monies were made available primarily for early childhood education, basic literacy and basic education programs rather than to institutions of higher education. As a result, Africa now has the world's highest rate of growth in high school education and one of the lowest levels of support for higher education. Universities are overcrowded, underfunded, and hotbeds of resistance. This creates turmoil and instability (Polgreen, 2007). However, there are signs of improvement. The World Bank, the International Monetary Fund, and the Partnership for Higher Education in Africa have pledged hundreds of millions of dollars to help universities in Africa over the next five years (Ibid., 2007).

Other nonprofit projects such as Microsoft's Unlimited Potential, are offering all developing countries deep price cuts for their hardware and software packages. Countries like Nigeria will benefit from deeply discounted bundles that would be made available to national, state, or local governments and then distributed to individuals (Lohr, 2007).

Aderinoye and Ojokheta (2004) provide an excellent background for open-distance education in Nigeria, and the role it has played in development and preparing students for work. They examine how education accomplishes changes in attitudes, values and behavior, particularly in the examples from Nigeria. They use the Capability Approach Theory and its developmental approach to education to examine how people make education relevant to their own values and lives. The authors emphasize the need for education to move beyond simply meeting economic needs through helping people achieve self-satisfaction, respect, and a sense of purpose and meaning to their lives. Thus education becomes a tool to increase peoples' capabilities and thereby enhance their quality of life. It is this opportunity for people to improve themselves that is a basic human right.

Social transformation is occurring in Nigeria and education is no longer available only to the elite or more fortunate. Distance education has been successful in spreading knowledge that leads to more democratic processes in the country. It is enabling students to get an education and prepares students for the workforce.

One of the most successful distance education projects has been the re-opening and re-establishment of the National Open University of Nigeria (NOUN) by Vice-Chancellor Dr. Olugbemiro Jegede. Under Jegede's leadership NOUN opened its doors in 2002 with 32,000 students. In an effort to reach the marginalized, the poor, and the under-educated of the country, the Nartional Open University was born. With lofty goals of providing education for all, and using ICT for Open and Distance Learning (ODL), Vice-Chancellor Jegede undertook a daunting task of offering education in a country where 70 percent lived in rural areas, and over 60 percent were under 15 years of age. Training teachers to reach the previously unreached and ever-expanding population in Nigeria was an admirable undertaking. As one of the fastest growing countries in the world, Nigeria's population of 120 million in 2001 is expected to double by the middle of the 21st century and become the third most populous country next to China and India (Jegede, 2002). In addition only 20 percent of those applying to institutions of higher education had received admission. Since Nigeria is committed to educating its entire population, Open and Distance Learning was selected as a vehicle for providing educational opportunities for all. The government, and Jegede, envisioned a technology-driven educational revolution.

A recent study by Ambe-Uva (2006) illustrates the success of Jegede's vision. Only four years after the first students were enrolled in NOUN, the program is graduating thousands each semester. The majority of students are male, and combine full-time employment with studies. Most chose to study at NOUN because of its innovative nature, its motto "work and learn" and the fact that programs are tailored to working adults. In a study identifying factors that predicted successful completion of courses at NOUN, access to materials and opportunities for social and intellectual interactivity were the most important predictors of success (Ambe-Uva, 2006). In its effort to reach the marginalized, the poor, and the under-educated of the country, the National Open University has been a resounding success. Its goals of providing education for all using ICT for Open and Distance Learning (ODL) are well underway. However, budgets, materials, technology, infrastructure and staffing all present obstacles to complete success.

Over the past two decades, Nigeria has experienced greater inequalities between well-resourced and poorly resourced areas of the country. This has translated into a widening gap between rich and poor households. Education suffers a similar fate in different regions where educational disparities are becoming more evident. As a result many people have been excluded from formal education, creating a situation of social injustice, high illiteracy, and low quality of education (Geo-Jaja, 2006). This situation results in injustice and economic misfortune.

Social injustice is a way of life characterized by poverty, high rates of illiteracy poor education and an unequal distribution of a nation's capital and resources. The growing trend to decentralization, leaving financing to local governments, depends on adequate financing for all stakeholders, and a supply of good resources. According to Geo-Jaja (2006) "Once again the resource-poor are asked to bear the brunt while the state spends national resources to build educational institutions that benefit the elite" (p. 131). Social policy that results in social injustice does not benefit the citizens and provides a disservice by leaving a significant number of citizens disenfranchised. Equitable availability of information using ICTs offers the potential of equalizing the disparity and offering educational opportunities to citizens.

One of the most frequently used technologies in Nigeria is the mobile phone. Mobile phone service has expanded much more quickly than land telephone services. Although telephone landlines have existed in the major cities since the late 1970s, service has been expensive and erratic. The use of cellular phones, on the other hand, has spread steadily since the late 1990s, and Internet service has expanded rapidly in Nigeria. In Cape Verde, on the other hand, geographic isolation, small country size and lack of a good telecommunications infrastructure has delayed the growth of cellular phones. Figure 7.2 illustrates those differences.

Global wireless technology is developing to the point that, where infrastructure is in place, Internet services can be accessed on relatively inexpensive hand held devices. Although many people have access to affordable mobile phone service, Internet service providers still control prices and services for retrieving information. In locations like Cape Verde, with few providers, this poses a great obstacle. For information to be widely available, governmental and local policies must be put in place to ensure equality of access to information resources available through ICTs.

In Nigeria, a number of initiatives are in place to help build digital technical capacity. The University of Iowa has a long partnership with Universities of Ibadan and Jos in NIgeria. Their slogan "knowledge makes a difference" highlights their mission to improve digital communication for people in developing countries. Over the last decades they have partnered with the University of Ibadan and the University of Jos, as part of their WiderNet initiative (http://www.widernet.org). Two of their current projects are "Training Technicians at Nigerian Universities" and "Coaching Nigerian University Decision Makers". Both projects aim at helping to build

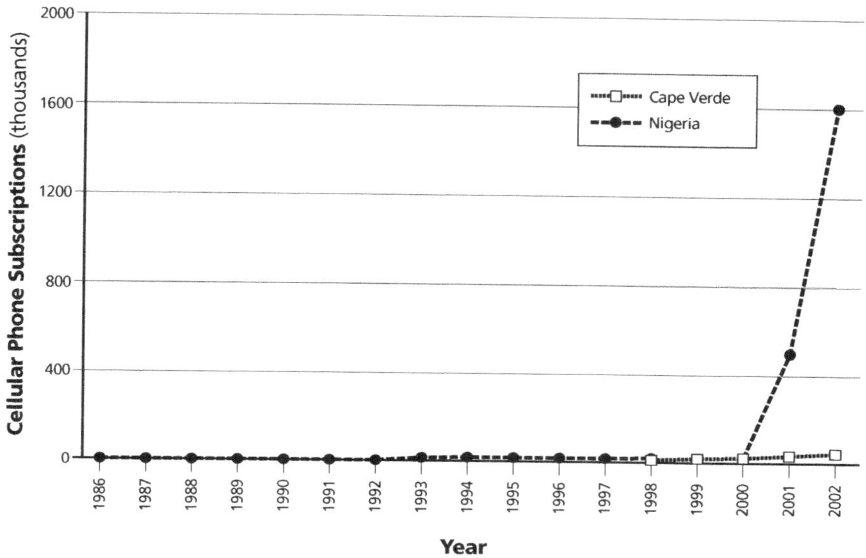

Figure 7.2 Cellular phone subscriptions (data from *Encyclopedia Britannica*, 2007).

digital capacity and collaboration with Nigerian educators, and educators around the world.

Investment in telecommunications infrastructure is growing quickly, particularly in Africa. The new generation of interactive networking tools, known as Web 2.0, may offer countries like Cape Verde and Nigeria an increased voice in user-generated knowledge building and social networking. Combining these networks with OER and OCW may, indeed provide global resources to those previously undereducated or marginalized.

CONCLUSION

The ultimate realization of the goals of EFA, MDG and WSIS depend largely on the ability of government and industry to join together to build a technology infrastructure that will deliver pedagogically sound content to teacher training institutions and teachers who will eventually guide young people to become independent learners. Issues of incompetence, corruption and greed will have to be overcome for these opportunities to succeed.

On June 28, 2007, The Open University's OpenLearn project announced that they were awarded a further $4.45 million grant to make more course materials freely available to anyone in the world. The William and Flora Hewlett Foundation approved the grant to the OpenLearn website to double the amount of free learning content by April 2008. The website will also have more learning support and collaboration tools to connect learners and educators online. The opportunity for everyone to have free or inexpensive access to knowledge is of utmost importance to develop informed citizens for a democratic society. OER and the development of OCW can help ensure our commitment to develop a knowledge-based economy and provide opportunities for all citizens to become well informed consumers of information with universal access and consumer rights.

OER and OCW can change the way people use and generate information. These activities underlie the current knowledge building movement. Social networking is a democratic, collective activity that emphasizes collaboration rather than competition, sharing rather than hoarding, and the provision of equality of access rather than privileged use. It depends on the collective power of individual contributions and is service oriented rather than product oriented. The opportunity for users to generate and contribute to the knowledge stream through blogs, Wikis, and other social networks can help to allay fears of further institutionalization of education and marginalization of the poor.

Global citizens need the skills and knowledge to be able to compete in an information society. To comply with UNESCO's Education for All initiative as well as the goals of the MDG for the year 2015, OER and OCW have the opportunity to make a difference in accelerating educational opportunities around the world. It may be possible to use our collective intelligence to solve educational problems in our poorest countries by promoting new jobs through education, the reduction of poverty, equality for women and minorities, and increasing educational opportunities for all.

Can we eliminate the digital divide by 2015 and provide education for all? Despite the promise of these new technologies, it is not the technologies that will make the difference. Education for all can only occur if:

- Content and instruction meet local needs,
- Instruction is pedagogically sound,
- Teachers are well trained,
- All stakeholders are involved,
- overnments make education a priority,
- Telecommunications industry provides affordable service.

Civil society can only develop if citizens become involved in contributing to a knowledge-base that helps build a democratic society, within which every voice is heard.

REFERENCES

Aderinoye, R., & Ojokheta, K. (2004, April 1). Open-distance education as a mechanism for sustainable development: reflections on the nigerian experience. *The International Review of Research in Open and Distance Learning* [Online] 5:1. Accessed May 21, 2007 from http://www.irrodl.org/index.php/irrodl/article/view/174/256

Ambe-Uva, T. (2006, July) Interactivity in distance education: The National Open University of Nigeria (NOUN) experience. *Turkish Online Journal of Distance Education.* 7:4 Accessed May 3, 2007 from http://tojde.anadolu.edu.tr/tojde24/pdf/article_9.pdf

Carson, S. (2006), Evaluation. Accessed May 20, 2007 from http://ocw.mit.edu/OcwWeb/Global/AboutOCW/evaluation.htm

Geo-Jaja, M. (2006). Educational decentralization, public spending, and social justice in Nigeria. *International Review of Education. 52*(1), 125–148.

Global Information Society Watch (2007). *Report.* Association for Progressive Education. Accessed June 20, 2007 from http://www.globaliswatch.org/

Hewlett Foundation (2007). *Open educational resources (OER)—Making high quality educational content and tools freely available on the web.* Accessed June 18, 2007. http://www.hewlett.org/Programs/Education/OER/openEdResources.htm

James, J. (2007) Cumulative bias in the new digital opportunity index: Sources and consequences. *Current Science,. 92*(1), January, 2007

Jegede, O. (2002*). An integrated ICT-Support for ODL in Nigeria: The vision, the mission and the journey so far.* Paper prepared for the LEARNTEC-UNESCO 2002 Global Forum on Learning Technology, Karllsruhe, Germany, 3–8 February, 2002.

Lohr, S. (2007) Software by Microsoft is nearly free for the needy, *New York Times,* April 19, 2007.

Millenium Development Goals Report, (2006). NY: United Nations. Accessed June 5, 2007 from http://mdgs.un.org/unsd/mdg/Resources/Static/Products/Progress2006/MDGReport2006.pdf

MIT Open Courseware. Massachusetts Institute of Technology (2007). Accessed May 2, 2007. http://ocw.mit.edu/OcwWeb/

Mueller,M.; Kuerbis, B. & Page, C. (2007) Democratizing Global Communication? Global Civil Society and the Campaign for Communication Rights in the Information Society. *International Journal of Communication, 1,* 1–31.

Ojo, D., & Olakulehin, F.(2006, Jun 5). Attitudes and Perceptions of Students to Open and Distance Learning in Nigeria. *The International Review of Research in Open and Distance Learning* [Online] 7(1). Accessed May 10, 2007 from http://www.irrodl.org/index.php/irrodl/article/view/313/496

Open Learn: online learning with the Open University (2006). Accessed June 12, 2007 from http://www.open.ac.uk/openlearn/home.php

O'Reilly. T. (2005). What Is Web 2.0? Design Patterns and Business Models for the Next Generation of Software. Accessed May 12, 2007 from http://www.oreillynet.com/pub/a/oreilly/tim/news/2005/09/30/what-is-web-20.html

Peña-López, Ismael. (2007) "World Information Society Report 2007 and Digital Opportunity Index 2007" In *ICTlogy*, #44, May 2007. Barcelona: ICTlogy. Accessed September 22, 2007 from http://ictlogy.net/review/?p=551

Polgreen, L.; Dickinson, E. (2007, May 20). Africa's Storied Colleges, Jammed and Crumbling *New York Times*.

UNESCO (2002a), *UNESCO Promotes New Initiative for Free Educational Resources on the Internet*. Accessed May 28, 2007 from http://www.unesco.org/education/news_en/080702_free_edu_ress.shtml

UNESCO (2002b) Education for All: Is the World on Track?" *EFA Global Monitoring Report*, Paris: Author.

UNICEF. 1999. *The State of the World's Children 1999: The Right to Education*. New York: Oxford University Press.

United Nations Development Programme. (2001). *Human development report 2001: Making new technologies work for human development*. New York: Oxford University Press. Accessed June 10, 2007 from http://hdr.undp.org/reports/global/2001/en/default.cfm

Wiley, D. (2006), *The Current State of Open Educational Resources*. Accessed May 25, 2007 from http://opencontent.org/blog/archives/247.

World Commission on Environment and Development (1987). O*ur Common Future, Report of the World Commission on Environment and Development,. Published as Annex to General Assembly document A/42/427, Development and International Co-operation: Environment August 2, 1987*. Accessed February 9, 2008 from http://www.un-documents.net/wced-ocf.htm

World Lecture Hall, University of Texas at Austin. (2006). Accessed May 20, 2007 from http://web.austin.utexas.edu/wlh

WSIS (World Summit on the Information Society) Geneva 2003–Tunis 2005, Tunis Commitment, (2005). Accessed June 10, 2007 from http://www.itu.int/wsis/docs2/tunis/off/7.html

Yusuf, M.O., and Falade, A. A. (2005) Media in Distance Learning: The Nigerian National Teachers Institute Distance Education Programme. *Turkish Online Journal of Distance Education, 6*(4). Retrieved June 5, 2006, from http://tojde.anadolu.edu.tr/tojde20/pdf/Volume6Number4.pdf.

PART 3

ICT FOR INCLUSION

CHAPTER 8

MOBILE TECHNOLOGIES

Current Practices, Future Possibilities

Tom Power
The Open University, UK

James Sankale
Ministry of Education, Kenya

INTRODUCTION

In this chapter, we seek to investigate the potential relationship between mobile technologies and professional learning for teachers through an analysis of global trends in increased access and use of mobile communications networks, particularly in Sub-Saharan Africa, and the implications of such trends for teacher professional development. Case studies are presented showing early examples of harnessing the potential of mobile devices for educational and developmental purposes, including the SEMA project in Kenya (Power & Sankale, 2007), and the DEEPER project in South Africa (Power & Thomas 2007). From these sources, we identify current practices and future possibilities for capitalizing on the mobile revolution as a tool for education

ICT for Education, Development, and Social Justice, pages 123–145

and development, with a particular focus on the professional knowledge and practices of teachers serving disadvantaged rural communities.

SURVEYING THE LANDSCAPES

The use of mobile phones and other handheld digital devices to support the professional development and practice of rural teachers is a relatively recent innovation, arising from the interaction between three overlaid "landscapes":

- The urgent and pressing challenges of providing quality universal primary education for all (Moon, 2007);
- The frustrations and failures of many "ICT suite" based educational interventions in developing nations (World Bank, 2003, p. 17);
- The global revolution of mobile communications networks or "Africa's great success story" (Gray, 2006).

The Educational Landscape

It is now accepted that the Millennium Development Goals are all about children.

—UNICEF 2005

Education lies at the heart of eradicating poverty, and it is now recognized to be the crucial core of the Millennium Development Goals (United Nations, 2000). In low-income countries, for instance, with each year of additional education, average earnings increase by 11%. People with literacy are best positioned to start their own enterprises and increase wealth (UNESCO, 2005). Globally, 77 million children, mostly in poor countries, still have no access at all to even the most basic schooling. Sub-Saharan Africa is home to half of the world's out-of-school children; even of those who enroll in school, only one in three will complete their primary education. The children most likely to be out of school live in rural areas and come from the poorest households (UNESCO, 2007).

In addressing the issue of providing universal primary education, the need for teachers is staggering. Sub-Saharan Africa as a whole will need to expand its teaching force by 68%. In some countries the crisis is even more severe—Ethiopia must double the number of its teachers; Chad will need almost four times as many, from 16,000 to 61,000 (UNESCO, 2006). It is calculated that 18 million teachers are still needed if the Millennium Development Goals are to be met (Global Campaign For Education, 2006). Perhaps surprisingly, the Millennium Development Goals make no mention of the need for teachers or teacher training. However, the Commission for Africa Report (2005) identifies teacher training and development as a key priority area for reducing poverty.

There are now further signs that the policy community has begun to concentrate attention on this key challenge (Moon, 2007, pp. 1–2), but practical policies remain under-developed—traditional "college based" methods of teacher education simply cannot meet the need. Imaginative and robust solutions are required which are high quality, relevant to local needs and school and classroom-based (Leach & Moon, 2002).

It is not simply a matter of training new teachers for new pupils (quantity), but also of upgrading the knowledge, skills and qualifications of the existing teaching workforce (quality). For example, a survey of eleven eastern and southern African countries indicated that a third were untrained (UNESCO 2000); a more recent survey of seven Sub-Saharan African countries found some teachers scoring lower than their pupils in basic numeracy tests (UNESCO, 2005a).

These problems are experienced much more acutely in the rural areas: 82 percent of children not in school in developing countries are located in rural settings (DevInfo, 2006). The scarcity of trained teachers is also greatest in the countryside (Mulkeen, 2005). Experienced practitioners largely avoid poor rural placements, or relocate to towns and cities as soon as they are able (Hedges, 2000).

The Educational Technology Landscape

Most governments in the global south are now investing heavily in new technologies, with strong arguments being made for the potential of ICT in education (e.g., Commission for Africa, 2005; Selinger & Gibson, 2004; Unwin, 2005). New technologies orientated for educational development, such as the $100 laptop, (MIT, 2006) are already available. Within this context, teachers are seen as key to the success and sustainability of ICT related educational strategies. Despite considerable rhetoric about the value of ICT in education, research shows that such educational ICT programs make few linkages to issues of quality teaching and learning (Unwin, 2005). Our own research has shown that such innovations largely mirror increasingly outdated practices from developed economies, based on a standard paradigm orientated to a resource rich, office-based practices, where computer suites are used to teach ICT skills often disconnected to the contexts and lives of those learning them (Leach et al., 2006).

Such approaches, disconnected from the identities, circumstances and practices of rural teachers, have been shown to be both culturally irrelevant in rural communities (Heeks, 2005) and generally unconnected to poverty reduction strategies (OECD, 2005), leading to what Unwin (2005) has described as the "computer tragedy": "piles of hardware accumulating in dusty corners, and "computers hidden under plastic covers that have rarely if ever been used" (p. 5). In reviewing for InfoDev the practical lessons learned about ICT, poverty and development over the previous decade, the World Bank (2003) reports that:

> Vast amounts of resources and energy have been invested into efforts to increase access to ICTs in developing countries and among the poor.... The results of these efforts are, thus far, inconclusive... because poverty and low growth remain seemingly intractable problems in so many countries, ICT s themselves have not proved to be the transformative tools that some predicted they would be. (p. 3)

The Mobile Technology Landscape

There has been an explosion in mobile phone use in developing nations, starting shortly before the new millennium, with Mobile phone use in Sub-Saharan Africa growing 5000% between 1998 and 2003 (BBC News, 2005). The ITU figures (Gray, 2006) document the exponential growth of mobile phone subscriptions in comparison to the increase in landlines (see Figure 8.1).

- In 2001, the number of mobile phone users overtook the number of landline users in Africa
- In 2004 alone, the African continent gained 15 million new mobile phone subscribers, being equivalent to the total number of telephone subscribers (landline and mobile) just 8 years earlier in 1996.
- By 2004, there were 3 mobile phone subscribers for every landline subscriber in Africa; in Sub-Saharan Africa, this figure rises to 4 mobile phone subscribers for every landline, the highest proportion for any region on earth.

One of the reasons for the relative figures for mobile subscriptions being so high is because of the incredibly low penetration achieved by landlines during the previous century, with landline subscription for the African continent as a whole only at 1.7% of the population by 1994. A detailed survey of 10 African countries (Gillwald, 2005) shows how even these figures mask the great inequalities found in landline access between urban and rural areas, with Ethiopia receiving special mention for not having any rural landline phones at all (see Figure 8.2).

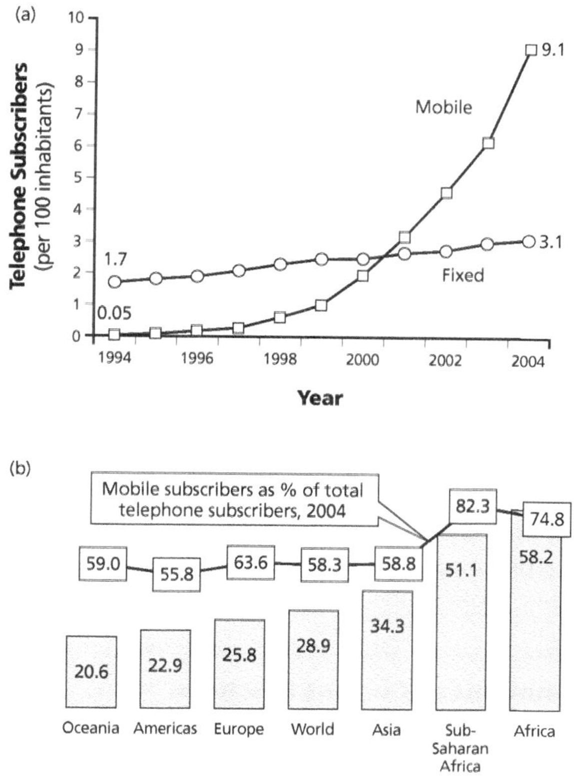

Figure 8.1 Mobile uptake in Africa, from Gray (2006). (a) Mobile and fixed telephone subscribers per 100 inhabitants in Africa, 1995–2004, and (b) annual average percentage growth in mobile network subscribers, 1999–2004, world regions.

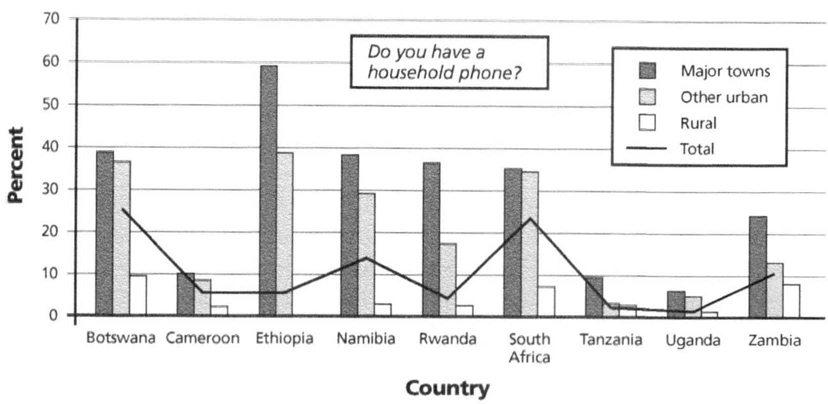

Figure 8.2 Household landline phone by survey location (Gillwald, 2005, p. 21).

THE LANDSCAPES SURVEYED

- There are severe challenges in creating meaningful education for all; these challenges are most severe for rural teachers, pupils, and communities in the global south.
- The educational potential of ICTs are widely recognized, but the dominant models of implementation and practice seldom fulfill this potential.
- There is a revolution in mobile ICT currently taking place in the global south: the mobile phone revolution; but this is not yet commonly harnessed for enhancing education.

Such an analysis raises the following questions:

- Can the mobile phones teachers possess be used to support their professional development and practice?
- How will the affordances of these devices change in the near future?
- What are the implications for future initiatives seeking to use ICT for teacher professional development?

Mobile Technologies—Current Practices

It is within these landscapes that we consider two case studies of mobile technologies being used to support teachers and schools serving disadvantaged, often rural communities in Sub-Saharan Africa. A recent DFID review of support for students on school-based primary teacher training programs in Sub-Saharan Africa identified six guidelines for the planners of distance education programs, two of which are of particular relevance here:

> Build the capacity of the entire delivery system and support network in a way that links the key stakeholders with one another... [and] prioritize student support as the key ingredient of success. (Mattson, 2006)

A number of Sub-Saharan African institutions have begun to explore the potential of SMS to meet this challenge, including the University of Pretoria, which has begun to use SMS to support ten thousand teachers enrolled through the unit for distance education (Hendrikz et al., 2006). The first case study presented here looks at an even larger scale program using SMS messaging to connect stakeholders and support teachers engaged in a national teacher professional development program in Kenya. Such programs are now able to operate on a large scale, using mobile phone technologies and networks that have become near ubiquitous in Sub-Saharan Africa over the last 8 years.

The second case study does not use the current "common" phone, but considers the potential of "pocket computers". Although these are currently uncommon, and for most teachers in the global south, unaffordable, their features and capabilities are now being integrated into "smartphones", and are likely to be found in the "common" phones such teachers will carry in the near future. Such devices have been described as "Trojan mice" (Soloway & Norris, 2005) relatively small tools that can bring about fundamental changes in educational settings.

Case Study 1: The SEMA project (SMS for supporting teacher professional development and schools in Kenya)

The Ministry of Education (Kenya) has implemented a large scale program, SEMA (2005) to explore the potential of mobile phone technology for facilitating communication between teachers and their peers and trainers, and between schools and the ministry. James Sankale was the coordinator (2005–2007) of the SEMA project. This was a part of the larger School Empowerment Program, which James also coordinated (2004–2007) for the Kenya Ministry of Education INSET unit.

The National Context

MOEST (2005), puts a clear emphasis on developing infrastructure and capacity, in particular human resources, in order "to develop the skills today which will be needed tomorrow". The government envisages education as the natural platform for equipping the nation with the ICT skills in order to create a dynamic and suitable economic growth. The ICT Scoping Study (MOEST, 2005b) highlights the inadequate number and capacity of computers, as well as lack of access to the Internet in Kenya. Most people in Kenyan society have no access to the Internet through landlines or computers; on the other hand, the mobile phone networks are far more available and accessible than any other form of ICT except radio, with many more people using mobile phones than the desktop computers. The low cost, high mobility and high utility of the mobile phone have contributed significantly to the high take up of these digital devices, compared to desktop computers (see Figure 8.3).

Survey data shows that over 17% of the Kenyan population possessed a mobile phone, with 65% of subscribers (especially the youth) being users of SMS services. On average, 3 million SMS messages are being sent each day in Kenya. Furthermore, when thinking of teacher professional

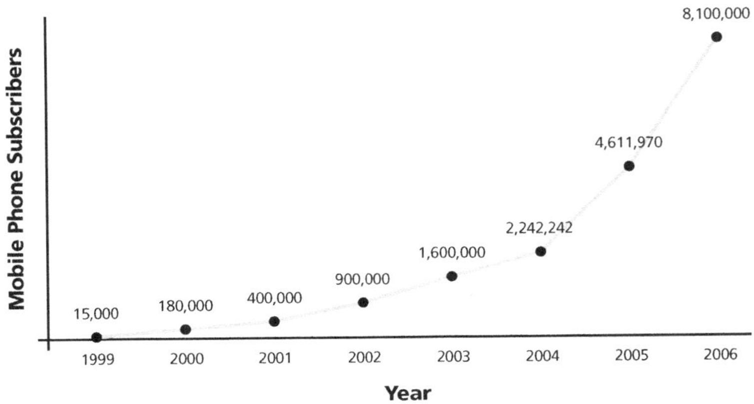

Figure 8.3 Number of mobile phone subscribers (Kenya), 1999–2006.

development programs, we were encouraged that the MOEST study also shows that teachers are early adopters of mobile technology; estimating that 80% of teachers in Kenya had already purchased their own mobile phones by 2005.

In other sectors, there is increasing evidence of SMS being incorporated into organizational information systems—for marketing and fund-raising, for communication among staff, clients and wider organizational networks, as well as for on-demand information services (Cheverest et al., 2003), with SMS messaging being used for administrative support, to communicate alerts and for mentoring. In popular culture, SMS use extends from public message displays to voting on Pop Idol. In this context, it seemed that the time was now right to begin exploring how to harness the potential of SMS for supporting large scale, national educational programs.

The SEMA Program

SEMA (School Education Management Application) is built around a powerful database driven back-office, connected to two mobile phone network providers in the country. Teachers and those supporting them in the program are all registered individually on the system, which enables SMS messages to be sent to individuals, schools, regional clusters of schools, or even to everyone with a specific role in a particular geographic region. The primary purpose of SEMA SMS service is to support School Empowerment Program (SEP)—a teacher in-service program which used a blended approach in its delivery (including the use of distance learning modules supported by video and audio recordings and broadcast radio productions). SEMA has used SMS to facilitate administration and communication within this professional development program, enabling one-to-one and one-to-group messages to be sent between participants.

SEMA seeks to explore how SMS can be used to cost effectively improve:

1. The organization and administration of teacher education workshops and programmes;
2. SEMA uses SMS to provide support, continuity, guidance, reminders and peer coaching within clusters of schools participating in the "School Empowerment Program" (SEP) of teacher professional development;
3. The efficiency, speed and accuracy of data collection, collation, storage and analysis.
4. SEMA collects data such as the number of boys and girls enrolled in each year, in every school, providing the MoE with more up to date and reliable data in relation to school enrolment, performance, support and funding, providing better quality information for decision making within the ministry.

SEMA aims to:

- Improve quality of in-service teacher training (INSET) through provision of information services;
- Enhance communication among various cadres within the education system;
- Improve education data collection for EMIS (Education management information System);
- Improve the efficiency, speed, accuracy, storage and analysis of data by setting up a simple system.

To date, SEMA has registered 3500 schools, with16,350 teacher participants being supported by 310 support personnel, including Quality Assurance and Standards Officers, as well as School Advisors.

Issues Experienced During the Implementation

For the data collection aspects of SEMA, users must send in specially formatted text messages that have a syntax the application can understand. The positive aspect of this is that each individual message can be very "data-rich" for its 160 character size, but the down side is that users must be trained in how to use this syntax, and then use it precisely. There were some technical issues related to the different models of mobile phone teachers were using, for example, some teachers could not locate some of the special characters required for the SEMA messages, such as the hash key. Some of the female teachers had problems with husbands wanting to be "in control" of the mobile phone, making it difficult of them to use it for school purposes. A minority of teachers tried using the "free" SMS sending facilities within SEMA to send private messages. Using a cascade model of training, there is always the danger of some of the lower levels not "getting as wet as expected", or of the training materials being interpreted in a way which was contrary to the original intentions.

Challenges

A major concern in Kenya and many developing countries is to provide quality education to its larger population especially in the arid and semi-arid lands. Most of the network coverage in Kenya is often found along major roads and cities; despite the rapidly growing uptake of mobile phone technology, the network coverage outside many of our major urban towns is limited and inadequate. Network coverage has affected how rapidly SEMA has been able to roll out. However, even though, most schools in the rural areas do not have coverage, and so cannot get messages immediately as expected, in most cases they have found creative ways to access the system. Many teachers have identified areas in their locality where a signal can be received (e.g., a corner of a particular room, up a certain tree or other high point); they have begun to call these locations "hot spots" or "Boothes" where they receive messages. Many schools and communities have begun to put up signs indicating the location of a "boothe." In other circumstances, teachers give their phones to colleagues residing in areas with coverage to pick messages and return phones next day. Power grid also tend to follow areas with high population densities. Lack of power supply means that teachers cannot charge their phones. Teachers have again found innovative ways to address this, such as through the use of solar chargers. Finally, there is a need to engage a greater range of policy makers to raise awareness of how recent changes in mobile technology can be leveraged to achieve policy goals. "Access to connectivity remains one of the major challenges facing many developing countries. . . ." Darkwa and Mazibuko (2000).

Summary

SMS text messages enhance communication among teachers and school clusters, encouraging peer support as well as contact with those supporting the teacher training programme; SEMA is finding such additional communication and administration tools a valuable form of support to the School Empowerment Program.

It has been possible to engage a large number of teachers (over 16,000) over a short period of time, because of the use of technologies that are already almost ubiquitous, rather than having to provide "new" technologies and then having to support them through extensive training and technical support. The use of the mobile phone as the core communications platform for SEMA is seen as particularly appropriate, and pro-poor; the OECD good practice paper on ICTs for economic growth and poverty reduction notes:

> The [mobile] telephone is a device which suites the voice culture of the poor, does not require much technical literacy, offers a variety of payment mechanisms that suit the flexible finances of the poor (including text as a cost-effective alternative to voice) and which is battery operated, almost eliminating the requirement of access to the electrical grid. (OECD, 2005, p. 67)

It is particularly noteworthy that the SEMA system also made sending and receiving messages free of cost to the teachers and schools (through central funding). This is in contrast to many ICT initiatives, where donors typically meet the upfront costs of providing equipment, but pass on the maintenance and use costs to the schools; earlier work (Power, 2006) suggests that such ongoing costs can be substantial, and a significant barrier to ongoing participation in ICT enhanced activities.

Although enabling infrastructure is patchy outside major urban centers and trunk roads, teachers have shown sufficient motivation to participate in the SMS supported aspects of the program, that in many cases they have found a variety of innovative ways to overcome poor access to power and communications networks. The uses of SMS has enabled the rapid and accurate collection of data from many schools, condensing a process that previously took up to a year into a matter of weeks. This has greatly enhanced the quality of information available to the ministry.

However, despite SEMA using the pro-poor technology of the mobile phone and ensuring project usage costs are not incurred by teachers or schools, some issues of social justice remain. Almost all schools that have participated in the project serve poor communities and lack the technologies and infrastructure that might be required for other kinds of ICT initiatives, yet even within these schools, it remains the case that the most disadvantaged demographics (women teachers, rural teachers) experienced the most difficulties and challenges in their freedom to access their professional networks through the SEMA system. Schools in rural communities away from major towns or roads were unable to participate in the program, as they still lacked the mobile phone infrastructure the project depends upon. Providing such infrastructure to the rural majority is a necessary next step towards equity of opportunity.

Case Study 2—DEEPER—Handheld Mobile Devices for Teacher Professional Development and Practice

The "DEEPER" research project (Power & Thomas, 2007) grew out of the DFID funded "DEEP" research project (Leach et al., 2006), which had become an umbrella for a number of research activities into teacher education, international development and innovative approaches to ICT (www.open.ac.uk/deep), co-directed by Jenny Leach and Tom Power at the Open University, between 2001–2007.

In DEEP, teachers from schools serving disadvantaged communities in Egypt and South Africa used a variety of forms of ICT, including ICT suites, laptops, internet cafes, digital cameras and digital video cameras, scanners and printers, both for their own personal and professional development, and for the teaching and learning of literacy and science. Additionally, all project teachers were provided with a then "state of the art", handheld computer, to help develop their familiarity with computers, and to facilitate professional study. Course materials were installed on these devices, including illustrated e-books, case studies, exemplar lesson plans, video clips of professional practice, illustrated poems and an audio file of Martin Luther King's "I have a dream..." speech.

The research showed that teachers found the handheld devices particularly useful for professional planning and administration:

> It saves time because at home I can prepare my lessons. I then download to the PC [at school]. This didn't happen before. This is better than using the pen! The whole process was easier than normal preparation. Preparing and planning lessons was routine, but now I came to be creative.
>
> This account is borne out by observations of two lessons and by the range of products in Saraa's electronic portfolio, including a workbook on how to teach place value in maths.

The creative teachers, seeing learning and classroom practice at the heart of their development, also used the devices extensively in their classroom practice. Below are examples from teacher quotes from the interviews:

> "Word for writing... I left the device to the students"
>
> "I used the camera many times to take photos related to the lesson I'm teaching and also to write some information"
>
> "listening to songs and watching song clips"
>
> "making various slides on some animal and its various characteristics"
>
> "We have used the [handheld] for sports days, for cultural days, for all the activities...in the classroom situation, we've taken pictures of our learners"

At the end of the project, most teachers reported that they found the handheld just as useful as the laptop computers. Those who expressed a preference identified the handheld computer as the best tool for supporting teacher professional development and practice, particularly liking of the portability, and the ability to capture images and sounds. Whilst many studies have investigated the use of handheld computers in classroom settings, most of these focus on pupil learning (e.g., Fung et al. 1998; Yarnell et al 2003). Soloway (2002) argues that handhelds provide an opportunity for making major changes in educational settings, though there is not yet a substantial body of literature on the potential of handhelds for teacher education.

The DEEPER Project, 2004–2006

Twenty-eight teachers, from the Eastern Cape province of South Africa, took part in the follow up study, which was facilitated by the provision of 25 iPaq H4150 "pocketPC" handheld computers from the then South African based charity, Bridges (www.bridges.org).

Project DEEPER sought to explore:

- What specific advantages do handheld computers offer teacher professional development?
- In what ways do handheld computers complement other professional resources?
- What curriculum developments are enabled by such devices/what software development would enhance their use?

The teachers themselves used the analytical framework for teacher professional knowledge developed by Banks, Leach and Moon (1999) to consider their own experiences with the handheld computers. (The methodology and research instruments are detailed in Power & Thomas, 2007). DEEPER professional development materials (literacy activities on local social history, and science activities for studying the local environment) were *only* provided in digital form on the handheld computers. Examples can be downloaded from the project web site (http://www.open.ac.uk/deep/Public/web/projects/extending.html).

As well as digital texts (eBooks), the project also provided video and audio resources (such as examples of classroom practice), and exemplar spreadsheets and other documents for teacher professional development. The project team had also hoped to link the handheld computers to participants' mobile phones to provide email and internet services, but the large variety of phones in use made this beyond the technical resources available.

Findings

During the evaluation workshops, participants used sketches to illustrate their thoughts, feelings and experiences. They then arranged these into groups of related sketches, trying to identify what the common themes were. Three of the emergent themes are presented here:

1. Feeling lost . . . For many, there was an initial period of feeling "lost" with the handheld. 40% of the teachers on the project had little or no previous experience of using computers of any kind, and even those teachers who had used handheld computers in the prior study found the differences between device, operating system and software packages confusing at first, taking most of the six months from launch to the interim workshop for teachers to be comfortable and familiar with the new tools.

Figure 8.4 Participant sketch.

2. Beginning to see new Possibilities . . . A second theme to emerge from the teachers own reflections was a sense of "seeing possibilities opening up"—of excitement and potential. Several teachers illustrated a moment of realization when they understood that the handheld computer really was "a computer"—that it had many of the programs and capabilities of the desktop and laptop computers.

Teachers put a number of sketches in this "discovery" theme, which relate to professional practices outside the classroom, such as planning, preparation and personal organization. Below are quotes from the teacher exit surveys:

> "It helped me to plan my lessons, based on what is on the PDA [the course resources]"

> "I use it to write some reports for our cluster"

> "It reminds me of the work I must do and the date of something I'm going to attend"

"Even my Curriculum Vitae is with the PDA, so for always move around with all that can be important..."

"It stores information and reminds me easily and makes my work easy. That's what I like—it's handy. I can go anywhere with my information on the PDA"

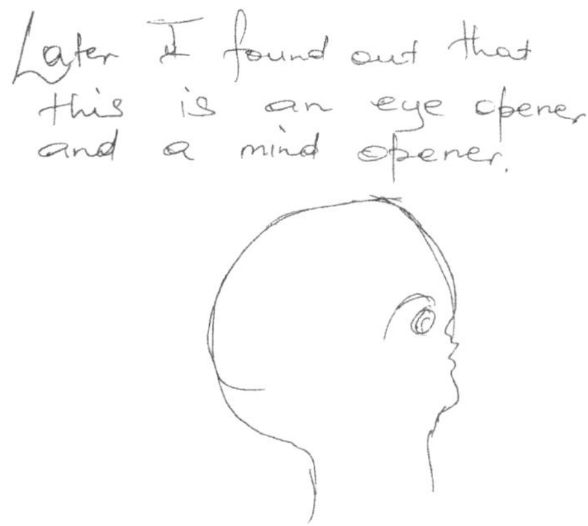

Figure 8.5 Participant sketch.

Exit survey results show that over 50% of the teachers had used the literacy materials, and over 50% used the science materials; almost 80% of reported the course materials on the handheld computers as "very useful" for their own study.

3. Exploring Classroom Practices. In the classroom:

- over 90% of the teachers had used the camera both to take photos and share them with others (pupils and peers) as part of their professional practice;
- 85% used the handheld as a calculator;
- 65% of teachers regularly used the dictionary as a tool for learners, and for themselves at home;
- 65% used the handheld as a word processor;
- 58% used the handheld as a voice recorder;
- 43% had used the handheld as data collection tool, using spreadsheets.

Part of the appeal of the handheld that, used with creativity and ingenuity by the teachers, it could "become" so many different resources: at one moment a planner, at another a mark-book, the next a dictionary, a calculator, a book to read, a tape recorder, word-processor or spreadsheet, a photo album of class experiences and the world outside, a music player, and so on and so on. Six of the teachers even used it as a Bible for religious instruction at the start of the school day.

Figure 8.6 Participant sketch.

Issues and Challenges

The prime challenge for future interventions using handheld computers or smart-phones is the extent of teacher training required, and the need to further develop a range of curriculum related practices to capitalize upon the capacity of such digital tools. The secondary challenge is around the development of appropriate educational software and resources, as the current feature-set is orientated to office environments and practices; for example: there is no software currently available that allows teachers or pupils to create multi-media documents directly on the handheld. If pupils want to put words to the photos of the fieldwork they have done, they must currently resort to a "proper" computer. Teachers saw this as one of the main limitations of the devices.

The main technical issue with these early handheld devices affected almost every teacher at some point: the volatile device memory caused information to be lost when the battery was drained. The course resources stored on the memory card were not lost, but the software to read the resources was installed on the device and was lost, leaving the resources inaccessible. Teachers also lost any of their own work not stored on the memory card. It would be hard to overstate the significance of such data loss, particularly in rural areas. Fortunately, more recent devices tend to have non-volatile memory, so this should not be as much of an issue in future initiatives.

There were a small number of much more minor technical issues detailed in Power and Thomas (2007).

Summary

This study used "handheld computers" that occupied a niche somewhere between the mobile phone and the laptop or desktop computer. These devices are not yet as pro-poor as the mobile phone: the rapid expansion of mobile phone access over the 21st century has been driven by demand; there is yet little evidence of similar scale of demand for "pocket computers", and accordingly, little evidence of a range of payment mechanisms that would enable the poor to access such technologies through the private sector.

The study deliberately set out to explore the use of these technologies with teachers from schools serving disadvantaged communities: the Eastern Cape is the poorest province with the widest poverty gap of any South Africa; of the fourteen schools participating, twelve were rural or peri-urban; of the twenty-eight teacher participants, twenty-four were female. Unsurprisingly, none of the teachers owned their own "pocket computer" at the start of the project. Because the technologies were unfamiliar to the teachers, the need for initial training and support was high; many teachers had a lengthy period of uncertainty before they began to feel comfortable with the technology.

By the end of the study, almost all teachers had used the handhelds for personal professional development, and for classroom practice with learners and two thirds of them reported the handheld computer to be as or more valuable to their practice than either laptop or desktop computers. The way the handheld can "be many things" and serve many purposes was highly valued by project teachers and 85% of the teachers said they would be willing to spend their own money to purchase a handheld computer to support their work. (At a subsequent informal meeting with several of the teachers a year after the project, all of those present had purchased mobile phones with color screens, internet and email access, and regularly used these features). The handheld devices used in this study do have a number of characteristics in common with pro-poor ICTs such as the mobile phone: the light-weight, long-battery life, highly portable nature of the devices is highly valued by teachers, especially those teaching in schools in rural communities.

Current Practices—Conclusions

In both case studies, there is a sense that the teachers highly valued the opportunity to use mobile digital tools; in both cases, teachers were not passive recipients gaining "access" to knowledge created elsewhere, but they actively used the technologies for purposes central to their professional identity and practice as teachers. Pryor and Amplah (2003, p xii) identify three factors that contribute to the successful integration of ICTs into rural educational settings:

- Recognition—people were able to see themselves and their way of life reflected [in the use of these devices].
- Association—they were able to communicate and associate as part of a prestigious global community [of users of ICT].
- Appropriation—the appropriation of skills allowing people to develop information and media literacy [for purposes that are valid and meaningful to them].

The first case study shows that, through using technologies that are already possessed by most teachers, it is possible to very quickly move to large scale adoption of such technologies to support professional development programs. The technical training demand is greatly reduced by such a strategy, with teachers already confident and familiar in using the tools, which typically offer only voice and SMS services. The communicative power of the mobile phone is highly valued, particularly in rural areas where network coverage exists (mainly within signal range of major roads and towns). This study used a range of ODL resources, including print, video cassettes, audio cassettes, and face to face workshops, supplemented by the limited affordances of basic mobile phones to support communication and administration.

The second study shows that providing new, more powerful, mobile technologies to teachers unfamiliar with them currently has a high training demand, as well as incurring costs in providing equipment; both of these aspects currently present barriers to large scale adoption of such technologies to support professional development programs in the global south. However, after a period of time, teachers came to highly value being able to use this "multi-tool" both for their own professional development and for their classroom practices, and rated such devices as preferable to either desktop or laptop computers. In this study, all the ODL resources, including text, video and audio assets, were made available directly to teaches through the digital handheld devices. Taken together, these case studies raise questions about the nature of "technology" being planned for in educational settings in the global south.

Currently "educational ICT" is often used as a shorthand for desktop or laptop computers; initiatives typically orient around donor or government led procurement with most expenditure going on equipment and networks; Pimienta's Law (Pimienta 2007) suggests that when:

- > 60% of expenditure is on such infrastructure, projects are likely to end in serious trouble due to deficiencies of educational content and training
- > 80% of expenditure is on such infrastructure, the project is likely to end in disaster
- 100% of expenditure is on such infrastructure, the project should be investigated for corruption.

Yet we are currently riding the wave of a global revolution in mobile technologies, where for the first time, mass access to digital communications networks and devices is becoming a reality, even for many of the rural poor. Just as strikingly, this access is largely the result of private sector activity, using flexible financing to make mobile phone technology affordable to people on very low incomes.

In the last three years, we are beginning to see a shift in the context of large scale educational interventions, from "providing" (alien) ICTs to schools to using the mass ICTs that teachers already own through their private purchase. Currently such interventions must be supported by other educational resources (such as books, video, audio) provided through non-mobile technology. As we move into the second decade of the 21st century, it is likely that the technologies and affordances of current handheld computers and "smartphones" will become features of "common" phones. (This is already occurring now, with cheap handsets from China offering colour screens, GPRS network connections, internet and email services at prices that would have been for "budget" handsets 12–24 months ago). When teachers carry in their pockets devices capable of playing and recording audio, video and still images, reading and writing text documents, and sending and receiving all of these over the internet, what are the implications for teacher professional development and classroom practice?

Currently, very little is yet known. The case studies here represent two early examples of exploring the possibilities. In order to move forward, it is necessary to establish:

1. The ways in which mobile devices can support good classroom practices;
2. The ways in which mobile devices can support best practices in teacher professional development programs;
3. The nature of infostructure (software and resources) development required to support 1) and 2).

There is an ongoing whirlwind of change in access to mobile networks, ownership of mobile devices and the capabilities of mobile devices. There remains much more that is unknown about whether and how such changes might be exploited to help equip teachers with the professional knowledge, tools, and resources that are desperately needed in the global south. But it seems clear that the educational technology world can no longer afford to ignore the mobile revolution.

REFERENCES

Banks, F., Leach, J. and Moon, B. (1999). New understandings of teachers' pedagogic knowledge. In Leach, J., & Moon, B. (Eds). *Learners and pedagogy*. London: Paul Chapman.

BBC News (2005). *Mobile growth 'fastest in Africa'*. http://news.bbc.co.uk/1/hi/business/4331863.stm, Accessed online January 2008.

Cheverest, K., Clareke, K., Fitton, D., Rouncefield, M., Crabtree, A., & Hemmings, T. (2003). *SPAM on the menu: the practical use of remote messaging in community*. Proceedings of the 2003 conference on Universal usability (p 23–29). Vancouver, Canada. http://portal.acm.org/citation.cfm?id=957205.957210.

Commission For Africa (2005) *Our common interest,* London. http://www.commissionforafrica.org.

Darkwa, O., & Mazibuko, F. (2000). Creating virtual learning communities in Africa: Challenges and Prospects. *First Monday,* 5(5). http://firstmonday.org/issues/issue5_5/darkwa/index.html.

Developments.org (undated). Mobile phone revolution. *Development Magazine.* http://www.developments.org.uk/articles/loose-talk-saves-lives-1/?searchterm=tanzania%20mobile, accessed January 2008.

DevInfo (2006). *The facts. You decide.* http://www.devinfo.org/facts_you_decide/2002.htm?IDX=13' , accessed January 2008.

The Economist (2005). The Real Digital Divide. *Technological Quarterly,* March 10th, 2005.

Gillwald, A. (Ed.) (2005). *Towards an African e-Index. Household and individual ICT access and usage across 10 African countries.* Johannesburg: Research ICT Africa. http://www.researchictafrica.net/images/upload/Toward2.pdf.

Global Campaign For Education (2006). *Teachers for all,* (GCE Briefing Paper). Johannesburg: Global Campaign for Education. http://www.campaignforeducation.org/resources/Mar2006/GCE%20Teachers%20For%20All.pdf

Gray, V. (2006). *The un-wired continent: Africa's mobile success story.* International Telecommunications Union. http://www.itu.int/ITU-D/ict/statistics/at_glance/Africa_EE2006_e.pdf.

Hedges, J. (2000). The importance of posting in becoming a teacher in Ghana. *International Journal of Educational Development,* 22, 353–366.

Heeks, R (2005). I-development not e-Development: Understanding and implementing ICTs in development. *Journal of International Development on ICTs and Development,* 14(1).

Hendrikz, J., Viljoen, J. M., & Adams, L. (2006). *Text messaging (SMS): Perceptions and usage patterns.* (Report for the Unit for Distance Education, Faculty of Education) Pretoria: University of Pretoria.

Leach, J., Ahmed, A., Makalima, S., & Power, T. (2006). *DEEP IMPACT: an investigation of the use of information and communication technologies for teacher education in the global south.* Researching the issues. (DFID Research Series No. 58) London, U.K.: DFID http://www.dfid.gov.uk/pubs/files/ict-teacher-education-no58.asp.

Leach,J., Makalima, S., Porteus, K., Power, T., Thomas, R., & Tshume,K. (2006). *New voices, new technologies, new communities: the role of ICT in rural schooling and development.* Unpublished strategy paper prepared for the Nelson Mandela Foundation's Unit For Rural Schooling and Development, Eastern Cape, South Africa.

Leach, J., & Moon, B. (2002). *Globalisation, digital societies and school reform: Realising the potential of new technologies to enhance the knowledge, understanding and dignity of teachers.* 2nd European Conference on Information Technologies in Education and Citizenship. Barcelona, June 26, 2002.

Massachusetts Institute of Technology (2006). *One lap top per child.* Massachusetts, U.S: MIT Multi Media Lab . http://laptop.media.mit.edu.

Mattson, E (2006). *Field-based models of primary teacher training. Case studies of student support systems from Sub-Saharan Africa.* Researching the Issues 63. (DFID Research Series); London, U.K.: DFID http://www.dfid.gov.uk/pubs/files/field-based-models-teacher-training-63.pdf.

Ministry of Education, Science, and Technology (2005). *Kenya education sector support programme 2005—2010.* Delivering quality education and training to all Kenyans. Nairobi: MOEST. http://www.education.go.ke/MOESTDocs/KESSP%20FINAL%20PT%201%20JUL%2026TH%202005.pdf.

Ministry of Education, Science, and Technology (2005b). session paper No.1, 2005: 77. Nairobi: MOEST.

Moon, B. (2007). *The global teacher crisis—meeting the challenge through new technologies and new modes of teaching and learning.* 12th Cambridge International Conference on Open and Distance Learning. Cambridge, UK. 28th September 2007. http://www2.open.ac.uk/r06/conference/BobMoonKeynoteCambridge2007.pdf.

Mulkeen, A. (2005). *Teachers for rural schools: A challenge for Africa* (Ministerial Seminar on Education for Rural Peoples in Africa: Policy Lessons, Options and Priorities) Addis Ababa, Ethiopia. September 7–9th 2005.

Organisation of Economic Co-operation and Development, (2005). Good practice paper on ICTs for economic growth and poverty reduction. *The DAC Journal,* 6(3). http://www.oecd.org/dataoecd/2/46/35284979.pdf.

Pimienta, D. (2007). *Digital divide, social divide, paradigmatic divide.* Santo Domingo, Dominican Republic: Funredes. http://funredes.org/mistica/english/cyberlibrary/thematic/Paradigmatic_Divide.pdf.

Power, T. (2006). *Using suites of 'free' refurbished computers may cost over four times more than buying and using 'state of the art' learning technologies.* BERA, Warwick, U.K. 6–9 September 2006 http://www.open.ac.uk/deep/Public/web/publications/pdfs/TPower2006-BERA.pdf.

Power, T., & Sankale, J. (2007). *In the palm of your hand: supporting rural teacher professional development and practice through the use of mobile phones and other handheld digital devices*. Meraka Innovate Conference, 18–20 April 2007, Johannesburg, South Africa.

Power, T., & Thomas, R. (2007). 'The classroom in your pocket?', *The Curriculum Journal*, 18(3), p. 373–388 http://dx.doi.org/10.1080/09585170701590031.

Pryor, J., & Ampiah, J. G.(2003) *Understandings of education in an African village: the impact of information and communication technologies* (Report on DFID Research Project Ed2000-88) London: DFID. http://www.dfid.gov.uk/pubs/files/understandedafricaedpaper52.pdf.

Samuel, J., Shah, N., & Hadingham, W. (2005). *Mobile communications in South Africa, Tanzania and Egypt: Results from community and business surveys in Africa: the impact of mobile phones.* (Vodafone Policy Paper Series, Number 3, March 2005). www.vodafone.com/etc/medialib/attachments/cr_downloads.Par.78351.File.tmp/GPP_SIM_paper_3.pdf.

Selinger, M., & Gibson, I. (2004). *Cultural relevance and technology use: Ensuring the transformational power of learning technologies in culturally defined learning environments.* Proceedings of World Conference on Educational Multimedia, Hypermedia and Telecommunications 2004, 5310–5317. URL: http://www.editlib.org/index.cfm?fuseaction=Reader.ViewAbstract&paper_id=11835.

Soloway, E (2002) "*Palm-sized devices are the personal computers of choice*", (Colloquium series; November 12, 2002) Massachusetts, USA: MIT Media Lab http://www.media.mit.edu/events/movies/video.php?id=soloway-2002-11-12.

Solloway, E., & Norris, C. (2005), *Mobile technology: the future of learning in your hands.* mLearn 2005: Cape Town, South Africa, 25–28 October 2005.

United Nations (2000) Resolution adopted by the General Assembly. 55/2 United Nations Millennium Declaration. New York, U.S.: United Nations. http://www.un.org/millennium/declaration/ares552e.pdf.

United Nations Children's Fund—UNICEF (2005) *Annual Report 2005*. New York, U.S.: UNICEF http://www.unicef.org/publications/index_34144.html.

United Nations Educational, Scientific and Cultural Organisation (2000) *Education for All 2000 Assessment*, (Statistical Document) Paris, France: UNESCO.

United Nations Educational, Scientific and Cultural Organisation (2005a) *EFA global monitoring report: Regional overview* (Sub Saharan Africa). Paris, France: UNESCO. http://portal.unesco.org/education/en/file_download.php/73a941d1b5f931d7beee73443402fed4sub_saharan_africa_ENG.pdf.

United Nations Educational, Scientific and Cultural Organisation (2005b) *Strategy for cross cutting theme: Eradication of poverty, especially extreme poverty.* UNESCO and Least Developed Countries: Medium Term Strategy, 2002–2007. Paris, France: UNESCO. http://www.unesco.org/ldc/stragey.htm.

United Nations Educational, Scientific and Cultural Organisation (2006) *UIS regional profile: Teacher supply and demand in sub-Saharan Africa.* Paris, France: UNESCO. http://www.uis.unesco.org/TEMPLATE/pdf/Teachers2006/Regional_Profiles/RegProfile_sub-SahAfrica.pdf.

United Nations Educational, Scientific and Cultural Organisation (2007) *The EFA global monitoring report 2008. Education for all by 2015. Will we make it?* Paris, France: UNESCO http://portal.unesco.org/education/en/ev.php-URL_ID=49591&URL_DO=DO_TOPIC&URL_SECTION=201.html.

Unwin, T. (2005) Towards a framework for the use of ICT in teacher training in Africa, open learning. *The Journal of Open and Distance Education, 20(2), 113–128.*

World Bank (2003) *Information and communication technologies, poverty and development: Learning from experience.* (Background paper) infoDev Annual Symposium, 9th–10th December, 2003, Geneva, Switzerland.

Yarnall, L., Penuel, W. R., Ravitz, J., Murray, G., Means, R., & Broom, M. (2003) "Portable assessment authoring: Using handheld technology to assess collaborative inquiry" *Education, Communication & Information,* 3(2).

CHAPTER 9

THE DIGITAL DIVIDE IN DISABILITY AND EDUCATION

Jason Brent Ellis
Carla Abreu-Ellis
Ashland University

Amber Ricker
Bowling Green State University

INTRODUCTION

According to the United States Census Bureau's 2005 American Community Survey, 6.5% of school-aged children (5–15 years of age) were identified with a disability. The United States Department of Education's Office of Special Education Programs (2006) estimated that special education services were provided to 6,813,656 children 5–21 years of age in the fall of 2005. As definitions and classifications of disabilities have been redefined, in terms of medical definitions and legislative amendments, and as awareness has grown of disability in society, what seems to be an ever increasing stream of individuals are being identified with disabilities.

ICT for Education, Development, and Social Justice, pages 147–167

Mitra (2006) defined the meaning of disability to the layperson as "*the inability to do something*" (p. 236). However, researchers in the area of disability studies identify the definition of disability as falling under different, opposing, theoretical frameworks. Rioux and Valentine (2006) stated that "how disability is perceived, diagnosed, and treated, scientifically and socially, is reflected in assumptions about the social responsibility toward people with disabilities as a group" (p.50). Two main frameworks in which to contextualize and understand disabilities are noted: the Medical Model and the Social Model.

The Medical Model sees disability from a biomedical approach. The individual is expected to assume "the sick role" since he or she is considered to have a medical condition that is unwanted. Pfeiffer (2003) notes the inadequacy of this model in stating that:

> In the medical model the individual has a condition (a deficit) which is unwanted or which the past caused something unwanted in the individual. As such the individual is viewed as being in the sick role, or as being sick.... The person in the sick role is [thus] exempt from everyday social obligations... [and] must follow the orders of the professional—your doctor's orders—in order to become "well" (p. 31)

This line of thinking explains the unjust segregation and institutionalization of individuals with disabilities.

Rioux and Valentine (2006) refer to the Social Model as the social pathology framework which assumes an environmental and human rights approach to understanding disabilities. From this perspective, "disability is not inherent to the individual. Rather, they assume that the disability is a consequence of the social structure" (p. 51). The Social Model of disability envisions disability as a social construct. Smart (2001) provided the following example of how the perceptions and inevitable acceptance of disability work within this model:

> Often termed "the universality of disability," the theoretical model of everyone in a community having the same disability helps us to understand the social construction of disability. For example, if no one could walk, the community would be completely accessible for wheelchairs. Even more important, there would be no stigma, prejudice, or stereotypes about people who could not walk. The community would adjust to the inability to walk, with both universal accessibility and the corresponding absence of prejudice and discrimination. (p. 7)

The Social Model focuses on the interaction between individuals and the environment, and assumes that if the environment is modified, people with disabilities can become active members of society. It is the premise of this chapter that school environment can be modified through instructional practices that successfully integrate Information and Communication Technologies (ICT), including Assistive Technologies, for accommodations in education.

In the United States of America, school districts are required under the law to provide appropriate technology to accommodate students with disabilities when it supports their acquisition of a free and appropriate public education (Individuals with Disabilities Education Act, 1997). In order to support the inclusion and participation of students with disabilities in regular education classrooms, all Individual Education Plan's (IEP) developed for children identified as needing special education services, must indicate that assistive technology (AT) has been considered to provide meaningful access to the general curriculum (Individuals with Disabilities Education Act, 1997). More specifically, the Individuals with Disabilities Education Act mandates that assistive technology devices and services must be made available to a child with a disability if required as a part of the child's: (a) special education; (b) related services; or (c) supplementary aids.

However, many assistive technologies are computer based; they necessitate access to computers to work. This access to technology infrastructure may be influenced by a digital divide in who gets access to technology in education. Hendrix (2005) noted that:

> Computers are becoming common tools in schools, often viewed as a democratic panacea despite the costs involved and despite the fact that the majority does not have access to computers and/or the Internet; this creates a digital divide for students, in which some are 'more equal' than others. (p. 63)

Schools serve an essential role for students who have access to computers from only one location. Although nearly all schools and classrooms have computers, most provide severely restricted access to the students and teachers (Bronack, 2006). In light that the digital divide has traditionally been associated with inequities in access related to race (Fairlie, 2004), gender (Cooper & Weaver, 2003), and social class (Cleary, Pierce, & Trauth, 2006), this chapter attempts to observe the digital divide through the lens of disability. Even though the authors have focused mainly on examples related to students with auditory based disabilities, principles and concepts discussed in this chapter are easily transferrable to other disabilities, equitable access to technology and information, and it implications to social justice in education.

ACCESS TO EDUCATION FOR INDIVIDUALS WITH DISABILITIES

The history of the education of individuals with disabilities has been marked by an increase in societal awareness of the reality that some children need modifications to learn and grow (Smith, 1998). Many educational historians trace the roots of special education to isolated attempts at educating children with disabilities in the eighteenth century, such as those made by Jean-Marc-Gaspard Itard, perhaps most famous for his efforts to educate Victor, the wild boy of Aveyron (Smith, 1998; Bryant & Bryant, 2003). Victor, an eleven or twelve year old boy, thought to be abandoned by his parents at an early age, was found in the Caune Woods in the Department of Aveyron in France (Itard, 1962), having suffered from environmental deprivation and thought to have been born with a cognitive disability (Smith, 1998). Itard attempted to educate Victor with the goal of achieving age appropriate educational outcomes related to language acquisition and behavior. He documented many of his beliefs and practices, some of which are still utilized in special education today.

Another major figure that helped increase societal awareness of the special educational needs of children with disabilities was Eduard Seguin, a student of Itard, who published *The Moral Treatment, Hygiene, and Education of Idiots and Other Backward Children* in 1846, deemed the first manuscript that truly addressed the needs of children with disabilities (Smith, 1998). Seguin, a trained physician like Itard, held the strong belief that individuals, even with severe intellectual disabilities, could be educated; a belief that was inspired by philosophers such as John Locke and Abbé de Condillac. Almost 100 years before Seguin's time, Locke had brought forth the idea that the newly born child's mind was much like a blank slate (tabula rasa) and thus any child could be nurtured into learning appropriate behaviors (Wood, 1992). Similarly, Abbé de Condillac wrote the Traité des sensations in 1754 that argued that external impressions, received through the senses, accounted for all ideas and all mental operations (Yousef, 2001).

Seguin established an explicit developmental program for individuals with intellectual disabilities, with the ultimate goal of "responsible functioning in society" (Ball, 1971, p.49). His "specific techniques are not only ingenious but, in many instances, are directly applicable to today's training problems" (Ball, 1971, p.49). Seguin also helped found the initial organizations that would eventually become the American Association on Mental Retardation; the oldest and largest interdisciplinary organization in the field of cognitive disabilities (Smith, 1998).

Maria Montessori is perhaps the most commonly associated name in influencing societal awareness in the education of children with disabilities. Seguin's work has been said to have "deeply influenced Madame Montessori, who at the beginning of her career worked with feeble-minded children and obtained remarkable results by the use of his system" (Humphrey, 1962, p. xvii). She notable postulated the view that "mental deficiency presented chiefly a pedagogical, rather than mainly a medical, problem" (Orem, 1969, p. 15).

By the beginning of the early nineteenth century, residential schools were being established for individuals with disabilities under the guidance of such historical figures as Thomas Hopkins Gallaudet and Samuel Gridley Howe (Smith, 1998). Special education classes began to appear in public schools for the first time in the late nineteenth century with specialized training for teachers of students with disabilities only appearing in the first decade of the twentieth century (Smith, 1998). Stainback and Stainback, (1996) noted that "by the 1950s and 1960s, the use of special education classes in public schools was the preferred educational delivery system for most students with disabilities" (p. 20), and further observed that it was "during this period...that public attitudes about the places of individuals with disabilities in schools and the community began to change" (p. 20), moving away from a model of segregation towards one of inclusion.

The initial premise set forth in educating children with disabilities was to make individuals *more normal* within society and thus help facilitate their inclusion into the community. In the late 1950s, *normalization* became the target of educational policy (Bloom, 1973). Normalization thus became an important issue in special education on the basis that "persons with disabilities had a civil right to live, attend school, and work in the same environment as others" (Winzer, 1997, p. 27). Thus, normalization became the act of "making available to all persons with disabilities or other handicaps, patterns of life and conditions of everyday living which are as close as possible to or indeed the same as regular circumstances and ways of life of society" (Nirje, 1985, p. 67). This concept of normalization served as the basis for the inclusionary model of education today (Winzer, 1997).

Within the inclusionary model of education, children with disabilities are "placed in classrooms they would attend if they did not have a disability" (Stainback & Stainback, 1996, p. 28). In essence, this philosophy of inclusion established the belief that individuals with disabilities should be equals in terms of access to place and space in schools. Stainback and Stainback, (1996) observed that inclusion gained much momentum in the 1990s and has been deemed a "cultural force for school renewal" (p. 31) in which family, student, and school staff become catalysts of change. However, inclusion does not simply happen by itself; school policy must reflect a climate that fosters inclusion and tools must be provided to students with disabilities that allow them the opportunity to gain access to the general curriculum.

Scherer (2004) noted that inclusion can be facilitated to a large degree by the utilization of technology to accommodate the individual needs of persons with disabilities. This genre of technology for accommodation of disability is widely known as assistive technology.

ASSISTIVE TECHNOLOGY AND THE EDUCATION OF INDIVIDUALS WITH DISABILITIES

Assistive technology was first broadly defined by the Technology-Related Assistance for Individuals with Disabilities Act of 1988 (PL 100–407) as any kind of device that assists persons with disabilities in the performance of daily tasks and activities (Carlson, Ehrlich, Berland, & Bailey, 2001). The scope of assistive technologies encompassed under this definition are a genre of devices and technologies, "ranging from 'low tech' mobility devices such as walkers and canes to 'high-tech' speech synthesizers and other augmentative communication devices" (Carlson, Ehrlich, Berland, & Bailey, 2001, p. 1).

The United States Congress noted that in 2004, over 54,000,000 individuals in the United States self-identified as having disabilities, "with almost half experiencing severe disabilities that affect their ability to see, hear, communicate, reason, walk, or perform other basic life functions" (29 USC 3001: Assistive Technology Act of 2004, p. 1). In education, Hasselbring and Glaser (2000) noted the importance of AT in inclusion in that:

> Not only can computer technology facilitate a broader range of educational activities to meet a variety of needs for students with mild learning disorders, but adaptive technology now exists than can enable even those students with severe disabilities to become active learners in the classroom alongside their peers who do not have disabilities. (p. 102)

In education, the goal of assistive technology is to provide meaningful access to the general curriculum for students with disabilities (Individuals with Disabilities Education Improvement Act, 2004). White, Wepner, & Wetzel (2003) observed that "there is an ever-increasing population of students who desire a full education and need technology to assist them in achieving their goals" (p. 27).

Little research has been performed measuring type of disability and amount of school assistive technology use (Carlson, Ehrlich, Berland, & Bailey, 2001). However, the education community has been challenged by barriers to successful technology integration to properly accommodate students with disabilities, and teachers have been viewed as unprepared to use available assistive technology resources (White, Wepner, & Wetzel, 2003). These challenges in integrating technologies to accommodate in schools manifests as two distinct forms of the digital divide; (a) a divide in accessing information through the instructional use of ICT by teachers in inclusive education and (b) a divide in access and training opportunities for individuals with disabilities.

THE DIGITAL DIVIDE IN INSTRUCTION AND ACCESS

Let us introduce first the digital divide in terms of instruction. Imagine yourself in a contemporary classroom with rows of desks aligned so they face the front of the classroom. You are a student in the class and the teacher is about to project a movie that she has found on an educational website that will provide a greater understanding of the topic of the day. The teacher tells the class that there will be a short quiz on the content of the video immediately following. You are excited at the promise of being able to get a concrete example for the theory you have just been taught. As you see the streaming video begin to appear on the screen you become saddened, disillusioned, frustrated, and angry. You see, you are clinically deaf. You can hear with your hearing aides, but since they pick up all the ambient sounds in the classroom, you also hear the rustling of papers from one of your peers two seats over, the hum of the florescent light that your teacher has left on at the back of the room, and the vague mumbling and merging sounds coming form the projector speaker. You remember that you are going to be tested on the material from the film immediately following its presentation, but are faced once again with not having the equivalent access to information that your hearing peers have been granted.

This is an all too familiar example of the digital divide in accessing information because pedagogically ICT has been used in an inefficient way. In essence, instruction has failed to provide access to a wide range of students' needs. To provide diverse students with equity of access to information, *Universal Design* (UD) principles should be incorporated into instruction.

Universal design is "the design of products and environments to be usable by all people, to the greatest extent possible, without the need for adaptation or specialized design" (Center for Universal Design, 2007, p. 1). Bowe (2000) describes seven principles of Universal Design, which included: a) equitable use, b) flexibility in use, c) simple and intuitive use, d) perceptible information, e) tolerance for error, f) low physical effort, and g) size and space for approach and use. In the example illustrated previously, the teacher could have made the instructional material available ahead of time to all students on the class website allowing them to watch the proposed video before class. This would benefit students with learning disabilities who require repetition in order to assimilate the content. In adopting UD principles, a transcription of the video should be made available on the class website as well as provided to students before the presentation of the video in class. This approach would benefit the student who is clinically deaf in that the student would be able to follow the material in a written format, as well as students who assimilate written information better than in an auditory manner. By providing the transcription of the video, students could listen, read, and visualize the material presented in the video by applying all three senses and accommodating the needs of all the student s in the class.

The digital divide is also related to access and training for students with disabilities. Unfortunately, not every individual within society has the financial resources to secure the technologies that would provide them appropriate accommodations in the classroom. Parents and advocacy groups relentlessly fight battles for children in attempting to secure funding and resources. What is of grand concern is that while these children are forced to wait for technology accommodations they are not allowed the educational production afforded to their peers without disabilities, but are expected to fulfill the same educational outcomes.

In the United States two laws current provide discourse on the educational expectations of students with disabilities, the No Child Left Behind Act (NCLB) of 2001 and the Individuals with Disabilities Education Improvement Act of 2004, which both "support the philosophy that all children, regardless of disability, should have access to the general education curriculum" and that within the context of these two laws "with few exceptions, students with disabilities are expected to meet the same high academic standards as their peers without disabilities" (Johnston, Beard, & Carpenter, 2007, p. 14). Johnston, Beard, and Carpenter (2007) noted that both of these complimentary laws have been said to have "thrust students with disabilities into the mainstream of general education in greater numbers" (p. 10), and as such "are expected to become proficient in subject matter, AT will provide access for them to become successful learners in the general education classroom" (p. 10). Closing the digital divide in disability may be the catalyst for meeting educational expectations outlined under these legislative mandates.

To provide a tangible example of how the digital divide plays out in disability, the following case was written by Amber Ricker; one of the authors of this chapter. It represents her personal narrative reflections of barriers in instruction and access she has experienced during her education. It provides insights into the lived experiences of a student, self- described as hard-of-hearing, in her plight to get equitable access to assistive technologies and access to information through sound pedagogical approaches in educational services. The narrative spans, in time frame, from early childhood through higher education. It is important to note that for the purpose of this chapter ICT encompasses instructional technologies and assistive devices that facilitate learning as well as allowing individuals with disabilities to live independently.

Amber's Story

My name is Amber Ricker and I am a 21 year old college student. I have a bilateral sensorineural hearing loss. I have three main contributing factors to my hearing loss: nerve damage due to a skull fracture in 1988, scar tissue from ear infections and ear surgeries, and hereditary factors. Basically, I am faced with the fact that my hearing will deteriorate as I age. I received my first hearing aid when I was in sixth grade.

In my freshman year of high school an IEP (Individualized Education Plan) was set up for me. With this, I was provided with an FM System which registered the teacher's voice through a microphone and transmitted the signal directly to my hearing aids.

Right after services had been established, in the middle of my freshman year in high school, I moved to another town because my parents separated. At first, I was not able to attend my new school since school administrators thought it would be best for me to be transported to and from my old school since they already had a program established for deaf and hard-of-hearing students. However, due to family conflicts, springing from my parent's pending divorce; it was decided best for me to be at the new school and a few weeks later services were transferred. Many teachers at this new school were not familiar with an FM System or how to work with students with hearing impairments.

I remember one day, shortly after I began attending the new school; I was walking in the hall between classes. This was a hectic time for me, especially since it was still the first few weeks at the new, larger school. I always shut the FM System off in the hallways. Apparently, a teacher had tried to get my attention and she thought I was ignoring her. So she proceeded to, as I was walking up the stairs, grab my arm and pull me into the office. I was so confused! I had no idea what was going on as I was not able to turn my FM System back on. She made me sit in the office while she got the principal. She was very upset. Apparently, the new school had a policy against wearing flip flop sandals at school, which I was wearing that day. The teacher thought that I was ignoring her as I kept on walking as she tried to stop me in the hallway. After much confusion, I received apologies from both the teacher and the principal.

The school year progressed with similar instances; it was a constant battle to have films with closed captioning and teachers who were not understanding of the limitations created by my disability. No matter how elaborately I explained it, teachers never seemed to understand that even with an FM System, I could not always understand them when they would turn to write on the chalkboards and speak while they were writing. When a teacher does this, Deaf or hard-of-hearing students are not able to read lips to differentiate between the ambient sounds and the teacher's voice.

Hearing aids and FM Systems have been very beneficial to me and I would have never gotten through high school without them. However, it is essential to know that they do not *fix* a student's hearing deficit. By the end of my high school career I realized that teachers' attitudes were what determined whether or not the semester would go well and whether or not my needs would be accommodated.

Technology has become a vital part of my ability to succeed in daily activities. I depend on my hearing aids for everything. Even though I am visual [can see], there are so many things that I need to be able to hear (such as teacher's voices or a fire truck's siren). While I was growing up I used hearing aids that were not the greatest for my type of hearing loss since the manufacturer primarily focused on adults with hearing loss due to aging. However, at the time they were a complete God-send because my family had no way to pay for the hearing aids. The company had a children's foundation which covered the large expense of the hearing aids since our insurance covered minimal expenses in this area.

Students whose parents are financially stable have an obvious advantage in accessing technology. A student's parents who are set financially are able to buy him or her hearing aids and have access to services such as speech therapists. As for lower income families, like mine, they must rely on organizations and public school systems to help provide their children with the technology and resources that they need. This process can take months, if not years in order to obtain support services.

Now I have hearing aids, which are top of the line. They are digital (programmable on a computer) and automatically filter sounds, which have both benefits and drawbacks. Analog hearing aids amplify everything. I would hear lights buzzing, people's voices, chairs screeching across the floor, and so many other sounds all at the same level. Analog hearing aids also have limited volume control. For instance, the analog hearing aids I was first fitted with, only had four volume level settings. With digital hearing aids, a computer can program the volume as needed. I went through five analog hearing aids before I finally received my digital hearing aids. Even with my profound hearing loss, my current hearing aids still can be adjusted should my hearing continue to decrease. With digital hearing aids, certain sounds can also be filtered out. I have one setting that works best in environments that are large, but not with a lot of people, and I have another setting that is primarily for when I am in a classroom that has many different ambient noises and people.

Another piece of technology that I depend on is my alarm clock. When I first started college, people would ask me if I had to have someone come to my room every morning to wake me up. I thought this was absurd. I have an alarm clock that vibrates my bed and flashes the lights in order to wake me up. I regularly use my FM System and closed captioning in a variety of settings. For instance, I go to larger movie theatres that have a headset to amplify sound, as well as a rear-view captioning system. Back when I got my first hearing aid when I was in sixth grade, I was unaware of these possibilities. For all I knew, I would never go to see a movie again. Apparently when you ask the neighbor next to you to repeat what you just missed, people get quickly annoyed. Who would have thought?

In the past, I did not have much experience with technology, since my disability was not emphasized in my family. I was never known by my disability. This can be both good and bad. It was good in a sense that I was not labeled "disabled" and placed within a segregated group, but at the same time, my technological and support services were delayed. By not being perceived as "disabled" I experienced little stigma in that people continued to see me as capable in school. However, by not being on an IEP until I was in high school and my family not recognizing my disability, my education was inhibited. When I graduated from high school my reading comprehension was approximately at a junior high level. If the proper services would have been in place, I could have received the necessary services and assessments, at which time I believe would have revealed the delay in my development.

When I became a delegate for the Ohio Governor's Council on People with Disabilities' Youth Leadership Forum, I learned about various services available to me such as: TTY (Teletype), hearing dogs, vibrating alarm clocks, and many other resources and forms of assistive technology available to individuals with hearing loss. I quickly learned, during my freshman year of college that I needed to advocate for myself. I knew that I needed to stand up for my rights as an individual with a disability.

It was not until I met other Deaf and hard-of-hearing individuals that I realized the importance of self-advocacy. I knew that my parents were not going to speak up for me in regards to my disability. Only I know what I need and when I need it. Seeing others stand up for themselves caused me to realize that I must do the same if I too want to become a successful person in life. Even after this epiphany, I had no idea of the difficulties I would encounter throughout high school and college to obtain proper and adequate support services. A lot of documentation is needed at the college level; you cannot just walk into class on the first day demanding an interpreter, usage of an FM System, notes, and preferential seating. Most instructors would either laugh in your face or not know what to say. A procedure must be followed in order to obtain services. However, once the proper documentation is in place, most services will quickly follow.

My freshman year of college though, I went to a small private liberal arts Christian school. I loved the aspect of faith being inter-mixed with my collegiate education; however, the disability services office did not meet my needs. The very first week I had a professor refuse to use my FM System. To this day I have no idea what was discussed or taught in that class.

Upon transferring to a different college in my sophomore year, I realized the gravity of my situation. I decided that I needed to be more proactive and adamant about the services I required to help me excel. Now, when I meet with my advisor in the disability services office we discuss the areas in which I am struggling and we come up with a concrete plan. For instance, I was struggling with my textbooks. I have great difficulties with reading comprehension still today; I would spend more than five hours reading one chapter of a textbook and not be done with it. After reading the material, I had no clue what I had just read. To make matters worse, due to other health problems my vision had become blurry and trying to read class materials became even more time consuming. I was to the point where I just stopped reading; and my grades plummeted. I finally went to disability services and explained everything to my advisor and we decided to start putting my textbooks on a computer format so that I could use text-to-voice software to read the textbooks to me. Yes, I am clinically deaf. However, with hearing aids I get much benefit from listening to the text. As well, the same software that reads the text also allows me to change the font size and highlight information to make it more accessible to my specific needs.

Self-advocacy is essential to obtain necessary services to aide someone in their educational experiences. The disability services office had no idea that I had the needs until I went and shared with them my concerns. Students must learn at an early age the great need for advocating for themselves. Parents need to work with their children and schools to set up support services. If money is an issue, do not push that child to the side. Rather, get creative and come up with a way to get the technology that would help the student to excel to their fullest potential. Above all, keep the child actively involved in the process; they will need the experience for later on in life once they reach high school, college, and/or the work force.

SUCCESSES AND CHALLENGES IN USING ICT FOR THE EDUCATION OF STUDENTS WITH DISABILITIES

Based on the information provided in the case study, the following discussion provides insights into the challenges and successes of educational access and ICT for individuals with disabilities. The available research literature in the area of disability and technology has been included to contextualize Amber's story. Regarding the performance of reflective narrative research, Denzin & Lincoln (1994) describe the process as "textual-discourse analysis" (p. 358). Within this frame of context "documents of experience can be content analyzed; that is, themes, issues, and recurring motifs within them can be isolated, counted, and interpreted" (p. 358).

A content analysis of Amber's narrative was performed to identify emergent themes. To derive themes, the following questions for reading narratives, outlined by Patton (2002) were considered:

> What does this narrative or story reveal about the person and world from which it came? How can the narrative be interpreted so that it provides an understanding of and illuminates the life and culture that created it? (p. 115)

These themes are discussed at length and related to current research literature in the following section of this chapter.

MOBILITY, CHOICE, AND ACCESS TO EDUCATION FOR INDIVIDUALS WITH DISABILITIES

Students with disabilities, including hearing impairments as illustrated in the case study, are being educated in public school settings with their peers without disabilities in ever increasing numbers (Schick, Williams, & Kupermintz, 2005). Marschark et al. (2005) observed that deaf students in K–12 mainstream classrooms have a teacher "who typically is unfamiliar with the implications of early hearing loss" (p. 729). A major concern within the research literature regarding students who are deaf and hard-of-hearing in mainstream education arises around their ability to fully participate in teacher and peer communications (Antia, Sabers, & Stinson, 2006). Within the case study included in this chapter, Amber observed that, when faced with moving schools, her school district had elected to keep her in the school, in which accommodations had been established. This was because they were prepared to provide appropriate services with staff members who were aware of the nature of her disability.

In transitioning to her new school, Amber described an inequity of accessing information due to the staffs' lack of awareness of disabilities and ICT used to accommodate students' functional limitations. For instance, she noted struggling to have access to closed captioned films that were shown in the classroom and the tendency for her teachers to speak with their backs to the students when lecturing. Once at university, she noted the outright refusal of a professor in using an FM system to broadcast his lecture to her hearing aids. As such, these instances mark sufficient grounds to state that Amber experienced an inequity in accessing information to which her peers, without disabilities, had ready access. In moving towards inclusive education, schools have assumed that students with significant hearing losses could access communication by sign language interpreters, real time text, and other forms of ICT and that "the structures of instructional materials designed for hearing students in a 'hearing' classroom are appropriate for the knowledge structure and the learning styles of deaf students" (Marschark et *al.*, 2005, p. 754).

A survey research measuring teachers' perceptions of barriers to assistive technology use in California indicated that teachers lack training in ICT when serving students with disabilities as Ashton (2005) found that special education teachers perceived that (a) having a deficit in knowledge related to assistive technology, (b) lacking resource materials, (c) having inadequate training time, and (d) lacking access to funding were issues that acted as substantial barriers to successful integration. Ashton also noted that special education teachers' responses indicated that they felt that their teacher education programs had not adequately prepared them for successful assistive technology use. Perhaps this sheds light into why Amber only came to the realization that technology could successfully accommodate her disability late in her academic career.

EQUITY IN ACCESS TO ICT FOR STUDENTS WITH DISABILITIES

In school, children compete; they are rivals for grades, the teacher's attention, and access to technology resources. The premise here is much like Charles Darwin's concept of survival of the fittest in that all living things compete for survival. As such, those organisms that are best adapted to changes in their environment have a better chance at survival (Delger, 1991). For students with disabilities, survival in the academic realm may be dependant on obtaining appropriate environmental adaptations through ICT.

In the case study, Amber discussed the fact that her family did not have financial resources to accommodate her disability through technology. She observed that she had luckily found a program through a hearing aid manufacturer that had provided her with her first hearing aids. Amber also noted that students with disabilities, whose parents have financial means to acquire appropriate technologies to make accommodations, have a much easier time in procuring technology that provides them with equity in access to curricular materials and information.

De Graaf (1986) noted that "inequalities in educational attainment due to race, sex, and region have decreased, but inequalities that can be attributed to parents' occupation and education have remained stable" (p. 237). In discussing the effects of parents' education and occupation on school experience, Anyon (1983) suggested that public schools in complex industrial societies, like the United States, make different types of educational experiences available to different social classes. She studied several different schools, catering to different social classes in the United States, and concluded that:

> Differing curricular, pedagogical, and pupil evaluation practices emphasize different cognitive and behavioural skills in each social setting and thus contribute to the development in the children of certain potential relationships to physical and symbolic capitol, to authority, and to the process of work. (p. 165)

In essence, children are taught at the level of their social status. What is critical is that these structures seem to reproduce themselves over time. Children who come from parents whom have positions of power and higher education thus have the means to provide the same educational experiences to their children and readily procure ICT to accommodate their children with disabilities. As Amber observed those who do not have the means to acquire ICT out-of-pocket may have to wait for months or years to find a means of acquiring the appropriate technologies.

Regarding access to ICT in schools, Natriello (2001) observed that "poor and minority families and their children have less access to a range of resources in society" (p. 260). This inequity in who gets access to technology has been coined the digital divide. As stated previously, the problem regarding technology to accommodate disability and appropriate access is one of academic survival. As Hasselbring and Glaser (2000) note this in stating that:

> Millions of students across the United States cannot benefit fully from a traditional educational program because they have a disability that impairs their ability to participate in a typical classroom environment. For these students, computer-based technologies can play an especially important role. (p. 102)

Thus, without appropriate technology access in schools for individuals with disabilities, and the absence of "multiple dimensions of educational settings and organizations configured to support learning for all students, learning will not be equitably distributed" (Natriello, 2001, p. 263).

Perhaps even more frightening is the fact that access in schools to appropriate ICT for individuals with disabilities may be marred by staff attitudes. In interviewing special education teachers about their perceptions of the digital divide in schools, Ellis (2007) found that professionals, providing educational services to individuals with disabilities, perceived that special education was treated as *lesser* education in terms of access to technology. In essence, teachers felt that there was a pecking order to technology access in schools, as manifest in a disparity between both access to existing, shared technology resources in schools, and the distribution of new technology resources. Means (1998) noted that technology infrastructure is often envisioned as the first step in successfully integrating technology into instruction, and as such, "large applications of public funds are likely to focus on infrastructure improvements, often with a formula for 'equitable' distribution of resources across all districts, schools, or classrooms" (Means, 1998, p. 6). Means (1998) subtly observed that there may not be much equality in a formula of equitable distribution of resources. As such, the disparity of the distribution of technology resources within schools may be seen as another of the "complex factors that shape technology use in ways that serve to exacerbate existing education inequalities" (Warschauer, Knobel, & Stone, 2004, p. 562). As Hendrix (2005) noted, within technology access, some students are clearly denoted as 'more equal' than others.

LEVELING THE PLAYING FIELD THROUGH TECHNOLOGY

The phrase "level playing field" is often used in discussing the utilization of accommodations for individuals with disabilities in education. It refers to the idea that if a field of play, for instance in soccer, is sloped toward the direction of one team's goal, there is an obvious disadvantage; as such a level playing field would offer fair or even competition, where no advantage is provided to either side. In terms of disability, ICT is seen as one means, along with other appropriate educational accommodations, of leveling the field of play for students with disabilities.

Amber noted reaching an epiphany that using technology in school and her daily living could equalize her chances at academic success. Indeed, she noted the successful integration of text-to-speech utilities to access print materials given her newly acquired visual impairment and challenge of decoding written text. She also observed how the use of an FM system in conjunction with her hearing aids provided her access to information, such as instructors' lecture materials, that would be difficult to access otherwise. In fact, even the example of her vibrating alarm clock is congruent with ICT in that it provides her access to information, in this case the time to awaken, which would not be accessible otherwise given her profound hearing loss.

With the benefits of technology also come costs and self-advocacy to acquire the appropriate ICT. Under current American legislation, students with disabilities are to be provided access to ICT in schools to accommodate the functional limitations of their disabilities and, in essence, level the playing field with their peers. However, schools are not required by law to provide the best accommodations to students with disabilities nor maximize the student's potential. In 1982, the case of the Board of Education of the Hendrick Hudson School District v. Rowley, the United States Supreme Court ruled that:

> The obligation to provide a FAPE [Free and Appropriate Public Education] did not mean a district was required to maximize a student's potential or provide the best education possible. The Court noted that the program must be

> based on the student's unique individual needs and be designed to enable the student to benefit from an education. (Hager & Smith, 2003, p. 45)

What the Supreme Court had decided was that students with disabilities must be provided sufficient accommodations to make educational progress, but at the same time if they could make educational progress through minimal, low or non-technological means, then that was sufficient. A hypothetical example would be that of a student who had the functional limitation of not being able to produce oral language. Assistive technology would be deemed appropriate in providing some means of communication and thus providing an accommodation for a free and appropriate public education under IDEA (1997). However, school district decision makers could easily argue for a minimal accommodation in the form a communication board in which the student points at pictures to communicate needs rather than technology that produced synthesized language that requires the provision of both computer hardware and software.

There has been little resolution in both research literature and legal discourse to the problem presented in the previous discussion; however parental advocacy has been viewed as essential in achieving inclusion in educational services, and this too may work for achieving appropriate technology accommodations (Burgstahler, 2004). Parent driven advocate groups have been essential to both enacting and changing legislation regarding disability and education (Turnbull, Trunbull, Erwin, & Soodak, 2006). In recent years many non-profit groups such as the Parent Advocacy Coalition for Educational Rights and the National Center on Access to Information Technology in Education have been formed to help parents in advocating for their children with disabilities. Barred successful advocacy, parents' other options include lodging formal complaints with the Office of Civil Rights and the more costly option of class action or other litigation (Hager & Smith, 2003).

CONCLUSION

Students with disabilities can benefit from ICT, principally in the form of assistive technologies, in order to enhance their academic experiences. However, an inequity exists regarding access to educational technology for students who lack self-advocacy skills, have parents who do not voice their opinions, and families from low economic status. Further, students with disabilities are challenged in their academic success due to teachers' lack of awareness of both disability and Universal Design principles in instruction. Technology services are supported by legislation; however, the quality of services each individual is to receive is not clearly defined under the law.

Therefore, in order to secure appropriate ICT for individuals with disabilities one must rely on their ability to fight for their rights and demonstrate that the technology is an essential requirement in order to gain meaningful access to the general curriculum.

Johnson and Hayes (2007) observed that "social justice matters in education and it matters most when students struggle to complete and succeed at school" (p. 371). For students with disabilities, social justice must be manifest in the form of equality of opportunity (Gale, 2000). More specific, to the central argument in this chapter, through equality of access to technology and information provided through instructional practices that utilize ICT.

True inclusion, and the social justice that comes with it for students with disabilities, necessitate shifting the focus away from "individual deficits to the environmental, structural and attitudinal barriers within institutions and society" (Allan, 2003, p. 176). As Thomas (1997) noted, changing societal opinions about disability in general may be a key ingredient for social justice in educational access and access to educational resources. In his perspective, inclusion should be viewed from an ethical juxtaposition rooted in "a philosophy of acceptance and about providing a framework within which all children (regardless of the provenance of their difficulty at school) can be valued equally, treated with respect and provided with equal opportunities at school" (Thomas, 1997, p. 103).

REFERENCES

Allan, J. (2003). Productive pedagogies and the challenge of inclusion. *British Journal of Education, 30*(4), 175–179.

Antia, S. D., Sabers, D. L., & Stinson, M. S. (2006). Validity and reliability of the classroom participation questionnaire with deaf and hard-of-hearing students in public schools. *Journal of Deaf Studies and Deaf Education, 12*(2), 158–171.

Anyon, J. (1983). Social class and the hidden curriculum of work. In H. A. Giroux & D. Purpel (Eds.), *The hidden curriculum and moral education: Deception or discovery* (pp.143–167). Berkley, CA: McCutchan.

Ashton, T. M. (2005). Perceived knowledge, attitudes and challenges of AT use in special education. *Journal of Special Education Technology, 20*(2), 60–63.

Assistive Technology Act (2004). *ATAP press release: Congress passes the assistive technology act of 2004.* Retrieved May 17, 2007 from http://www.ataporg.org/AT-pressrelease.pdf.

Ball, T. S. (1971). *Itard, Seguin, and Kephart: Sensory education, a learning interpretation.* Columbus: Charles E. Merrill Publishing Company.

Bloom, B. (1973). *Normalization and educational policies.* Downsview, Ontario : National Institute on Mental Retardation.

Bowe, F. G. (2000). *Universal design in education: Teaching nontraditional students.* Connecticut: Bergin & Garvey.

Bronack, S. (2006). Learning unplugged: The internet divide in American schools. *Electronic Magazine of Multicultural Education,* retrieved May 23, 2007 from http://www.eastern.edu/publications/emme/2006Spring/bronack.pdf.

Bryant, D. P., & Bryant, B. R. (2003). *Assistive technology for people with disabilities.* Toronto: Pearson Education, Inc.

Burgstahler, S. (2004). *How can parents promote the use of accessible technology in schools?* Seattle: National Center on Accessible Information Technology in Education.

Carlson, D., Ehrlich, N., Berland, B., & Bailey, N. (2001). *Assistive technology survey results: Continued benefits and needs reported by Americans with disabilities.* Austin: National Center for the Dissemination of Disability Research.

Center for Universal Design. (2007). *About universal design.* Retrieved September 12, 2007 from http://www.design.ncsu.edu/cud/about_ud/about_ud.htm.

Cleary, P. F., Pierce, G., & Trauth, E. M. (2006). Closing the digital divide: Understanding racial, ethnic, social class, gender and geographic disparities in Internet use among school age children in the United States. *Universal Access in the Information Society, 4*(4), 354–373.

Cooper, J., & Weaver, K. D. (2003). *Gender and computers: Understanding the digital divide.* Mahwah, NJ: Lawrence Erlbaum Associates.

De Graaf, P. M. (1986). The impact of financial and cultural resources on educational attainment in the Netherlands. *Sociology of Education, 59*(4), 237–246.

Delger, C. N. (1991). *In search of human nature: The decline and revival of Darwinism in American social thought.* New York: Oxford University Press.

Denzin, N. & Lincoln, Y. (1994). *Handbook of qualitative research.* Thousand Oaks, California: Sage Publications, Inc.

Ellis, J. B. (2007). *The digital divide in special education: Where do my students fit in?* Presented at the International Study Association for Teachers and Teaching Conference, July 9, 2007: Totems and Taboos. St. Catharines, ON.

Fairlie, R. W. (2004). Race and the Digital Divide. *Contributions to Economic Analysis & Policy,* 3(1), retrieved May 26, 2007 from http://www.bepress.com/bejeap/contributions/vol3/iss1/art15.

Gale, T. (2000). Rethinking social justice in schools: how will we recognize it when we see it? *International Journal of Inclusive Education, 4*(3), 253- 269.

Hager, R. M., & Smith, D. (2003). *The public school's special education system as an assistive technology funding source: The cutting edge.* Neighborhood Legal Services Inc. Retrieved May 15, 2007 from http://www.nls.org/pdf/special-ed-booklet-03.pdf.

Hasselbring, T. S., & Glaser, C. H. (2000). Use of computer technology to help students with special needs. *Children and Computer Technology, 10*(2), 102–122.

Hendrix, E. (2005). Permanent injustice: Rawls' theory of justice and the digital divide. *Educational Technology & Society, 8*(1), 63–68.

Humphrey, G. (1962). *Introduction to the wild boy of Aveyron.* New York: Appleton Century Crofts.

Individuals with Disabilities Education Act of 1997, 20 U.S.C. § 1400 *et seq.* (Lexis 2005).

Individuals with Disabilities Education Improvement Act. (2004). P.L. 118–446. (Lexis 2007).

Itard, J. M. G. (1962). *The wild boy of Aveyron* (C. Humphrey & M. Humphrey, Trans.). New York: Appleton-Century-Crofts (Original work published 1894).

Johnson, K., & Hayes, D. (2007). Supporting student success at school through teacher professional learning: The pedagogy of disrupting the default modes of schooling. *International Journal of Inclusive Education, 11*(3), 371–381.

Johnston, L., Beard, L. A., Carpenter, L. B. (2007). *Assistive technology: Access for all students.* Columbus: Pearson.

Marschark, M., Pelz, J. B., Convertino, C., Sapere, P., Arndt, M. E., & Seewagen, R. (2005). Classroom interpreting and visual information processing in mainstream education for deaf students: Live or Memorex. *American Educational Research Journal, 42*(4), 727–761.

Means, B. (1998). *Models and prospects for bringing technology-supported education reform to scale.* Presented as part of an interactive symposium, Educational Technology for School Reform: Ways to Win (and Ways to Lose) at the annual meeting of the American Educational Research Association, San Diego, CA.

Mitra, S. (2006). The capability approach and disability. *Journal of Disability Policy Studies, 16*(4), 236–247.

Natriello, G. (2001). Comment: Bridging the second digital divide: What can sociologists of education contribute? *Sociology of Education, 74*(3), 260–265.

Nirje, B. (1985). The basis and logic of the normalization principle. *Australia and New Zealand Journal of Developmental Disabilities, 11*(2), 65–68.

Orem, R. C. (1969). *Montessori and the special child.* New York: Capricorn Books.

Patton, M. Q. (2002). *Qualitative research and evaluation methods.* Thousand Oaks: Sage Publications.

Pheiffer, D. (2001). The conceptualization of disability. In S. N. Barnartt & B. M. Altman (Eds.), *Exploring theories and expanding methodologies: Where we are and where we need to go* (pp. 29–52). New York: Elsevier Science, Ltd.

Rioux, M. H., & Valentine, F. (2006). Does theory matter? Exploring the nexus between disability, human rights, and public policy. In D. Pothier & R. Devlin (Eds.), *Critical disability theory: Essays in philosophy, politics, policy, and law* (pp. 47–69). Toronto: UBC Press.

Scherer, M. J. (2004). *Connecting to learn: Educational and assistive technology for people with disabilities.* Washington: American Psychological Association.

Schick, B., Williams, K., & Kupermintz, H. (2005). Look who's being left behind: Educational interpreters and access to education for deaf and hard-of-hearing students. *Journal of Deaf Studies and Deaf Education, 11*(1), 3–20.

Smart, J. (2001). *Disability, society, and the individual.* Gaithersburg, MD: Aspen Publishers, Inc.

Smith, D. D. (1998). *Introduction to special education: Teaching in an age of challenge.* Toronto: Allyn and Bacon.

Stainback, S., & Stainback, W. (1996). *Inclusion: A guide for educators.* Baltimore: Paul H. Brooks Publishing Co.

Thomas, G. (1997). Inclusive schools for an inclusive society. *British Journal of Special Education, 24*(3), 103–107.

Turnbull, A., Turnbull, R., Erwin, E. J., & Soodak, L. C. (2006). *Families, professionals, and exceptionality: Positive outcomes through partnership and trust.* Columbus: Pearson.

U.S. Census Bureau. (2005). *2005 American community survey: Disability characteristics.* Washington, DC: U.S. Census Bureau.

U.S. Department of Education. (2006). *Children with disabilities receiving special education under Part B of the Individuals with Disabilities Education Act, 2005.* Retrieved September 13, 2007 from https://www.ideadata.org/PartBdata.asp.

Warschauer, M., Knobel, M., & Stone, L. (2004). Technology and equity in schooling: Deconstructing the digital divide. *Educational Policy, 18*(4), 562–588.

White, E. A., Wepner, S. B., & Wetzel, D. C. (2003). Accessible education through assistive technology. *T H E Journal, 30*(7), 24–27.

Winzer, M. (1997). *Special education in early childhood: An inclusive approach.* Scarborough: Prentice Hall.

Wood, N. (1992). Tabula Rasa, Social Environmentalism, and the "English Paradigm." Journal of the History of Ideas, *53*(4), 647–668.

Yousef, N. (2001). Savage or Solitary? The wild child and Rousseau's man of nature. *Journal of the History of Ideas, 62*(2), 245–263.

CHAPTER 10

SCHOOL–COMMUNITY ICT-MEDIATED LINKAGES

The Southeast Asian Experience

Cher Ping Lim
Edith Cowan University

John Hedberg
Macquarie University

INTRODUCTION

Since 1995, many countries have spent billions of dollars to bring information and communication technologies (ICT) into classrooms as part of school reform initiatives to change the way schools operate and the way students learn. The primary motivation for such investment is the belief that ICT supports students' constructive thinking, allows them to transcend their cognitive limitations, and engages them in cognitive operations that they otherwise may not have been capable. In many of the Southeast Asian countries, master plans for ICT in education were launched to help schools integrate ICT into their curriculum and consequently to develop a culture of thinking, lifelong learning, and social responsibility. More recently, the

ICT for Education, Development, and Social Justice, pages 169–179

initiatives have attempted to connect schools to their communities through ICT. Here we explore several case studies of such initiatives in Indonesia, Malaysia, Singapore, and Thailand, and discuss the nature of the connections that are taking place and the benefits that have resulted from these initiatives.

SCHOOLS AND ICT IN THE SOUTHEAST ASIAN COUNTRIES

In the last decade, the spectacular proliferation of ICT use in the workplace, home, and school has fuelled the creation of a global information environment. ICT impact every aspect of everyday life from communication with friends and families to shopping, banking, and entertainment. In many Southeast Asian schools there has been recognition that ICT has the potential to play an important role in facilitating the linkages between schools and their communities, and this has led to some important innovations. The first stage of our investigations into how these linkages operate involved our taking account of the educational and technological landscape of the school systems in Indonesia, Malaysia, Singapore, and Thailand. This is necessary to provide a context for the examination of the case studies of how ICT is being used to facilitate linkages between schools and their local, national, and global communities.

A central goal of the school system in Indonesia is to equip children with the skills, attitudes, and knowledge to participate in the modern nation state, including its bureaucracies, its morals, and its ideological foundation. In 1993, the Indonesian government declared a nine-year compulsory basic education program: six years of primary education followed by three years of junior secondary education. For primary education, Indonesians between seven and twelve years of age can choose between state-run, non-sectarian public schools supervised by the Department of Education and Culture or private/semi-private schools supervised and financed by the Department of Religious Affairs. After primary education, students may choose between vocational and pre-professional junior and senior high schools, where each level is three years in duration.

The goal of the Malaysian education system is to develop the potential of individuals in a holistic and integrated manner. Compulsory education is only at the primary level for six years. The national education system consists of pre-school education for three years, primary school education for six years, secondary school education for four years, and post-secondary education for two to three years. For the primary schools, most are national or national-type schools. At the secondary level, there are the academic schools, technical and vocational schools, and religious national schools.

The vision of the education system in Singapore is "Thinking Schools, Learning Nation." This motto describes a nation of thinking and committed citizens capable of meeting the challenges of the future, and an education system geared to the needs of the 21st century. Compulsory education in Singapore is similar to Malaysia's—six years of primary education. At the primary level, students go through a four-year foundation stage, Primary One to Four, and then a two-year orientation stage from Primary Five to Six. Almost all primary schools are government or government-aided schools. For secondary schools, students go through four years before being admitted to pre-university colleges or the polytechnics. There are four types of secondary school: independent, autonomous, government-aided, and government schools.

The aim of the Thai education system is to develop Thailand into a knowledge-based society based on the principle of "Education Builds the Nation, Empowers the Individual and Generates Employment." The Thai school system comprises four levels: three years of pre-primary education, six years of primary education, three years of lower-secondary education, and three years of upper-secondary education. Compulsory education is similar to that in Indonesia with six years of primary education and three years of lower-secondary education. Most of the primary schools are under the Office of the National Primary Education of the Ministry of Education, while most public secondary schools are under the Department of General Education, Ministry of Education.

Regardless of the differences in the education systems, all of the four countries have formulated a national ICT plan in education and have also focused on the technological challenges of buying an appropriate learning management system, getting sufficient bandwidth allocated to e-learning, and obtaining state-of-the-art learning tools and materials. Although the technological infrastructure may vary in the four countries (with Singapore and Malaysia being the most developed), all four have established reasonable infrastructure and processes for the professional development of educators and flow-on training for students and parents in the use of ICT.

HOW ICT IS EMPLOYED IN DEVELOPING COMMUNITIES

Linkages between schools and their communities take the form of formal and informal online communication among principals, teachers and parents, online collaboration among students and the local and international community, and online sharing of ideas, problems, and information between schools and parents. These linkages are facilitated by e-mail communication between teachers and parents; updated school websites to provide parents with information about school policies, programs and activities; login accounts for parents to access their children's progress records via the school online administrative system; online discussion forums for teachers, principals, and parents to engage in dialogue about the vision and activities of the school; and synchronous online communication for parents who are too busy to meet teachers face-to-face.

The home-school link in using ICT has been a topic of discussion among educators. Research studies suggest that there is a gap between computer use in the home and the school in terms of frequency of use, type of technology, software used, and style of interaction. Mumtaz (2001) conducted a study in England with primary school students to find out children's enjoyment and perception of computer use in the home and the school. She reported that the most popular activity on the home computer is playing games. It was found that there are gender differences with boys spending more time than girls playing computer games. She also reported that the most frequent activity at the school computer was word processing, which pupils considered boring. Based on these findings, the author suggested that schools should learn from what works at home and enable children to engage in activities they find valuable, motivating, and worthwhile.

In another study, Harris (1999) reported on secondary school students' use of ICT at home in England. While the study found that the majority of the students had access to a personal computer at home, students did use computers to complete their schoolwork and study using educational programs. They also used computers to surf the Internet and play games. The two applications which students indicated they used most were games/adventures and word-processing. She found that boys spent the majority of their time using games/adventures. The gender differences were consistent with Mumtaz's (2001) report. Harris also focused on the students' motivation for using computers at home, where students reported that they used computers at home because they enjoyed playing computer games, and because the computers helped them with homework.

Sutherland and colleagues (2000) reported the Screen Play project which investigated how context shaped the use of computers in out-of-school settings. Interviews with the participating children indicated that having computers at home assisted the children's learning in school, made up for perceived shortage of up-to-date technology in schools, supported children to prepare for a technology-rich future world of work and leisure, kept their children at home and provided entertainment through access to games. The authors described the application of computers as cognitive tools and supporting communication between people using email and chat. In addition the technology was viewed as a medium for supporting collaboration in educational contexts. These authors suggested that children's approaches to home computing have implications for the use of computers in schools that have yet to be fully explored. However, the claims suggest that there is a complimentary role between school and home use of computing technologies. The home school link can increase the amount of involvement or interaction between the school and children's parents. ICT thus offers the potential for schools to create websites that parents and the community can access. Many parents found that information provided by the schools was beneficial for the community as a whole.

Lewin, Mavers, & Somekh (2003) pointed out that since early 1990, teachers have planned and facilitated online collaboration between students and their local and international communities. The case studies in this chapter illustrate continued evidence of this kind of activity with some expansion into community linkages that were not previously occurring. For example, there are collaborations such as e-mail exchanges between international or local experts/researchers and students; asynchronous and synchronous communication among students from different parts of the world to work on an online project; and online collaboration between students and local enterprises or organizations to help the community.

LINKAGES BETWEEN SCHOOL AND COMMUNITY IN SOUTHEAST ASIAN SCHOOLS

The case studies in Indonesia, Malaysia, Singapore and Thailand illustrate the links being forged between schools and their communities. In this section we describe the benefits of forging such linkages and illustrate the nature of the interactions that are occurring in each of these places:

1. ICT Bridges and Strengthens the Home–School Connection and, if Properly Harnessed, Promotes Parents' Activities and Involvement in the School

Although there has always been a need for information exchange between schools and parents, both parties are often denied critical information about the children (both at home and in the school) due to outdated modes of home-school communication. Such communications once focused mainly on formal, scheduled school activities that have been offered to all parents, such as parent-meet-teacher days or back-to-school nights (Weiss, Kreider, Levine, Mayer, Stadler, & Vaughan, 1998). The informal channel of communication, if any, was confined to suggestion boxes situated outside the school general office or telephone calls when a student was hurt or had repeatedly committed an offence. As a result of this lack of home-school communication, parents and teachers are often deprived of making informed decisions about children that will better meet their needs (Epstein, 1996).

ICT have made a fundamental change in this antiquated mode of communication; it has facilitated the linkages between schools and homes by enabling teachers and parents to play a greater role in the students' learning experiences. The bond between school and home can be strengthened through increased interaction and communication:

Malaysia: One of the deliverables of the Smart School Integrated Solution is a feature in the computerized Smart School Management System that enables parents to access their own children's school records remotely and to keep track of their progress. This integrated management software covers nine areas of school management: financial, student affairs, educational resources, external resources, human resources, facilities, school governance, security, and technology. The feature for parents became available in late 2002, but it has yet to be fully utilized by parents, particularly those who have no Internet access.

Singapore: A wide range of school activities involve parents and the community, due partly to school-industry partnerships and the autonomy given to schools in the ICT in education master plans. Moreover, with better connectivity linking the school to the home and community, peers, teachers, and parents are able to play a more active role in the students' learning. One example is the "Learning Village" project in Outram Secondary School under a MOE-IBM Collaboration, a School-Community Web Collaboration System using the Internet to foster home-school-community connection and partnership. By connecting various stakeholders of education, the Learning Village has strengthened the school's effort to achieve its mission: "An Intelligent School and a Caring Family". In another example, the Radin Mas Primary School has set up a Parent Link website to promote rapport among parents and between the parents and the school, as well as to foster mutual support in shaping the overall character of the students.

2. When Parents Are Encouraged to Participate in and Contribute to Change Management Activities within a School's ICT Master Plan, Change Occurs More Quickly

Several research studies have shown that what parents think and believe about various school reforms can affect the effectiveness of change management activities (Tobin & Dawson, 1992; Konzal, 1997). Where positive attitudes of parents towards reform initiatives are developed, it is likely that their support and participation in these activities will be encouraged. With respect to the use of ICT in schools, most parents have a positive attitude towards it; but, there needs to be a better understanding of parents' views of how ICT should be used in schools for teaching and learning (Scott & Hannafin, 2000). A key task for schools is then to involve parents in the formulation and implementation of the school ICT master plan.

Singapore: Outram Secondary School, an old neighbourhood school was chosen to pilot the Learning Village project, a Ministry of Education and IBM joint venture. The web-based project combines a set of Internet applications to allow communication and collaboration within the school and beyond it. Parents are given passwords to log in to the site from their homes and offices. Parents can go to an events calendar to check the whereabouts of their children, or visit teachers' home pages to find out more about their teaching methods, students' grades achieved in class, assignments, homework, and also lessons for independent study. Parents can also participate in online "meetings" with teachers and also be involved in their children's online discussions. With this mode of communication and collaboration, parents can offer their ideas for the schools' development and influence its policies even to the point of soliciting their views about the school's opening hours.

Malaysia: Pilot schools in the Smart School Project are encouraged to include parents and the community in their change management activities. Parent-teacher associations (PTA) have taken a keen interest in the development of the Smart School Project and helped to sponsor trips to the Multimedia Development Corporation (MDC) for an inside view of the work of the Multimedia Super Corridor (MSC). The MSC is a regional launch site for companies developing or using leading multimedia technology and the MDC is a one-stop shop created to manage and market the MSC. Other PTAs sponsored talks by ICT personnel, and facilitated the schools' participation in ICT-related competitions. The Smart School Pilot Project Team also organized a national seminar for representatives of PTAs from non-pilot schools as part of the Smart School Outreach Programme. In addition, the team has given talks and presented papers at seminars, conventions, and meetings to help disseminate information about the Smart School Project.

Thailand: In most cases, parents, alumni and PTAs are great school supporters. School committees comprising students, parents, and teachers are established across grade levels to work together on the students' learning and to prepare proposals to obtain support from the school board or PTA. Parents not only provide hardware and software, but have also become resource people. Some private schools have offered ICT training to parents so that they can guide their children in the use of technology or even learn together.

3. As ICT Opens Opportunities to Collaborate with Different Organizations and People in Local and International Communities, Schools Are Able to Use These Opportunities to Strengthen Their Students' Personal and Social Development

With appropriate support and autonomy, schools are capable of innovative ICT-based projects to improve the bonds between themselves and their communities (Kerawalla & Crook, 2002).

Indonesia: Schools in Indonesia were involved in several projects in the Asia-Europe Classroom Programme. An example is the Ndolalak and Hambo project (the title refers to the names of two dances from Sweden and Java that symbolise cultural life in the two countries) created to provide opportunities for cultural understanding and exchange. The Senior High School 7 in Purworejo on Java (Indonesia) and Torsbergsgymnasiet in Bollnäs (Sweden) are attended by students of approximately the same age—about 18 to 19 years. The purpose of the project was for these students to learn about cultural varieties in Java and Sweden with the aim of their making friends and developing understanding, respect, and positive attitudes across cultures. The Swedish group of students belonged to a class who were pursuing cultural studies (art, literature, music, dance, traditions and the like); they already had personal pen friends in other countries. The Indonesian class, on the other hand, was new to online communication and received a lot of support from their teacher and technical officer. Through e-mail exchanges and online bulletin boards, the students designed websites and created videorecordings for one another.

Malaysia: In the "Face 2 Face" project under the Asia-Europe Classroom Programme, students from Helsinki Business College in Finland and the Garden International School in Malaysia planned to visit each other during the course of the project (October to June). In preparation for these visits, they communicated with one another via e-mail and bulletin boards, and shared various aspects of their cultures through the web pages that they designed. They also planned the itinerary for their visits using an online open forum. Another project, Multicultural Exchanger–A Newspaper On Line, involved Malaysia, Finland, Sweden, Indonesia, France, China, Singapore, and Portugal. The students researched, planned, and exchanged information before designing the website for the online newspaper.

Singapore: Parents, industry experts, and academics are invited to work with Singaporean schools to make meaningful contributions to the community (Soh, 2002). One example is the service-learning programme at Crescent Girls' School (www.crescent.edu.sg) in which students use ICT in innovative ways to make a difference in the lives of less fortunate members of the community. In 2000, a group of secondary three students set up an e-commerce project, "Very Special Bazaar," together with members of Peacehaven (Home for the Elderly), the Movement for the Intellectually Disabled of Singapore (MINDS), and the Very Special Arts Singapore. Arts and craft pieces were put on sale via the web with an e-commerce engine and the proceeds went to the elderly and the physically and intellectually challenged in these organizations. Two other projects by the school involved the Singapore School for the Deaf where hearing-impaired students and Crescent's students cooperatively designed digital art cards to raise funds. They also wrote, illustrated, and translated some works into sign language to enrich teaching and learning resources for the hearing-impaired members of the community.

Again in Singapore's Radin Mas Primary School, there were also many community projects made possible by ICT. One such project, entitled "Shangri-la for the Seniors," was begun in 2001 by Primary five students. The main objectives of the project were to encourage students to care for the elderly and engage them in entrepreneurial pursuits to help the elderly. The students communicated and interviewed directors of Senior Citizen Centres overseas and locally via e-mail, together with grandparents and teachers who would be retiring. With that information and the help of the three-dimensional software, the students designed a Senior Citizen Centre for the elderly.

ICT also opens opportunities to collaborate with organizations and people in local and international communities. Outram Secondary School students can use the site to work together on projects, not just with each other, but with counterparts in other schools, even other countries. Official "mentors" who may have the special expertise or experience to contribute to the school can do so from around the world. Recently, a class was given the opportunity to put questions to a mountaineer climbing Mount Everest.

These examples demonstrate the nature of the links that are connecting schools and communities through innovative uses of ICT. With support from the ministry, community, and commercial sectors, it is likely that opportunities for productive and creative interactions between school and community will expand.

CONCLUSION

These examples of how the ICT has been used in schools around the Asia-Pacific region have illustrated the advantages and usefulness for parents, students, and their communities, locally, within their own contexts and globally. As ICT advances, more and more homes will be connected to schools, and this will provide many more opportunities for stakeholders. For parents, such links will provide up-to-date and better information about their children's education and opportunities to understand more fully the efforts taken by the school to improve learning. Home-school connections also provide parents with ways to help their children learn. Using communication channels for this purpose can improve students' academic motivation and engagement in learning tasks which in turn may lead to increased learning and to a higher level of school attainment (Tracey, Penn, & Fowler, 1999).

The use of ICT to connect communities and schools improves the professional growth of teachers and support staff. Connections of this kind allow the creation of professional links with like-minded staff, thus establishing a community of practitioners. These networks can be used to discuss issues relating to curriculum and assessment, or to share and explore issues that arise. With the linkages, these professional exchanges and collaborative interaction are likely to be helpful. Greater interaction with parents also allows staff to see things from a parent's point of view and better understand and empathise with them. Using ICT in these ways also allows staff to access a wide range of resources that can enrich the delivery of lessons.

The range of interactions reported here suggests that a reciprocal culture of appreciation is under construction in Southeast Asian communities. The observed benefits for each of the stakeholders—parents, students, local staff, and those from global organizations—are considerable and the efforts deserve support.

REFERENCES

Cuban, L., Kirkpatrick, H., & Peck, C. (2001). High access and low use of technology in high school classrooms: Explaining an apparent paradox. *American Educational Research Journal, 38*(4), 813–834.

Epstein, J. L. (1996). Advances in family, community, and school partnerships. *New Schools, New Communities, 12*(3), 5–13.

Fullan, M. (1993). *Change forces: Probing the depths of educational reforms.* London: Falmer Press.

Gullickson, P. (2000). The promise and challenge of a connected world. *Technological Horizons in Education (THE) Journal ONLINE, 27*(8).

Harris, S. (1999). Secondary school students' use of computers at home. *British Journal of Educational Technology, 30*(4), 331–339.

Henderson, J. G., & Hawthorne, R. D. (1995). *Transformative curriculum leadership.* Englewood Cliffs, NJ: Merrill.

Kerawalla, C., & Crook, C. (2002) Children's computer use at home and at school: Context and continuity. *British Educational Research Journal, 28*(6), 751–772.

Konzal, J. (1997). *Attitudes: How parental attitudes may influence classroom instructional practices.* Paper presented at the American Educational Research Association Annual Meeting, Chicago.

Lewin, C., Mavers, D., & Somekh, B. (2003). Broadening access to the curriculum through using technology to link home and school: A critical analysis of reforms intended to improve students' educational attainment. *The Curriculum Journal, 14,* 23–53.

Lim, C. P. (2004). Engaging learners in online learning environments. *TechTrends: For Leaders in Education and Training, 48*(4), 16–23.

Mumtaz, S. (2001). Children's enjoyment and perception of computer use in the home and the school. *Computers and Education, 36,* 347–361.

Scott, B. N., & Hannafin, R. D. (2000). How teachers and parents view classroom learning environments: An exploratory study. *Journal of Research on Computing in Education, 32*(3), 401–416.

Soh, V. (2002, September-October). MP2: The next masterplan for IT in education. *Education,* 30–33.

Sutherland, R., Facer, K., Furlong, R., & Furlong, J. (2000). A new environment for education? The computer in the home. *Computers and Education, 34,* 195–212.

Tobin, K., & Dawson, G. (1992). Constraints to curriculum reform: Teachers and the myths of schooling. *Educational Technology Research and Development, 40*(1), 121–140.

Tracey, K., Penn, C., & Fowler, J. H. (1999). Developing an infrastructure to support communities of learning. *BT Technology Journal, 17*(1), 98–110.

Weiss, H., Kreider, H., Levine, E., Stadler, J., & Vaughan, P. (1998). *Beyond the parent-teacher conference: Diverse patterns of home-school communication.* Paper presented in the American Educational Research Association Annual Meeting, San Diego, CA.

PART 4

ICT FOR CULTURAL UNDERSTANDINGS

CHAPTER 11

ONLINE GAMING

Building Bridges that Enhance Cultural Understandings

Mary A. Kayler
Debra Sprague
George Mason University

Chris Dede
Harvard University

INTRODUCTION

In our current state of global affairs, multiple conflicts simultaneously confront our world. Cultural and political wars, environmental issues, and military conflicts often polarize populations, undercutting ways to learn and understand from one another. Online gaming provides a unique opportunity for diverse individuals from all over the world to interact virtually with one another in real time. This interactive, immersive medium potentially offers ways that individuals who have different culture, ethnicity, race, gender, socioeconomic status, and educational level can collaborate, cooperate, and compete within a structured framework designed by a gaming community.

ICT for Education, Development, and Social Justice, pages 183–200

Our research explores the psychosocial implications of online gaming in terms of building (or undercutting) cultural understandings. We are attempting to delineate ways in which designers of and participants in online games can help diverse individuals to develop and work towards common goals. We are also studying how the processes of online gaming can contribute to forming meaningful friendships based on the appreciation of differing cultural experiences among individuals separated by geography and worldview.

The purpose of this chapter is to address the ways in which online gaming works to strengthen and deepen individual understandings and acceptance of diverse worldviews across potential divides such as culture, race, ethnicity, gender, socioeconomic status, and education level. The research questions that guided our study were: a) In what ways, if any, has online gaming the potential to strengthen cultural understandings among diverse populations? b) What design structures and community mores hinder or enhance diverse participants evolving and working towards common goals? c) What are the ways in which online gaming can help participants to understand their own cultural worldview?

THEORETICAL PERSPECTIVE

The most profitable use of the Internet, next to pornography, is massively multiplayer online role-playing games (MMORPG) (Snider, 2002). DFC Intelligence, a game-industry research company, reported that in 2005 subscription revenue from online games was $2 billion (Thorsen, 2006). MMORPGs are graphical immersive games played online, allowing participants to interact not only with the gaming environment, but also with each other through the use of computer-created representations called "avatars."

Participants in MMORPGs come from all walks of life and from all over the globe. These individuals engage in a virtual world that is often created around a fantasy narrative, where the players are free to act within the rules, structure, and culture of that particular scenario. For example, in a swords-and-sorcery world, one might slay ogres, lay siege to castles, or barter for goods in town. In such worlds, allegiances are made and teams or clans are formed. In military style games, players join a Division and form Companies as they gain rank, move up the military chain of command, and work to defeat their opponents. Given their engaging nature, their profitability in the entertainment industry, and their growing popularity with people of all ages, ethnicities, and nationalities, MMORPGs "are quickly becoming *the* form of entertainment and a major mechanism of socialization for young and old alike" (Steinkuehler, 2004, p. 1).

As with any society, MMORPG virtual worlds are governed by intricate rules and etiquette. These rules are developed by the designers and players and are based on fundamental principles of fair play and socially acceptable behavior. Many MMORPGs, such as Desert Combat, Future Conflict and Battlefield 2, encourage and facilitate the forming of Divisions and several-individual Companies that play important roles in the storyline. Survival and ultimately victory depend on the strength of the Division and Companies working in unison to defeat their opponent. Through peer mentoring, such a form of teaming can allow players to achieve higher levels of game play and to gain experience quickly. However, forming successful teams (or clans as they are referred to in some MMORPGs) is not easy, since this involves inventing a viable shared culture and requires cross-cultural social skills to be successful. Dysfunctional teams die off quickly in this type of virtual world, while teams who know how to work together and divide tasks among the skills and accomplishments of individual members are more successful at negotiating the game space (Humphreys, 2003).

For many, it is the development of these social networks, or teams, that makes MMORPGs engaging. The social networks can keep players engaged long after they have mastered the intricacies of the game (Herz, 2002). Kolo and Baur (2004) researched the social dynamics of members of a MMORPG called *Ultimate Life.* Thirty-four percent of the players who responded to their survey knew one-quarter or more of their fellow players offline. These players reported they had made new friends, had become more sociable than they were before participating in the MMORPG, and felt that barriers to communication with unknown people had been significantly reduced.

Could the team structure of MMORPGs be used to strengthen cultural understandings among diverse populations? A virtual environment that encourages collaboration and team work has the potential to help players create a viable culture through a structured gaming environment, shared rules, common language, and norms of participation. Game playing moves from individual game play to groups of individuals working in tandem, learning from and with each other as they work towards common goals. What design structures and community mores hinder or enhance diverse participants evolving and working towards common goals? What are the ways in which online gaming can help participants to understand their own cultural worldview? These are the questions this research attempts to answer.

CONTEXT

Our work centers around one MMORPG online gaming community. This community claims to be the "largest online Battle Field 2 (BF2) gaming community for organized play," (made up of approximately 350 active members). Members can join for free or can pay $5 to join a division of their choice. This community centers on a military style tournament where players participate in simulated wars using the tournament's own "modded" (modified) version of BF2. The tournament includes commanding officers, divisions, and a battle map on the tournament home page showing the progress of the war from week to week. Weekly, 12 hour battles on weekends occur during the 8–12 week campaign season.

This community is composed of a diverse population in terms of geographic location, race, ethnicity, socio-economic, education levels, age, and time spent gaming. Participants are required to have internet access and to have installed TeamSpeak (free software that allows real time talk) and Battlefield 2, the game of this particular community. Participation within the community is voluntary, and the amount of time individuals' play varies.

TOURNAMENT STRUCTURE AND RANKING SYSTEM

A chain of command-style of play is used within this gaming community to encourage teamwork and provide a structure for an organized team play environment. Once players join and are assigned to a particular company, they can determine their level of activity and engagement within their assigned Divisions and Companies in a variety of ways (e.g., attend practices and battles, design avatars, contribute to map intelligence, devise strategies, conduct practices, and build company morale). Company Captains promote players within their companies to hold various ranks and assume leadership roles based on their company and division contributions, performance, and leadership abilities. During the campaign, players are awarded virtual medals and receive recognition.

Two communication features of this tournament are the use of Division/Company forums and TeamSpeak. Tournament forums provide a space for players to read and post on topics and discussion related to the tournament. Each company has its own forum along with an HCO/officers forum to discuss battle strategy, practice schedules, and the like. A company "mess hall" is created for topics not related to battle discussions. TeamSpeak provides players with an opportunity for synchronous communication with other players around the world.

The tournament owners provide servers and a website for the tournament. Tournament owners also incorporate the use of modified maps, game play, and equipment. A group of players, both volunteers and appointed members (a "modding team"), work to create new maps, modify game play and equipment to provide novel challenges for each campaign. While some players are appointed to hold a few high ranking slots and roles within the tournament, it is the owners that hold all power related to the tournament in general: rules and regulations, forum moderation, and overseeing of all day-to-day operations.

METHODS

Data Sources and Analysis

This mixed methods study provides authentic evidence as to the ways in which online gaming can work towards peace and reconciliation. One author [I would identify that author by initials here] has been involved in this online gaming tournament for four years and has held a variety of leadership roles (private—general) within the community. She has firsthand knowledge and served as an informant, allowing us to gain access for data collection.

An open-ended survey was conducted to explore gamers' experiences with online tournament gaming and the ways in which gamers negotiate cultural differences. A voluntary call to participate was posted by a tournament administrator within the tournament forums inviting gamers to complete the survey (approximately 15–30 minutes), available online for three months. Survey questions focused on the players' experiences, as well as game processes and structures that hindered or promoted gaming experiences and cultural understandings. There were 57 respondents with a relatively low 16.28% rate of return; however, our findings suggest patterns of interactions and themes.

Two researchers independently conducted an analysis of survey responses, developing codes/categories from participants' responses. Survey responses were entered into a database and coded for categories using the constant comparison method (Bogdan & Biklen, 1999). For example, the code of *structure* was assigned for survey responses that referenced the military format and overall organizational format of the tournament. The code of *administrators* was assigned to participants' references to the interactions between administrators and players related to tournament play. Additional coding categories were created within each of the emergent themes.

The researchers met and discussed coding responses and collapsed some codes into broader categories. This process served as a reliability check and worked to address one researcher's "insiders" experience, providing an additional check from a non-participant's perspective in terms of coding and findings. Demographic information, findings, and emergent themes are reported below.

FINDINGS

Gamers

Survey respondents for this study were all males, ranging from 18–54 years old, and who spoke English as their primary language (the tournament uses English as the language for discussions and forum postings). There are three female players within the tournament, but none responded to this survey. The average age of respondents was 29 years. The majority of players (53%) reside in the United States, speak mainly English and reported having limited fluency with other languages. Other respondents reported living in Canada (15%), United Kingdom (11%), Germany (8%), Russian Federation (2%), Serbia (2%), Norway (2%), Denmark (2%), Northern Ireland (2%), Netherlands (2%) and Colombia (1%). These respondents reported being comfortable using English (in varying degrees) and fluent in the language of their native country. Respondents reported the following ethnicity or nationality: Caucasian, Hispanic, Serbian, British, and German.

Gamers reported a wide range of experiences in online gaming in terms of types of games played, including first person shooter, role playing, MMORPG, racing, strategy, and board games. Players' online gaming experience ranged from less than one year to twelve years, with an average of seven years experience. Respondents reported belonging to this tournament for one month to four years, with an average of one to two years of tournament involvement.

FINDINGS

The first research question asked was "In what ways, if any, has online gaming the potential to strengthen cultural understandings among diverse populations?" Two open-ended questions on the survey were included to answer this question. The first question asked participants to reflect on what their specific group (called Company in the game) does to promote a better understanding of each other's culture. Table 11.1 shows the themes and percentages of responses. (It should be noted that percentages may exceed 100% because some statements were coded in multiple themes.)

Survey findings reveal that talking with others was the primary way participants' learned about each other's cultures. Respondents provided information about the openness and acceptance of others as a way to enhance understandings, appreciate differences and create a feeling of acceptance within the gaming community. For example:

TABLE 11.1 Engagements That Promote Understanding

Themes	References	Coverage
Talking to each other	29	62.1%
Providing access to others	17	49.0%
Acceptance/ openness	11	26.7%
Censorship/discouraged topics	5	18.5%
Culture is not present in the game	4	12.5%
Fun outside the tournament/game	5	7.4%

- "We have people from all backgrounds and walks of life and from other countries. The internet makes physical distance irrelevant. Everyone starts off as only being a name and a voice, but we get to learn who people are by talking with them. Since we are all here because of our common interest, we get to know people for who they are and are not hindered by misconceptions and prejudices common in our culture in the real world."
- "As a multinational company I find that just taking the time to talk to your team mates helps, as discussion normally moves to non-tournament issues. Although the forum policy of banning talking about certain subjects (politics, religion, etc.) seems to subconsciously pass over onto other methods of communication (TeamSpeak) not directly moderated like the forums, there is still a lot to learn about other portions of a persons' culture. I also know people that have been learning a foreign language that have found someone on their team that speaks it and have worked with them to help their education."
- "If we are ever on TeamSpeak we are normally discussing the differences between, some forms of system within our society. Whether that's educational, healthcare, or law enforcement."
- "There are a variety of cultures represented in our company, and everyone I have spoken to about their culture has been happy to share their views and experiences.... If not for this tournament I would not have dreamed of being able to speak to someone in Germany, England, Australia, and Columbia all at the same time."

One responsibility of the tournament administrators is the oversight and moderation of the forums. They monitor and censor (delete) postings that they feel are inappropriate or not in the best interest of the tournament. For example, postings related to religion and politics are considered inappropriate topics for tournament forums. Players reported how limiting discussion topics in the forums allowed for players to develop cultural understandings of others by not focusing on topics that could be controversial. Respondents indicated:

- "One item that I think prevents problems more than anything is that discussion of hot button topics such as politics is discouraged. While these are certainly subjects worthy of discussion and debate, they can become highly charged emotionally. Because our community is not face to face, it would be too easy to become disconnected from the human end and say things in the heat of debate that would be later regretted."
- "Most players are mature and respect each other's values, discussion of hot topics such as religion and politics are frowned upon which allows us to concentrate on playing our game and having fun."
- "We tend to keep political/religious discussions to a minimum. This helps avoid the conflicts that such topics usually create. Occasionally when one member is causing a problem, by insulting or degrading another individual, our command structure allows for the quick removal of that individual from the environment."

The second question asked the participants to name a feature of game play that kept them engaged and participating on a regular basis. Table 11.2 shows the themes and percentages of responses.

Players identified friendships and a sense of community as important aspects of game play and participation. It is common for Divisions, Companies and players to develop a sense of pride in their collective and individual accomplishments. For example:

- "The camaraderie that comes playing a war style game, where you win or lose as a team really enhances the experience."
- "Most people are welcoming and helpful to new players. A lot of players aren't only on TeamSpeak for tournament activities so it is easy to meet people and arrange non-tournament activities. If a member is in trouble in real life (for example, illness) then the whole tournament, irregardless of affiliation, bands around and provides support and encouragement. The tributes to members that have passed away are also very touching."
- "The people that surround me have always been for the most part supportive and in hind sight very close friends. I have made some friends that I myself would actually consider meeting and trusting; who says the reality we live in is the only truth in the world. Now-a-days through communities like this one it's possible to meet people you wouldn't.... I've made some excellent friends."

TABLE 11.2 Features of Game Play

Themes	References	Coverage
Sense of community	18	30.2%
Friendships	20	28.4%
Military features	3	9.9%
Structure of the game	6	9.7%
New features added to game	5	8.9%
Recognition	3	7.2%

Players reported on the value and enjoyment of working in a Company and Division. It is at this level that players made meaningful connections through the day-to day-operations and campaign cycle. Respondents indicated that using a military structure provides new players a framework within which to engage others. For example:

- "Having effective company leaders goes a long way to make everyone involved feel comfortable. I for instance tend to take non-native English speakers under my wing a little bit to make them feel more comfortable. I use in game tasks to help them get past any communication roadblocks. This not only lets them feel more comfortable speaking English, it also gives the English speakers a chance to adapt to the newcomers accent/way of speaking."
- "The company level is the one I enjoy the most, since you develop better relationships with people in that same company. Despite that, people still make friends across their whole division and even make friends with people on the opposing division."

In summary, time spent together and players having access and opportunities to virtually meet and "talk to each other" were crucial components to enhancing individual players' cultural understandings and creating meaningful friendships. Forum censorship and guidelines of appropriate discussion topics contributed to a sense of acceptance by allowing players to get to know each other as individuals. A sense of community supported players in developing meaningful friendships.

The second research question asked "What design structures and community mores hinder or enhance diverse participants evolving and working towards common goals?" To answer this question, four open-ended questions were included on the survey. The first question asked participants to reflect on the design structures of the tournament that enhanced their participation. Table 11.3 shows the themes and percentages of responses.

TABLE 11.3 Design Structures That Enhance Participation

Themes	References	Coverage
Military format	18	47.5%
Community atmosphere	14	20.4%
Overall structure of the game	10	13.6%
Using TeamSpeak	9	8.2%

In addition to experiencing a sense of community and developing friendships within the tournament, respondents reported on the ways in which having an organized and military structured gaming environment supported their participation and engagement. Players indicated that this promoted a sense of realism:

- "I like the military structure and organization. It adds to the immersion of the game and it keeps everything organized."
- "The fact its set up with a real military structure, with a command staff, separate line companies, air force company and armor company, its just a really interesting and unique kind of tournament to be a part of and continues to be fun even after a year of playing the same game almost every day."
- "The long and large scale battles with the idea of a team of 30 people fighting against 30 opponents. The overall structure of 1 large "team" or Division broken down to smaller units or companies, all working as a team to overcome the enemy, keeps me playing."

Other players noted how using a military structure organized and enhanced game play by providing order, multiple opportunities for game play during the week, and a structure to negotiate their way within the tournament. For example:

- "This helps create a sense of belonging as well as set a structure to adhere to, there is no wondering 'where do I fit in?' . . . It also allows you to explore different aspects of relating to one another as 'cyber' friends/peers. With structure and rules the tournament can take shape and help develop strong players."
- "The organized structure of weekly practices and competitions are very appealing and offer many opportunities to participate in the tournament and make friends."

The second question asked participants to reflect on the design structures that hindered their participation. Table 11.4 shows the themes and percentages of responses.

TABLE 11.4 Design Structures That Hinder Participation

Themes	References	Coverage
Lack of accountability	4	33.5%
Weekend battles	7	31.5%
Synchronous aspect of the game	6	12.6%
Quality of decisions made	6	11.4%
Administrators in charge of the game	10	11.1%
Various game features	5	3.9%
No hindrance	5	0.5%

Some respondents reported on the ways in which the administrators of the tournament hindered their enjoyment:

- "The leadership in almost any online community will drift towards 'benevolent totalitarianism' in which the original founders, and those who pay the expenses of the community, wield absolute control over all aspects of the group, in whatever way they deem just. In this particular community, many of the decisions and rules that are made often seem to directly favor other divisions of the tournament over the one I participate in, and this leads to a lot of unrest and a lack of respect for the administration from the lower ranks."
- "In some areas there is an 'old boys club' mentality. The two main issues this raises are: 1) the development of fresh talent is hindered as they are looked over for someone who is not necessarily more skilled than them, but who know the 'right people.' 2) That some people think they are automatically deserving of respect for participating in the tournament for a long time."

A third question asked participants to reflect on the community mores that enhanced their participation. Community mores were defined as the conventions, customs, habits, and rituals that players engaged in during the gaming experience. Table 11.5 shows the themes and percentages of responses.

Friendships, a sense of community, and rituals enhanced players' experiences. For example, at the tournament level two rituals (Love/Hated forum thread, after battle pictures) were identified as playing a role in enhancing players' experiences. For example:

- "Love/hated discussions are a great way for both sides to share stories, post personal victories, and share common elements of the day's [battle] events. It is a great community building element."

TABLE 11.5 Community Mores That Enhance Participation

Themes	References	Coverage
Sense of community/family/friendships	17	38.6%
Weekly schedule	12	15.6%
Recognition	3	13.6%
Military structure	10	9.3%
Discouraged topics	3	8.6%
Rituals	6	8.4%

- "The love/hated threads. One of the rare occasions, to see the battle from the enemy's point of view."
- "After battle screenshots. It stops me from sleeping because I want to be there to celebrate with the others."

At the Company level, rituals also play an important role. Individual company leaders and members create their own company culture by drawing upon members' strengths or company identity to build community among players. Players noted:

- "One player's signatures and cartoons. It takes some time to get recognized by him but somehow I did it and I got a short appearance in one of his strips."
- "Our community sometimes has fun day where its hunt the admin/HCO or HCO/Admins vs. all, that's quite fun and makes me attend on weeks where there's nothing planned in the tournament."
- "Our community has a number of customs and rituals that are rewarding. Outstanding participation and skill are recognized by awards and promotions. There are also a number of habits or customs (battle cries, shared jokes, procedures) that help make the organization unique which allows individuals to more easily identify themselves with the company."

Players acknowledge various personal reasons for playing within the tournament such as, receiving individual recognition. Players shared:

- "I play this game for the teamwork experience. I enjoy training new individuals and then working with them in a cooperative environment."
- "Playing with more or less the same people regularly, as you get to know each other the gaming experiences improves, and you can make friends. The size of the community is what keeps me around."

- "I work at a large company and as a supervisor I have found that just a little recognition for a job well done works wonders. This community and our company specifically, does a good job in recognizing those who do their best to help the group. There are no tangible rewards involved yet a simple "good job" is wonderful to give and get. In this light I like the reviews that are done at the end of each battle day with some recognition passed around as well as reviewing what went wrong/right that day."

The fourth question asked participants to reflect on the community mores that hindered their participation. Table 11.6 shows the themes and percentages of responses.

Respondents indicated several areas related to tournament administrators that negatively impacted their play and enjoyment in a variety of areas. One area was related to heavy forum moderation and a lack of openness to different opinions and beliefs. Players shared:

- "I personally think that the tournament forums are overly censored. While I understand the reasoning of banning certain topics of discussion (e.g., politics, religion, etc.) for the sake of maintaining harmony (as they can be very touchy topics), I think it is going a little too far, and that discussion of them should be allowed. The vast majority of people here, in my experience, are mature and the wide range of cultures that the tournament draws its membership from gives a prime opportunity for many different opinions and points of view to be aired and discussed."
- "The way they [administrators] censor everyone's opinions on the tournament, even constructive criticism."
- "Intolerance of any political belief apart from the rigidly held political/religious beliefs of the tournament owners/administrators."
- "There are sexist comments, gay bashing comments and excessive cursing."

TABLE 11.6 Community Mores That Hinder Participation

Themes	References	Coverage
Administrators in charge of the game	20	40.6%
Amount of time invested	6	27.3%
Weekly schedule	5	11.0%
No hindrance	12	7.9%

Another area concerned tournament administrators' lack of accountability, unclear or changing rules, and lack of opportunities for player input. Players wrote:

- "The lack of accountability for those leading the tournament. There are many volunteers who run the community and spend countless hours making it work but if they [administrators] get too tired of an issue or just don't feel like addressing something they don't."
- "Inconsistent application of rules, and the lack of any deciding voice from the playing community in regards to the direction of the tourney, or the rules.... If players express the opinions or suggestions in a manner not generally approved by tournament staff, they are subject to censure or given warnings (3 strikes and you're out)."
- "The disregard for written rules in questionable situations."

In summary, respondents valued the organized military structure of the tournament. Such structure enabled them to developed friendships and a sense of community. Tournament and division level rituals enhanced players' gaming experiences and worked to create a shared culture among players. Active participation on a regular basis and personal recognition were important to the survey respondents. Tournament administrators were cited as a source of dissatisfaction within the tournament and hindered players' participation in a variety of ways, from lack of consistency, ruling decisions, and not listening to players input. Some respondents felt that the structure of the tournament hindered their gaming experiences by limiting opportunities for leadership within the community.

The third research question asked "What are the ways in which online gaming can help participants to understand their own cultural worldview?" Two open-ended questions were included to address this research question. The first question asked participants to reflect on what could be done to enhance players' gaming experiences when interacting with others from a different background. Table 11.7 shows the themes and percentages of responses.

TABLE 11.7 Enhancing Interaction

Themes	References	Coverage
Talking to others	12	38.5%
Have more participants/access to others	6	29.1%
Acceptance/openness	11	22.1%
Question is not applicable	15	17.3%
Culture is not present in the game	3	8.4%

TABLE 11.8 Would Like to See Changed

Themes	References	Coverage
Administrators	22	62.6%
More participants	11	13.5%
Question not applicable	6	12.1%
Mod issues	8	6.2%

Players indicated that more opportunities to talk with others and acceptance of others would further enhance their gaming experiences and provide additional opportunities to learn about each other.

- "Talking about where they are from, and how life is in that area."
- "Open minds and understanding that everyone is different."

The second question asked participants to name one thing they would like see changed. Table 11.8 shows the themes and percentages of responses.

Respondents provided practical suggestions and shared ideas of ways in which to enhance tournament play. For example:

- "I think we could have a place in the forums people could describe their favorite food specific to their location or describe their flags (state, national, etc)."
- "I would like to see some of the HCO staff voted for. It seems like it is a popularity contest with the Admins of the tournament... I would also like to see the average player have more rights when it comes to disciplinary actions. Currently there is no real oversight when it comes to people being kicked out of the tournament due to arguing with a self-righteous administrator or HCO."
- "Getting the 'veterans' more involved in helping retain players: to kind of build up the next generation so the community doesn't fade away."

Respondents provided suggestions on how to enhance the operating structure of the tournament to encourage a more conducive playing environment. Players' acknowledged how opportunities to talk with others support building friendships with others.

DISCUSSION

Online gaming plays an important role in helping individuals enhance their cultural understandings. Opportunities to talk with others supported players in developing friendships and enhance their gaming experiences. Gamers reported on the value of learning about each other as individuals; enhancing their own cultural understandings and their appreciation of other people's experiences. Common ground is collectively built over time as players talked and played alongside individuals of different backgrounds and beliefs.

Designers of tournaments and the people in charge of running them play a large role in the ways in which players' gaming experiences are impacted (either enhanced or diminished) and the opportunities for cultural interactions among players. The structures and processes put into place within an online gaming community shape the ways in which individuals interact with one another. Creating an organized structure with clear guidelines and enforced rules provides an environment that maximizes players' interactions in a fair and consistent manner. Communication between players and administrators can enhance players' experiences and build a strong foundation for player commitment. When players perceive the people in charge of the tournament as vested in optimizing their gaming experiences, players stay longer, developing meaningful relationships with others that they may not come into contact with in real life.

It is important to have opportunities to get to know each other as individuals before representing oneself as a member of a particular culture. In order to promote cultural understandings, there need to be multiple ways and opportunities for players to talk with each other. Designers need to build these opportunities into the gaming community. Guidelines of appropriate forum topics can provide a framework for discussions. However, censorship limits players' opportunities for meaningful discussions about topics they find interesting, thus limiting learning about cultural differences. Regular contact, synchronous chats and posting of forums all potentially support the development of friendships across a more global society.

Rituals and personal recognition increase players' sense of belonging in a community, which in turn increases an individual's comfort level, allowing one to open up and share life histories. Players who valued individual recognition, company culture and divisional pride reported spending more time within the gaming community. Time spent with others creates opportunities for learning about differences.

From a design perspective, the tension between top-down structure and bottom-up evolution of the gaming environment is very interesting. The structure plays important roles in sustainability (players enjoy the shared combat experience, the collaborative design of new challenges, and the opportunity to interact with each other in ways that preclude divisive topics). Based on the experiences of those who have created online discussion forums solely focused on serious topics, a less structured environment that did not include a high degree of entertainment would likely founder fairly quickly. It is somewhat ironic that a military-gaming environment provides structures, rules, and motivations that seem to foster a greater chance of peaceful interactions among cultures.

On the other hand, players clearly resent many aspects of these structures and rules, finding them oppressive and rigid. Whether a more open-ended game setting would better foster cross-cultural understandings, or whether such a situation would simply bring forward a different set of issues players did not like, is an excellent topic for future design experiments. For example, allowing optional discussion forums that did address sensitive topics would be an interesting experiment, as would moving the game towards a more democratic decision-making process about rules and structures. Probably, in terms of fostering cross-cultural understandings, some "happy medium" exists in the degree and type of structure for these environments, balancing top-down constraints with bottom-up evolution.

One weakness of our study is that our findings are unique to the military style structure of the gaming community. These players' experiences within this military structured tournament may not be representative of other online gaming communities. Our data does not represent other gaming environments and there is the need to closely examine other gaming contexts and structures to see if there are similar findings related to the ways in which cultural understandings, friendships and a sense of community among players is shaped by the process and structures unique to that gaming culture. Another weakness is related to the limited diversity in survey respondents. Diversity in this study was related to age, geographic location and languages spoken. It is interesting to note that respondents reported an absence of culture within the tournament. Dominant English language speakers were more likely to report an absence of culture than bilingual players in their survey responses.

CONCLUSION

Our study illustrates gamers' voices and experiences within a multinational online gaming community, adding to the literature using authentic data, which have been lacking in most current scholarship on this topic. Our work captures the ways in which one online gaming community supported and hindered players in developing meaningful cultural understandings and appreciation of differences among players.

REFERENCES

Bogdan, R. & Biklen, S. (1999). *Qualitative research for education: An introduction to theory and methods.* Boston: Allyn and Bacon.

Herz, J. C. (2002). Multi-player worlds online. In L. King, (Ed.) *Game on.* London: Laurence King Publishers.

Humphreys, S. (2003) Online multiuser games: Playing for real. *Australian Journal of Communication 30*(1),79–91. Retrieved Dec. 12, 2006 from http://eprints.qut.edu.au/archive/00000237/01/Humphreys_Online.PDF.

Kolo, C., & Baur, T. (2004, November). Living a virtual Life: Social dynamics of online gaming. *The International Journal of Computer Game Research, 4*(1). Retrieved Dec. 12, 2006 from http://www.gamestudies.org/0401/kolo/

Snider, M. (2002, May 23). Where movies end, games begin; Industry mimics studio techniques and profitability. *USA TODAY,* p.D03. Retrieved June 1, 2002 from http://www.usatoday.com/

Steinkuehler, C. A. (2004). *Learning in massively multiplayer online games.* Retrieved Dec. 12, 2006 from http://labweb.education.wisc.edu/curric675/readings/SteinkuehlerICLS2004.pdf.

Thorsen, T. (2006, March 9). *Online game subscriptions up 43 percent in 2005.* Retrieved, Dec. 14, 2006 from http://www.gamespot.com/pc/rpg/worldofwarcraft/news.html?page=1&sid=6145712.

CHAPTER 12

COMPUTER-SUPPORTED COLLABORATIVE INTERCULTURAL EDUCATION

Creating Bridges for Palestinians and Jews in Conflict

Zvi Bekerman
Gabriel Horenczyk
School of Education and the Melton Centre
The Hebrew University of Jerusalem, Israel

INTRODUCTION

Numerous studies have confirmed Gordon Allport's (1954) claim that "prejudice . . . may be reduced by equal-status contact between majority and minority groups in the pursuit of common goals" (p. 24). Allport supported social change through extensive integration towards the achievement of social stability and harmony. Allport's influential initial articulation of the contact hypothesis has throughout the years evolved into a complex taxonomy of conditions for "good contact" to be possible. The main prescrip-

ICT for Education, Development, and Social Justice, pages 201–211

tions recommended in the contact literature include the following: Contact should be regular and frequent; it should involve a balanced ratio of in-group to out-group members while allowing for a genuine "acquaintance potential"; it should occur between individuals who share equality of status, and while being institutionally sanctioned it should be organized around cooperation toward the achievement of a superordinate goal.

Computer supported collaborative learning (CSCL) in its multiple facets has been trumpeted as being able not only to revolutionize the structural settings in which education takes place but also to recondition and improve learning and teaching options. Over the last decade new functionalities (Braa, Sorensen, & Dahlbom, 2000) have emerged from the media enabled by the new technologies. This has meant the creation of technological platforms with the potential to support the dynamic distribution and organization of educational material and to support more flexible forms of interaction, e.g., chat-rooms, computer conferences and news groups (Wolfe, 2000; 2000b). Numerous studies (Cole, 1996; Meyrowitz, 1985; Sproull & Kiesler, 1992; Wasson & Morch, 2000) have shown how the use of electronic media is not merely a neutral improvement in educational efficiency (Svensson, 2002) but, rather crucially, changes and restructures learning situations with respect to the social and cultural resources available to participants involved in the activity. These changes can have a profound influence on educational practice.

In this chapter, we suggest that CSCIE (Computer-Supported Collaborative Intercultural Education) can serve—under certain conditions—as an optimal means for the improvement of intergroup relations, particularly in conflict-ridden areas, where psychological—and sometimes real—barriers often prevent face-to-face intergroup contact. We will describe a recently developed project, Yad2Yad ("Hand-to-Hand" in both Arabic and Hebrew), aimed at bringing together, through virtual contact, school-age children attending Jewish and Arab schools in Israel.

THE ARAB-JEWISH CONFLICT IN ISRAEL

The Israeli-Palestinian conflict can be traced to the beginning of Zionist colonalization of Palestine, claimed by Jews as the land of their birthright, towards the end of the ninetieth century. The seemingly intractable conflict resulted from at least two dominant ideological discourses (one Jewish, one Palestinian) concerning the control of the land and recognition of group sovereignty. Historically, the region was never autonomously controlled, having a long history of colonial and imperial rule (Khalidi, 1997). The 1948 war, called the War of Independence by the Israelis and the Naqbe (the Catastrophe) by the Palestinians, was the first open military clash between the Zionist and Palestinian nationalist movements. Palestinians in Israel (20%) are an indigenous minority, who formed the majority in Palestine (two thirds of the population) until 1947.

The ongoing violent Israeli occupation of the Gaza strip and the West Bank since 1967 and the Intifada outbreaks in 1997 and 2000 brought about events that shattered the optimism for a peaceful solution that emerged after the Oslo agreements between the Israeli Government and the PLO in 1993. It remains to be seen whether the recent disengagement from the Gaza strip holds any promise for the future. The 2006 second Lebanese war and the recent takeover by Hammas of the Gaza area of the Palestinian Authority leave little room for optimism.

Israel, since its inception, and as is clearly stated in its Declaration of Independence, has been committed to full political and social equality for all its citizens irrespective of their religion or ethnic affiliation. Yet, even the Israeli government agrees that it has not been fully successful in implementing this ideal and has, for the most part, implemented segregationist policies towards its non-Jewish minorities, policies which only recently are starting to be challenged in the courts of justice (Gavison, 2000). In general, the Palestinian Israeli population is geographically segregated and institutionally and legally discriminated against (Al-Haj, 2002; Kretzmer, 1992).

In spite of Israel's declared goals of offering equal opportunity to all its citizens through the educational system, the gap between the Jewish and Palestinian sectors remains. For example in 1991, 45% of Palestinian and 67% of Jewish children earned a matriculation diploma, while in 2001, the percentage increased to 59% and 70%, respectively (Israel, 2001).

Not only are the school systems segregated, but so too are the curricula. Even today, Israel has no official multicultural educational policies. The Jewish curriculum focuses on national Jewish content and Jewish nation-building and the Palestinian curriculum is sanitized of any national Palestinian content (Rouhana & Korper, 1997). While Jewish students are called to engage in the collective Jewish national enterprise, Palestinian students are called on to accept the definition of Israel as a Jewish Democratic state (Al-Haj, 2005). All in all, the Palestinian educational system in Israel lacks the preferential support given by the government to the Jewish educational system, thus creating an enormous gap and leaving the Palestinian educational system behind.

At the psychological level, a consistent pattern of negative intergroup perceptions (Stephan & Stephan, 2001) can be seen as both the product of, as well as a major contributing factor to, the persistence of the conflict. Due to generalized mutual suspicion and fear, contact between Jews and Arabs—in the areas of work, tourism, and education—has diminished drastically during the last two years.

(VIRTUAL) CONTACT AND THE REDUCTION OF INTERGROUP CONFLICT

Lack of sufficient contact between Jews and Arabs is generally perceived as a factor exacerbating negative intergroup attitudes between the two national groups in Israel. It was only in the mid-1980s that intergroup encounters, designed to overcome distrust and hostility and contribute to co-existence, were initiated (Helman, 2002). The immediate stimulus seems to have been the publication of a survey (Zemach, 1980) disclosing anti-democratic attitudes and feelings among Jewish Israeli youth towards the Palestinian minority. This disclosure fanned fears that Israeli society might reject its democratic character (Katz & Kahanov, 1990; Maoz, 2004) and brought about the formation of what Rabinowitz (2000) defined as the "coexistence sector" which focused on the development of formal and informal educational dialogue activities, geared towards the recognition of otherness and co-existence (Maoz, 2002; Suleiman, 2004). In the era of the 1990s, the efforts towards educational co-existence activity mostly guided by dedicated NGO's strengthened with the Oslo Accords. Their activities focused on questions of the conflictual relations among the national groups and the possibility of coexistence and reconciliation (Bar & Bargal, 1995).

Most of these projects share the basic premises of the "contact hypothesis," which suggests that intergroup contact tends to contribute to the reduction of prejudice, if and when certain conditions are met. As mentioned above, early formulations of the contact hypothesis specified four such conditions: cooperative interaction, equal status among the participants, individualized contact, and institutional support. Many variables were added throughout the years. Stephan and Stephan (1996, 2001) categorized them into two broad domains: societal factors and person factors. More relevant to our analysis of CSCIE are the societal variables, which can be further divided into those related to the larger societal context and those related to the more proximal situational context. The former include, among others, aspects of social structure and stratification, historical relations between the groups (e.g., degree of conflict, sizes of groups), and current intergroup relations at the societal level. Among the situational context variables, Stephan & Stephan (1996) list the nature of the interaction (e.g., purpose, whether voluntary or coerced, duration, frequency), group composition (e.g., size of whole group and relative size of each subgroup), relative statuses, and task (goals interdependence and outcomes).

The Yad2Yad project seeks to enable and foster virtual, rather than face-to-face, contact between Jewish and Palestinian Arab students in Israel, trying to maximize the conditions that are likely to contribute to the improvement of relations between the two national groups. We suggest that virtual intergroup contact, within the framework of collaborative educational work, has unique beneficial features, which render CSCIE an additional valuable educational tool for conflict resolution. CSCIE is especially useful in cases when the two groups are unable—because of psychological or real obstacles—to meet face-to-face. This is currently the case in Israel, where spontaneous and planned interaction between Arab and Jewish youth and adults has diminished drastically. At this time, computer-supported interaction is perhaps the only way to overcome imagined or real distances. The importance of creating such bridges was stressed by Martin Luther King a few decades ago:

> Men hate each other because they fear each other. They fear each other because they don't know each other. They don't know each other because they can't communicate with each other. They can't communicate with each other because they are separated from each other.

THE YAD2YAD PROJECT

The basic structure of the Yad2Yad environment is similar to that of CD-Golem (Bekerman & Horenczyk, 2002)—a project designed to create a virtual learning community, in light of the perceived needs of a Diaspora group's attempt to impart its youth with a sense of belonging and continuity. CD-Golem (http://cdgolem.huji.ac.il) brings together students from Jewish schools worldwide, for collaborative work on activities mostly related to issues of culture and cultural identity. Yad2Yad (http://yad2yad.huji.ac.il) is an integrated educational and research project aimed primarily at fostering a dialogue between Jewish and Palestinian Arab children in Israel in order to promote a culture of mutual understanding and tolerance. The target population consists of students between the ages of 13 and 16, although it may also be appropriate for slightly younger or older age groups. Yad2Yad is a closed and secure site: Participating students are given login names, usernames, and passwords through their schools, enabling them to work from school and from home (the "guest login" option allows touring the site, but not to write in it).

Activities in Yad2Yad are designed to encourage Jewish and Palestinian Arab children to share with each other ideas primarily related to culture, identity, and common citizenship. Yad2Yad is a completely bilingual site: All activities are displayed in both Arabic and Hebrew, side by side, and some of them can also be viewed in English. Participants can also write in Hebrew or Arabic. The bilingual nature of the site (which required considerable technological and financial investment) reflects our strong commitment to complete equality between the two cultures in Yad2Yad. As to the actual language of communication in Yad2Yad, this will be left to the participating students for intra-group and inter-group negotiation, as it is in the "real" world. Much of the communication within each cultural group is likely to be conducted in the group's language; intergroup communication (which the program strives to encourage) can be held in a rather "neutral" language (such as English) or in any other arrangement agreed upon by the participants themselves.

The activities are grouped under categories, or "worlds." Yad2Yad is a dynamic site, with new worlds and activities been added continuously. At present, there are six worlds in Yad2Yad: "Groups and Communities," "Social Action," "The World of Writing," "Think about it!," "Culture and Tradition," and "Who is Toth?". The world "Groups and Communities," for example, includes the "Face2Face" activity that encourages and assists the participants to create personal and group "homepages," and to share them with other communities. The specially designed templates, which help participants and groups to present themselves, emphasize social and cultural aspects of self and community. The "Yad2Yad Gazette" (not surprisingly in the "World of Writing") is an electronic magazine offering the participants (again, as individuals or in groups) tools for engaging in journalism. They can write their own stories based on suggested themes (or on themes raised by the participants themselves), they can report on interviews (real or fictitious) with famous local, international, or historical figures. The "My Imaginary Country" activity, part of the "Think about it!" world, allows participants (as individuals or in groups) to create their own country: to design its flag, to plan the nature and location of its various institutions, to establish its rules and norms, to deal with minority groups within the country, to discuss issues of linguistic diversity. Students will be then asked to comment on each other's countries.

The "Think about it!" world also invites the students to take part in dramatized court cases, stimulating collaboration and argumentation towards cultural, intercultural, and ethical problem-solving. One simulation, for example, deals with issues of group loyalty, partiality, and intergroup relations. It depicts a person who is asked to donate an organ for transplant to one of two persons in urgent need; one of them is a member of his group, and the other not. After hesitation, the protagonist donates the organ to the in-group member, and the relatives of the other person decide to sue him. Yad2Yad students are asked to set up the court deliberation: One group takes the role of the prosecution, and the other group that of the defense. They are instructed to develop their argument in favor or against the protagonist's decision by searching different kinds of sources (legal, bio-ethical, traditional, religious). This process reaches its climax in a synchronous virtual meeting between the groups, where the simulation takes place.

As to the question: Who is Toth?. He (or she) is a mythical cyber-persona, who functions as an "educational agent or manager," navigating, supporting, motivating and challenging the participants throughout the program. Toth, similar to the Golem in the CDGolem project, can be thought of as one of the "partners" in the Vygotskyan Zone of Proximal Development (Cole, 1996; Wertsch, 1998), encouraging and assisting participants in their evolving performance. Participants are encouraged to send e-messages to Toth, who promises to answer most of the questions and queries. This is done through Yad2Yad's internal Communication Center which also allows students to write to each other. The Center also includes discussion forums (general and activity-specific), closed chat-rooms, and a "pager" option that allows the participant to send short messages to other participants currently logged to the system.

Discussion

Yad2Yad has been developed, and is in the initial phases of operation, as a program aimed primarily at improving intergroup relations between Palestinian Arabs and Jews in Israel. As such, it can be seen as joining a growing trend toward the use of computer technologies for conflict resolution purposes. Stuart (1997), for example, described the "Shalom/Salaam" initiative, a CSCCR (Computer-Supported Collaborative Conflict Resolution) program designed to foster a community of practice, focused on Palestinian-Jewish conflict resolution and the making of shared meaning. Along similar lines, (Hart, 1998) suggested that ICCMC (Intercultural Computer-Mediated Communication) can contribute to the reduction of cultural misunderstanding and conflict. Working in another conflict-ridden area, Northern Ireland, Austin (Austin, 1997) argued that information technology has a role to play through computer conferencing in conflict mediation by developing participants' skills in using discourse. He suggested that computer conferencing can offer an electronic mask to transcend a number of factors that tend to delimit participation.

By introducing Computer-Supported Collaborative Intercultural Education (CSCIE) we are not just adding a new acronym to the list. CSCIE, as exemplified by the Yad2Yad project, strengthens the collaborative learning component by providing structure for intercultural contact. The computer-based communication offers a virtual space to complement the "real" contact, and to provide an alternative when such face-to-face contact is not feasible. The design and implementation of Yad2Yad meet, to a considerable extent, the conditions specified by the "contact hypothesis," listed earlier. It does not merely offer a virtual space for unstructured contact between the groups; rather, it provides a semi-structured framework for cooperative interaction and collaborative learning on issues related to culture, identity, and common citizenship. The condition of equal status is also seriously sought after in our program. At the level of participants, serious efforts are devoted to including an equal number of Arab and Jewish schools in the system at any given period of time. This condition is also met by the assignment of equal status to both languages, Arabic and Hebrew. This is of paramount importance to our project, since language clearly plays a crucial role in the transmission of cultural and social values (Fishman, 1970, 1997; Safran, 1999). As a symbolic system, language not only constructs social identity but also may solidify or revitalize national/ethnic identities and loyalties (Haarmann, 1986, 1995; Smith & Bond, 1998). In a recent study of a bilingual program in Israel, we (Bekerman & Horenczyk,2002) showed the centrality of the equality in language use to the success of the educational project.

Individualized contact, albeit virtual, is also encouraged in Yad2Yad. Although the focus is on intergroup communication and dialogue, participants are also invited to share with each other their personal home pages (created using the "Face2Face" tools). An additional "keypals" activity creates "mixed" dyads: The Palestinian Arab and the Jewish kid first share personal information (family background, hobbies, and the like) and then discuss—in a semi-structured way—cultural and social issues. It should be noted that recent research suggests—perhaps counter-intuitively—that anonymity within Computer-Mediated Communication tends to enhance, rather than ease, intergroup hostility. As indicated by Postmes, Spears, and Lea (Postmes, Spears, & Lea, 1999), "there is a mounting evidence that anonymous communication increases the influence of social stereotypes on perceptions and on behavior, the derogation of outgroups and ingroup favoritism" (p. 179).

We also place heavy emphasis on institutional support . Teachers and principals play central roles in the project; periodic meetings and training workshops are conducted to increase the involvement and the enthusiasm of school staff with the project. Other societal, situational, and also personal variables thought to increase the effectiveness of the intergroup contact (e.g., duration and frequency of contact, historical relations between the groups) are also given consideration in the Yad2Yad project.

The weakening of negative stereotypes and the reduction of prejudice are not the only objectives of Yad2Yad toward the broader goal of improving intergroup relations. We have argued (Horenczyk & Bekerman, 2002) that the intergroup encounter can serve, and often does serve, as an optimal arena for the exploration, construction, and reconstruction of group and cultural identities. This rests on the assumption that these processes are essential for the creation and strengthening of more harmonious and fairer relations between majority and minority groups so as to foster a sense of, and commitment to, common citizenship among all groups. CSCIE in general, and Yad2Yad in particular, have also the potential to offer a "virtual arena" for such important "identity work."

Educational technologies hold a promise for peace education, but they are just in their infancy. Future research efforts need to inquire on multiple issues which have not been yet investigated. Among these are a) what strategies, within what contexts, can prove effective in integrating the study of peace across the curriculum; and b) how motivated individuals might make use of leading edge technologies to enhance their voices in the global conversation?

ACKNOWLEDGEMENTS

We are very grateful to the Truman Center for Peace and to the Melton Centre for Jewish Education, both at the Hebrew University of Jerusalem, for their continuous and generous support of the Yad2Yad project. We are also thankful to the Yad2Yad staff (Debi Katz, Gaby Fachler, Mohamad Turk, and Tirtsa Harif), and to our co-director Michael Karayanni, for their dedication and commitment. The present chapter is a revised and extended version of a paper presented at the International Conference on ICT's in Education, Badajoz, Spain, 2002.

REFERENCES

Al-Haj, M. (2002). Multiculturalism in deeply divided societies: The Isreali case. International Journal of Intercultural Relations(26), 169–183.

Al-Haj, M. (2005). National ethos, multicultural education, and the new history textbooks in Israel. *Curriculum Inquiry,* 35(1), 48–71.

Allport, G. W. (1954). *The nature of prejudice.* London: Addison-Wesley.

Austin, R. (1997). Computer conferencing: Discourse, education, and conflict mediation. *Computers and Education,* 29(4), 153–161.

Bar, H., & Bargal, D. (1995). *Living with conflict: Encounters between Jewish and Palestinian Israeli youth. Jerusalem,* Is: Jerusalem Institute for Israeli Studies.

Bekerman, Z., & Horenczyk, G. (2002). Golem, from Prague to cyberspace: The uses of CSCL in cultural education for diasporas. In G. Sthal (Ed.), *Computer support for collaborative learning: Foundations for a CSCL community,* (pp. 144–151). Hillsade, NJ: Lawrence Erlbaum Associates Inc

Braa, K., Sorensen, C., & Dahlbom, B. (2000). *The planet internet, challenges facing informatics.* Lund, Sweden: Studentlitteratur.

Cole, M. (1996). *Cultural Psychology: A once and future discipline.* Cambridge: Belknap Press of Harvard University Press.

Fishman, J. A. (1970). *Sociolinguistics.* Rowley, Mass.: Newbury House.

Fishman, J. A. (1997). Language and ethnicity: The view from within. In F. Coulmas (Ed.), *The handbook of sociolinguistics* (pp. 327–343). Oxford Blackwell.

Gavison, R. (2000). Does equality require integration? *Democratic Culture,* 3, 37–87.

Haarmann, H. (1986). *Language in ethnicity: A view of basic ecological relations.* Berlin: Mouton de Gruyter.

Haarmann, H. (1995). Europeanness, european identity and the role of language. *Sociolinguistica,* 9, 1–55.

Hart, W. B. (1998). Intercultural Computer-Mediated Communication (ICCMC). The Edge. *The E-Journal of Intercultural Relations.*

Helman, S. (2002). Monologic results of dialogue: Jewish-Palestinian encounter groupes as sites of essentialization. *Identities: Global Studies in Culture and Power, 9,* 327–354.

Horenczyk, G., & Bekerman, Z. (2002, April). *Perceptions of group identities in Arab-Jewish short-term encounters.* Paper presented at the Interactive Conflict Resolution Conference, Jerusalem.

Israel, C. B. o. S. (2001). *Statistical abstract of Israel.* Jerusalem: Central Bureau of Statistics. Document Number)

Katz, L., & Kahanov, M. (1990). *A survey of dilemmas in moderating Jewish-Arab encounter groups in Israel.* Megamot, 33(in Hebrew), 29–47.

Khalidi, R. (1997). *Palestinian identity: The construction of modern national consciousness.* New York; NY: Columbia University Press

Kretzmer, D. (1992). The new basic laws on human rights: A Mini-revolution in Israeli Constitutional Law? *Israel Law Review, 26*(2), 238–249.

Maoz, I. (2002). Conceptual mapping and evaluation of peace education programs. In G. Salomon & B. Nevo (Eds.), *Peace education: The concept, principles and practices around the world* (pp. 185–197). Nahwah, NJ: Lawrence Erlbaum Association.

Maoz, I. (2004). Coexistence is in the eye of the beholder: Evaluating intergroup encounter interventions between Jews and Arabs in Israel. *J Social Issues,* 60(2), 437–452.

Meyrowitz, J. (1985). *No sense of place: The impact of electronic media on social behaviour.* New York: Oxford University Press.

Postmes, T., Spears, R., & Lea, M. (1999). Social identity, normative content, and 'deindividuation' in computer-mediated groups. In N. Ellemers, R. Spears & B. Doosje (Eds.), *Social identity: Context, commitment, content,* (pp. 164–183). Oxford, UK Blackwell.

Rouhana, N. N., & Korper, S. H. (1997). Power asymmetry and goals of unofficial third party intervention in protracted intergroup conflict. *Journal of Peace Psychology, 3,* 1–17.

Safran, W. (1999). Nationalism. In J. A. Fishman (Ed.), *Handbook of language and ethnic identity* (pp. 77–93). Oxford: Oxford University press.

Smith, P. B., & Bond, M. H. (1998). *Social psychology across cultures.* London: Harvester Wheatsheaf.

Sproull, L., & Kiesler, S. (1992). *Connections: New ways of working in the networked organization.* Cambridge, Massachusetts: MIT Press.

Stephan, W. G., & Stephan, C. W. (1996). *Intergroup relations.* Dubuque, IA: Brown & Benchmark.

Stephan, W. G., & Stephan, C. W. (2001). *Improving intergroup relations.* Thaousand Oaks CA: Sage.

Suleiman, R. (2004). Planned encounters between Jewish and Palestinian Israelis: A social-psychological perspective. *J Social Issues, 60*(2), 323–337.

Svensson, L. (2002). *Interaction repertoire in a distance education community.* Paper presented at the Computer support for collaborative learning: Foundations for CSCL community, Boulder Colorado.

Wasson, B., & Morch, A. (2000). Identifying collaborative telelearning scenarios. *Journal of Educational Technology and Society, 3*(3), 12–22.

Wertsch, J. V. (1998). *Mind as action.* New York, NY: Oxford University Press.

Wolfe, C. R. (2000a). Creating informal learning environments on the world wide web. In C. R. Wolfe (Ed.), *Learning and teaching on the world wide web* (pp. 91–111). San Diego, CA: Academic Press.

Wolfe, C. R. (2000b). Learning and teaching on the world wide web. In C. R. Wolfe (Ed.), *Learning and teaching on the world wide web* (pp. 1–21). San Diego, CA: Academic Press.

Zemach, M. (1980). *Attitudes of the Jewish majority in Israel towards the Arab minority.* Jerusalem: Van Leer Foundation. Document Number)

CHAPTER 13

ICT FOR PEACE AND RECONCILIATION

Constraints and Possibilities in Cambodia and Tibet

Edward J. Brantmeier
Colorado State University

Jayson W. Richardson
University of Minnesota

INTRODUCTION

In the context of technological globalization, how are information communication technologies (ICTs) used as a means for reconciliation and peacemaking? In an era of condensed space and time, technology holds the potential to bring diverse people and divergent interests together to work toward common goals. The power of ICTs is being harnessed, in varying ways and degrees, by people and institutions around the world. The people of Tibet and the people of Cambodia have been influenced both by totalitarian rule and by isolating governance. ICTs are currently aiding Tibetans

ICT for Education, Development, and Social Justice, pages 213–236

and Cambodians to find new ways to promote peace, to attempt to reconcile their conflict-ridden pasts, and to reconstruct a more prosperous future. In this chapter, we first present two case studies. We then explore the theoretical underpinnings behind peace and reconciliation and discuss broadly the concept of ICT for peace and how ICTs can be used for reconciliation. An overview of the literature on ICT for peace and reconciliation is presented alongside an author-generated model for how ICTs can be used as catalysts to aid conflict transformation. Finally, this chapter will examine how ICTs are being appropriated for strategic educational ends by the Tibetan Government in Exile in India and the people of Cambodia to foster reconstruction efforts and to build peace within those situated contexts.

WHY TIBET? WHY CAMBODIA?

Our rationale for choosing Cambodia and the Tibetan Government in Exile as case studies is largely rooted in personal and professional experiences in those contexts. On two separate occasions, the first author had the opportunity to work in Tibetan schools for refugees in India. The first experience was in 1997 as a volunteer English language teacher in McLeod Ganj, home of the Tibetan Government in Exile in the foothills of the Himalayas in Northern India. While in McLeod Ganj in 1997, he quickly noticed the lack of technological infrastructure; it was very difficult to check e-mail and the telephone connections to the United States were spotty at best. In fact, the only place he could find access to the Internet was at the headquarters of the Tibetan Youth Congress, a political and cultural activist group dedicated to Tibetan independence (http://www.tibetanyouthcongress.org). Three years later when working as a co-leader of ten U.S. college-age students on an experiential education tour in India, he and the group traveled to McLeod Ganj to co-develop and to present environmental education workshops to local Tibetan schools as well as a Hindu school. He was surprised to see a plethora of Internet cafés, some established by Tibetans and others by members of the local Hindu population. In just three years, it seemed there was an ICT explosion in McLeod Ganj.

Generally speaking, non-violent practices and values based in a Tibetan Buddhist ethical framework were reinforced through both the curriculum and instruction observed at the Tibetan Children's Village, a school established to serve Tibetan orphans—orphans in relation to Chinese invasion of Tibet. On one occasion in 1997, Tibetan orphaned children performed a choreographed dance for the Dalai Llama at the Tibetan Children's Village in Upper Dharamshala. The children, first marching and then dancing in unison, were as strong and poised as a well-trained army. The first author reasoned that because of deep non-violent value frameworks and their approach of non-violence in daily life, these children were learning peace. The Dalai Llama promotes peaceful and nonviolent interactions with the Chinese Government. These Tibetan refugee children just as easily could be taught violence. It was then that he understood that a nonviolent approach to conflict transformation requires forgiveness, compassion, and wisdom. The impetus for the for the interpretive analysis of how ICTs are being used to promote peace and reconciliation by the Tibetan Government in Exile in this chapter stems from his personal connection to the struggle of Tibetan people for political and cultural autonomy amid colonization efforts by the Chinese Government.

The second author worked on an UNESCO ICT in education project in Phnom Penh, Cambodia in 2006. He traveled throughout the country gaining and in depth understanding of ICT needs at the national and grassroots level. He was amazed to see the coverage of ICTs not only in the education system, but in life in general. Pay-as-you-go mobile phones were literally everywhere. The cellular phone connections were clearer than in the U.S. and he never had a dropped call—even when making an international phone call. Computer kiosks were on every street corner. Computers were literally set up on the sidewalk and were covered with a tent that protected them from the elements.

The second author traveled to the Thai-Cambodian border and visited Buddhist run elementary schools. Most of these villages had no permanent source of electricity, only generated power. The monks as well as the general public could be seen talking on their cell phones. He was amazed at the reach of ICTs. Speaking with Cambodians, he gained a sense that discussing the Khmer Rouge and that time period was taboo. This experience triggered thoughts into how were or how could these omnipresent ICTs be used to reconcile Cambodia's violent past, sustain peace, and reconstruct a nation that was once the region's superpower. The combined personal and professional experiences of the first author in Tibetan communities in India and the second author in Cambodia provide real world footing for this interpretive analysis of the constraints and possibilities of ICTs for peace in those contexts.

ICT FOR RECONCILIATION: A CONCEPTUAL OVERVIEW

Peace is not created with a one-time act: the cease-fire, accord, or reconciliation is just a public point on a timeline between war and durable peace. True peace is built over time, with many different processes and approaches that move conflict into lasting, peaceful relationships. It requires actions at many different levels, by different people, in different ways, and at different points in a conflict (Cole & Crawford, 2007, p. 1).

Both the peace process and attained peace are ridden with obstacles and with milestones of hope. Reconciliation can be thought of as any process in a conflict that works to mend a breakdown in communication that has led to the severing of relationships that bind peoples across groups, nations, or regions. Reconciliation by nature is a *process* of forgiveness; it is not a single fixed point in time. As such, in an ideal form, reconciliation requires that individuals are at liberty to freely and openly interact, have the freedom to communicate via means and processes that aim to establish common understanding, have the ability develop a respect of differences, and ultimately learn to forgive. A very real constraint to the reconciliation process is obviating the asymmetrical power differentials between parties involved in the conflict. Surely, some parties possess more economic, political, social, and military power than others. Some parties in a conflict have considerable more power over others.

Andrews (2000) claimed there are two models of forgiveness. The first model is *negotiated forgiveness* where "forgiveness transpires through actual dialogue between the wrongdoer and the wronged" (p. 76). This model includes three steps for the wrongdoer: confession, ownership, and repentance. The second model is *unilateral forgiveness.* This "is a process which is contained entirely within one individual; it neither engages with nor is in any way dependent upon the position of the wrongdoer" (p. 76). Without dialogue, this unilateral forgiveness lacks depth, understanding, and empathy; it is one-sided forgiveness. Andrews however noted that "the act of forgiveness, which re-establishes severed ties between us, must be built on recognition of our interconnectedness. The forgiver and the forgiven need one another for justice to be enacted" (p. 86). Thus, within Andrews' polar definitions, dialogue remains a prerequisite for reconciliation in our conception here. The notion of forgiveness requires dialogic exchange, mutual engagement, and an understanding of the interrelatedness of both or several parties involved in a conflict. Ideally, the process of reconciliation is both healing and transforming for all parties involved; win-win outcomes are possible when common ground is established. Though there are considerable obstacles such as lack of genuine intention and effort by both parties in a conflict scenario, ICTs offer immense potential for serving as catalysts in the process of reconciliation. Perhaps reconciliation processes can begin with one-sided forgiveness. Over time, it cannot be one-sided proposal or even a geopolitically bounded event if sustainability is desired. Reconciliation processes can cross borders, can cross social groups, and can cross political lines that have been drawn by national atrocities and unthinkable horrors. ICTs are being harnessed to promote dialogue, and in some cases reconciliation, between citizens of nations that are often in political and/or military deadlocks. ICTs by nature have the potential to be transdialogic, transdisciplinary, and transnational. ICTs are an ideal tool in the process of reconciliation. ICTs are not the end, however. They are simply a means to facilitate the process to reach the end result–forgiveness. Andrews (2000) noted,

> Forgiveness is indeed based upon a change of heart, but a change of heart not only of offender or offended but of both parties, in consultation with each other... Forgiving an action is in measure influenced by our ability to understand it (even if the offense is not something which we can imagine ourselves doing). Accepting one's adversaries for who they are—a precondition to understanding their action—can only come about in dialogue with them. (pp. 81–82)

Thus, forgiveness is rooted in dialogue and the free flow of information that allows people to engage in such conversations. The free flow of information is an ideal that often meets hierarchies laden with asymmetrical power differentials among groups within local political, economic, and social systems. Changes of heart are hard won given the power to enact change often lies within the hands of the historical oppressors and not the oppressed. Also, who oppresses and who is oppressed can change over time. Forgiveness in reconciliatory processes is complex when role changes between oppressed and oppressor occur and when dominant and subordinate power dynamics serve to reinforce the inequality between the oppressed and the oppressors.

ICTs have the potential to mitigate inherent power differentials among parties engaged in reconciliation processes, but the potential should not be left uncritically scrutinized. Recent media coverage of Buddhist monks protesting on the streets of Myanmar provides a snapshot of how the Internet can be used to globalize political uprisings against a totalitarian government. However, the military regime in Myanmar quickly shut down Internet cafés and phone lines in order to isolate the voice of protesters from reaching the outside world (National Public Radio, 2007). As is evidenced in Myanmar, ICTs can be used as a means for both global political coverage of anti-governmental protests and for governmental control of information for strategic political ends.

In its ideal form, dialogic exchange works to construct knowledge and (re)build social capital. Bourdieu (1983) defined social capital as being tangible and intangible resources, real or potential, that bond a group together. This social capital is an aggregate, "it is not to be reduced to a discontinuous series of instantaneous mechanical equilibria between agents who are treated as interchangeable particles, one must reintroduce into it the notion of capital and with it, accumulation and all its effects" (p. 183). Cultural capital and social capital, in Bourdieu's conception of them, are linked to economic capital and the reproduction of the existing social order. Bourdieu situates his theory of cultural and social reproduction within a class based analysis of social stratification; those who do not possess economic capital often do not possess the *correct* linguistic, cultural, and social capital necessary to access elite circles of power where decisions concerning public policy are often made. Thus, economic capital is often paramount in sustaining unequal power relationships. Those who have access to technology are able to use it as a means for political, economic, and social ends. Those who do not have access to technology are left out of the conversation. A focus on the divide between these digital 'haves' and 'have-nots' is critical for ascertaining the true power of ICTs in peace and reconciliation processes.

Ideally, dialogue and connections made through ICTs provides opportunity for people to rebuild the social capital that has been previously lost in an attempt to find true and lasting forgiveness. Emmison and Frow (1998) noted "a familiarity with, and a positive disposition towards the use of, the burgeoning technologies of the information age can be seen as an additional form of cultural capital" (p. 44). If access to a broader range of ICTs (e.g., Internet, listservs, blogs, interactive radio, forums, and the like) was widened and a free flow of information was secured, ICTs would provide a powerful means for peace and reconciliation efforts aimed at establishing common ground and positive political and social change.

THE POTENTIAL OF ICTS IN PEACE PROCESSES

The term peacebuilding gained international credibility as a result of the 1992 United Nations Secretary General's report entitled, An Agenda for Peace: Preventive Diplomacy, Peacemaking and Peacekeeping (United Nations, 1992). In that document, peacebuilding was defined as "action to identify and support structures which will tend to strengthen and solidify peace in order to avoid a relapse into conflict" (p. 3). Peacebuilding, in this light, is understood as efforts that focus on comprehensive rehabilitation of social, political, economic, and ideological structures (i.e., pro-human rights orientations) necessary to support and sustain both negative peace (absence of direct violence) and positive peace (absence of indirect violence) in a post-conflict community.

The United Nations (1992) conceptualized peacemaking as "action to bring hostile parties to agreement," which usually involved a third party in the resolution of a conflict (p. 6). On the other hand, peacekeeping was defined as the deployment of UN troops in order to prevent conflict and to promote peace. Peacekeeping in this sense is understood as conflict prevention through a show of military strength; peace through strength or the threat of violence that is understood as a deterrent to actual violence. Applied on a macro level, peacekeeping, peacebuilding, and peacemaking have been framed globally within the context of United Nations efforts.

In an ideal world, ICTs can be used for both peacemaking and peacebuilding because they obviate challenges of space and time. In other words, cell phones, interactive radio, and Internet-based technologies such as podcasts, blogs, chat rooms, and file sharing as well as other creative ICTs bridge both physical and temporal distance and they bring people together into dialogue—one of the hallmarks of diplomacy and the foundation for (re)building of social capital. ICTs provide a vehicle for otherwise voiceless citizens who operate with limited knowledge of social, political, economic, and environmental conditions in their respective countries and in the world. ICTs can provide information from multiple vantage points that helps to counter ideological campaigns of the ruling elite within nations. In essence, ICTs can be harnessed and used to enhance social capital and rebuild connective relationships between and among citizens.

ICTs can be and are being used as counter-hegemonic means to disrupt both ideological campaigns and control of information by groups of people in positions of power. These technologies are also being used by governments to promote solidarity, reconciliation, and political mobilization for various causes and initiatives. Amid the struggle for information dissemination, reconciliation requires truths presented from multiple vantage points in order to include diverse interests and agendas. ICTs can thus provide the means to reconciliatory ends.

Hattotuwa (2004) noted:

> The possibilities of using ICT for peacebuilding dovetails seamlessly into ... conflict transformation, since it can augment the efforts of peacebuilders by enhancing channels, avenues and possibilities for communication, information and knowledge sharing, collaboration, empowerment and discussion in virtual spaces, even when physical, real world meetings are impossible on account of geographical distance or political sensitivities (p. 10)

OVERVIEW OF ICTS FOR PEACE

In-depth case studies of ICT for peace are rare since the union of ICT and peace and reconciliation is still in its formative stage. Organizations like ICT4Peace (www.ict4peace.org) are quickly becoming repositories for germane literature, but their main role is that of advocacy, not research. The news media hence provides the best evidence of ICT for peace cases. For example, in 2002, cell phone text messaging, or SMS, helped topple the president of the Philippines. "Demonstrators used it to mobilize protests, dodge authorities, and fire off political spam" (Hong, 2005, p. 1). The same ICT was used in Seoul, Korea to organize a 400-person student protest against the existing college-entrance exam. Voices of Reconciliation (VOR)

(2007) uses voice radio in Sri Lanka to promote "social, political, and cultural cohesion" (p. 1). These are a several recent examples where ICTs were used to promote peace, social change, or stability within a country. Clearly ICTs are being used in political protest and peacekeeping contexts to promote vested political interests of social groups and countries in the above examples.

Recent history also points to ways ICTs have been used in the formal reconciliation process. For example, during the truth and reconciliation process in South Africa, Gibson (2006) maintains that public radio broadcasts were effectively able to "pierce the consciousness of nearly all South Africans" given the widespread availability of radio technology in the country (p. 416). Gibson elaborates:

> The process made known, in highly personalized and excruciating detail, the suffering of thousands of individual South Africans. The atrocities committed during the struggle over apartheid were not abstractions but were, instead, deeply human losses that resonated with South Africans of every color. (p. 416)

Radio broadcasts were a major contribution to the success of the South African process; they were used to publicly voice stories of atrocities as part of reconciliation and renewal processes. As an insider to the process, Desmond Tutu (1999) reiterates the importance ICTs in saturating most of South Africa during the Truth and Reconciliation Commission proceedings: "In large measure it [high regard for the hearings] was because the media played a splendid role—radio, TV, the newspapers gave the TRC [Truth and Reconciliation Committee] and its victim hearings (as they did the amnesty hearings) saturation coverage" (p. 111). ICTs were effectively used to publicly and widely voice atrocities committed under Apartheid and this provided necessary national saturation for a society to begin the healing process.

MODELS AND DOMAINS OF ICTS FOR PEACE AND RECONCILIATION

Cole and Crawford (2007) found that ICTs can and have been used in peacemaking in six ways. Table 13.1 details the peacemaking goals and lists applicable technologies being used to achieve those goals.

1. ICTs can help to disseminate information to help people gain a true understanding of the situation.
2. ICTs can help people process information by helping to turn information into knowledge.

3. ICTs can help improve decision making skills by presenting critical details and creating an understanding of the repercussions of certain decisions.
4. ICTs can help alleviate resource scarcity by providing real-time data to key constituents.
5. ICTs can help maintain existing relationships and forge new relationships.
6. ICTs can increase peoples' understanding of culture, language, and view points.

Hattotuwa (2004) wrote "the overwhelming majority of populations do NOT participate in ICT interventions. While itself is not necessarily an

TABLE 13.1 Ways of Using ICTS for Peace and Reconciliation and Examples of Applicable ICTs

Ways of promoting peace and reconciliation through ICTs	Examples of ICTs
Provide information	• Internet connectivity • Mobile phones and personal data assistants (PDAs) • Geographic information systems (GIS) • Satellite imagery • Listservs and forums • Radio • Chat
Help people process information	• Websites and portals • Data visualization tools • Online dispute resolution tools • Virtual command centers
Improve decision making	• Games and simulations • Online dispute resolution tools
Reduce scarcity	• Mobile phones • Handheld portable devices
Support relationships	• Social networking tools • Online collaboration tools • Mobile phones • Virtual reality • Telecentres
Help people understand each other	• Translation software • Blogs • Social networking tools • Multimedia

Note: Adapted from *Building peace through information and communication technologies* by R.S. Cole and T. Crawford, 2007, retrieved September 21, 2007, from http://www.idealware.org/articles/peace_through_ICTs.php

impediment to the usefulness of ICT in peacebuilding, to forget this fact would be folly" (p. 22). The authors of the current study sadly understand that the digital divide remains immense. Although thorough coverage of the digital divide is beyond the scope of this chapter and is the subject of other chapters in this volume, it is necessary to note that it may be the most disenfranchised who are excluded from using ICTs as a mechanism for peace and reconciliation. For example, in researching the peace process in Sri Lanka, Hattotuwa (2006) noted "the use of ICT in the context of peacebuilding enables marginalized actors to participate more fully in peacebuilding processes" (p. 3). Disenfranchised people in Cambodia and in the Tibetan diaspora may lack access, and they may lack education on how to use these ICTs for peacemaking.

ICT for peace in the coming decades will not be centralized around access, but on the missing and integral component of education. Surman and Reilly (2003) noted there exists five challenges to appropriate networked technologies for social and political change:

1. Equity: There exists a north/south digital divide.
2. Impact: Little is known about the impact of ICTs on the stakeholders.
3. Trust: Social capital is fragile and difficult to navigate. Many societies in less developed nations have not developed a culture of collaboration.
4. Sustainability: Little is know about how to sustain ICT for social change projects.
5. Enclosure: There exists a threat to the open nature of the Internet (e.g., closed and proprietary networks, repressive intellectual property regimes, technology surveillance).

Surman and Reilly emphasize the point that crossing these hurdles is not restricted to infrastructure, but rather centers on creating awareness and understanding. Therefore education about how to use ICTs for political consciousness raising, mobilization, and engagement in the initial stages of the reconciliation processes becomes a critical component for subordinated groups in societies.

In Table 13.2, we offer our own model for how ICTs can be catalysts for deeper social and political change. We argue that ICTs can be used to: raise consciousness within a community; help to politically mobilize constituents to be active agents of change; to open dialogue between many parties in attempts to reach forgiveness; and to establish a new understanding that will empower both sides to create win-win transformations. In this model, we propose that reconciliation is not always possible, however other domains of peaceful conflict transformation do exist.

TABLE 13.2 Domains of ICT for Catalyzing Peaceful Conflict Transformation

Domain	Acts toward peaceful conflict transformation
Consciousness raising	Information dissemination.
Political mobilization	Organizing protests, marches, e-campaigns, and activism.
Dialogue	Truth recovery, establishment of perspectives, change conditions, and common ground. Knowledge creation.
Reconciliation	Establishment of common ground and forgiveness
Renewal	Social, political, cultural, and economic transformation.

Source: Brantmeier & Richardson (2007).

The concept of using ICTs in less developed nations is sometimes criticized as being culturally homogenizing or an act of colonization. As noted by Zembylas and Vrasidas (2005) however, this "paradox characterizes all educational interventions" (p. 67). Zembylas and Vrasidas urged that to get beyond this limitation one must look at ICTs as a mechanism for critical pedagogy. In other words, to truly embrace the power of critical pedagogy to foster change, critics of ICTs for peace must move beyond the myopic focus of colonization and focus on the possibility of positive change. It is through this lens of criticality that the current authors position themselves.

Case Study of Cambodia

Cambodia is a Southeast Asian nation struggling to rebuild after the atrocities of the Khmer Rouge. The Khmer Rouge, under the control of Pol Pot, was a totalitarian party that ruled the country from 1975–1979 and established what was then called Democratic Kampuchea. This regime closed schools, factories, banks, and hospitals and outlawed religion in an attempt to build a utopian agrarian nation. Under this regime, an estimated 1.7 to 2.2 million people, roughly a quarter of the population, died through forced labor, were executed, or starved to death (Etcheson, 2005, p. 1). Khmers associated with the government, education, religion, or wealth were exterminated. In October 1991, 18 countries and the four warring Cambodian political parties signed the Paris Peace Agreement which essentially began Cambodia's current era of peace, reconstruction, and reconciliation.

Publicly, directly, and formally addressing the Cambodian genocide may take years to come to fruition. The up-front costs for a Cambodian reconciliation tribunal are projected to be USD $61.6 million including in-kind costs to the Cambodian government (Etcheson, 2005, p. 5). In 2005, the Japanese government agreed to fund the majority of Cambodia's share for this tribunal. However, there remains much pessimism that political and legal reconciliation mandated through a tribunal will ever occur considering many of the leaders under the Khmer Rouge remain in positions of power today. Thus, many of those in control of the nation have a lot to loose from actively pursuing overt and public steps toward reconciliation. As evidenced by the many people who continue to pay homage to Pol Pot's grave, the nation has yet and may never agree on which elements of the Khmer Rouge represented hope and which ones represented despair. Although formal truth and reconciliation may be a distant hope in Cambodia, the people of Cambodia are indeed engaging in the initial domains of consciousness raising and the power of ICTs, for use in other domains as described in Table 13.2, is a glaring potential.

Walking the streets in most Cambodian towns it is obvious the Khmer people are actively seeking ways to participate in an ICT-infused world. For example, Cambodia was the first nation to have more cell phones than landlines. This reality indicates Cambodia's willingness and ability to leapfrog old technologies and embrace modern, more efficient, more locally responsive technologies. Additionally, Internet kiosks are not hard to locate and the array of ICT related shops is breathtaking. ICTs are helping Khmers communicate with the outside world, develop a formal and informal economy, run a country, and educate the populace. These ICTs are not static or one-sided, however. The same ICTs Cambodians increasingly embrace to meet personal, political, economic, and educational means are also being used to meet reconciliatory ends. We will next explore how these ICTs are being used in the government, educational, and private sector.

E-Government

Cambodia is currently strategically planning and implementing various e-government initiatives. The Royal Government of Cambodia (2004) created a strategy for national growth and noted that good governance is focused on anti-corruption, legal and judicial reform, public administration reform, and demobilization and should be implemented in an environment of peace, stability, and social order. To assist in this reform, the government created the National Information Communications Technology Development Agency (NIDA) whose mission is to bring the government closer to the people and to bring the people closer to the government.

NIDA (2006) reported that the government of Cambodia adopted the Government Administration Information System (GAIS) project to implement the following core applications: electronic approval system, real estate registration, resident registration, and vehicle registration. GAIS was also an attempt to create a presence of the government on the Internet. NIDA noted how "the GAIS project has achieved the initial objectives of revenue generation, better government image and services" (p. 20).

Creating transparent and easily accessible government records and systems, gives the citizens of a nation a sense of confidence in a system they may no longer trust due to past wrongs. Rightly so, many Cambodian continue to harbor a sense of distrust in their government and governmental processes. In a report funded by USAID, Calavan, Briquets, and O'Brien (2004) found that bribing and corruption within Cambodia remain a pandemic problem. Although government corruption decreases year by year, there remains a general malaise across the country that many government transactions are not completely legitimate. This sense was echoed internationally when the World Bank (2006) threatened to pull loans due to issues of fund misappropriation. Cambodia's e-government initiatives allow the Khmer society and the global society access to a range of government data and government resources. If the citizens of Cambodia are given open, transparent, honest, and free access to such information and systems, building confidence in the government will increase at both the local and international levels.

The government created a national website (www.cambodia.gov.kh) where static information about the king, the country, and the political structures is housed. The site also hosts a library where visitors can, among other things, download Khmer fonts, the national anthem, and a national law database. This site allows visitors to post opinions regarding the Cambodian government.

At this particular government site it is evident that the posts are filtered. In all fairness however, a Ministry website is not the ICT outlet Cambodians seek to be critical of the government. Reports are published frequently in the local Cambodian newspaper, the *Cambodian Daily*, of reporters being jailed for speaking out against the government. Electronic means of posting opinions (e.g., SMS, chat, email, blogs, and the like) are more fluid and semi-anonymous. From this angle, ICTs in Cambodia are providing a safe outlet for dialogue and consciousness raising where government censorship in the public realm is prevalent.

To reconcile the past and to forgive the government, people must be able to voice their dissention and discuss their concerns all the while building confidence in their newly developed government structures. In the Cambodian case, ICTs are being harnessed by the government to promote a sense of national unity, solidarity, and renewal. Although this propaganda does perpetuate a certain ideology, it is also a start to a national social capital rebuilding effort that is necessary for the doors of reconciliation to open. With that said, to fully embrace these nation-building efforts, the average Cambodian will need other ICTs outlets to take this national information and balance it against other perspectives to produce genuine knowledge. That is the great power of ICTs in Cambodia . . . to take information from various angles and produce genuine knowledge that will raise the country and the individual out of the mire of the past.

While in Cambodia, Jayson heard anecdotal reports of political parties traveling to the rural areas to give the poor food or livestock during election times. This, in essence, is a bribe. Since the people cannot investigate this person or are not exposed to the views of other candidates, they assume the gift-giving candidate is good, just, and benevolent. In Cambodia's case, access to political information, consciousness raising, and dialogue are imperative. Some of the current governmental leaders enacted violent acts against the nation under the Khmer Rouge, yet due to an inability for information to surface, the general population sees nothing beyond the most recent gift. For the poor to go through their own process of reconciliation, free access to information is needed. With added ICT outlets coupled with critical education at the grassroots level, the Khmer people can research, watch, and stay informed of the political events pertinent to their nations and make well-informed decisions. Again, ICT for peace is not about access, it is about creating knowledge by using ICTs as a mechanism for social or political change where full reconciliation is but one possible outcome.

As noted above in the case of Myanmar, governments can also attempt to control the flow of information or stop the proliferation of certain technologies. Reuters (2006) reported that the Cambodian Prime Minister Hun Sen "banned 3G [third generation] mobile phones after a complaint from his wife and her friends about receiving pornography on them" (1). These 3G telephones allow for the broadcasting of the Internet over mobile phones. Prime Minister Hun Sen noted that "we can wait 10 more years [for this level of technology] until we have managed to improve morality in society" (p. 1). Attempts to control the use and dissemination of new technologies and thus the free flow of information and dialogue are counter productive not just for technological advancement, but in building trust of the government, however nefarious that information may be toward individuals in the government. Suppression of technological use by the government might be counter-productive and halt the building of a common ground. Trust building is difficult if not impossible in a cloud of suppressed information. Without trust, social capital cannot truly be harnessed for peace building.

ICT in Education Policy

Considering that a central atrocity of the Khmer Rouge was the mass extermination of educated people and the closing of all schools, post-conflict rebuilding is urgently needed in regard to this system. In December 2004, the Cambodian Ministry of Education, Youth, and Sport (MoEYS, 2004) adopted a policy entitled *Policy and Strategies: Information and Communication Technology in Education in Cambodia.* Through the use of ICT, this policy aimed to increase access to basic education, improve the quality of basic education, and create a globally competitive workforce. Through this policy, Cambodia is entering into a state of education renewal.

According to UNESCO (2006), as of the summer of 2006, all teacher training colleges in the nation were outfitted with a computer lab and many had Internet access. These ICTs are currently being expanded into the secondary schools. As of the summer of 2007, the Cambodian government had not attempted to restrict or control information gained via the Internet into these educational institutions. This is a promising step in the reconstruction process. Students and teachers across the nation increasingly have access to resources where they can research and interact with the realities of the past. Allowing the Khmer people these outlets signals that the nation is ready and willing to allow dialogue and increase consciousness raising.

Reconciliation is also about replacing hopelessness with promise. Bernard Krisher, a journalist turned philanthropist noted that "before the kids in my orphanage [in Cambodia] knew how to use the Internet, their fate would have been being prostitutes or cycle drivers, now they want to be computer teachers" (Chon, 2001, p. 2). It is obvious that ICTs are increasing the economic potential of Cambodia. These same ICTs allow Cambodians to individually reconcile the past and replace a negative self-image with a renewed, positive self-image driven by the prospects of the future.

ICT for Cambodian Reconciliation Projects

The Internet has become an outlet for dialogue, political mobilization, and consciousness raising both within Cambodia and abroad. A group out of Fresno, California in the U.S.A. started the Cambodian Reconciliation Committee (CRC) (www.crcfresno.org). The CRC is a non-profit organization that serves Khmer-Americans and attempts to build cohesion among Cambodian people by placing their efforts on education. Their website is an outlet for this small community to remain connected and unified.

The Cambodian Genocide Project (www.cambodiangenocide.org) is based out of Yale University. It is a student-led organization that researches, trains, and digitally collects Khmer Rouge survivor stories to be used at any future tribunals. The Documentation Center of Cambodia (DC-CAM) (www.dccam.org) was founded after the U.S. Congress passed the Cambodian Genocide Justice Act in 1994 and became an independent Cambodian research institute on January 1, 1997. Based in Phnom Penh, Cambodia, the center's goals are to record and preserve the history of the Khmer Rouge regime and to collect data that may serve as evidence in any future tribunals. DC-CAM currently has 155,000 pages of documents and more than 6,000 photographs (DC-Cam, 2007).

These projects are using the Internet as a means to collect and disseminate information pertinent not only to the atrocities of the Khmer Rouge, but also reunification of the Khmer people. These sites offer Khmers and non-Khmers the opportunity to dialogue, share, and understand experiences and in essence to rebuild social capital through consciousness raising. As is evidenced in these projects, opening dialogue via ICTs dissolves borders of nations and cultures. This dialogue is the first step to forgiveness.

PREL (2003) found there remain constraints to the use of ICTs in Cambodia. These constraints include a lack of financial resources, weak telecommunication policies and infrastructure, a lack of basic education infrastructure, a lack of ICT human capital, and the slow pace of creating a Khmer UNICODE. These constraints directly impact technologically driven reconstruction and reconciliation efforts. Without free access to information and the ability to communicate that information, Cambodia will continue to have only pockets of true reconciliatory acts. However, if the present interest in ICTs continues, these acts will grow in number and power through people-people, people-government, and government-government connections.

The nation of Cambodia and the Khmer people have made tremendous strides and progress since the dark days of the Khmer Rouge. It has taken nearly three decades for the government, the education system, and the people to attempt to find their own definition of reconciliation. These acts would not have been possible had it not been for the proliferation and adoption of ICTs in Cambodia. Through ICTs, not only has access to information increased, but dialogue has increased and truth is surfacing. Forgiveness is happening, albeit at the level of the individual. Through this ICT-dependant dialogue, reconciliation is occurring under the umbrella of nation-building. Other nations, such as Tibet, are also using ICTs in a move toward reconciliation. Tibet's use of ICT for reconciliation however is quite unique from the Cambodian case. For Tibet, the use of ICT is not about nation-building, but rather dialogic exchange and information proliferation.

Case Study of Tibet

In 1949, the Chinese government deployed military forces into Tibet. The Chinese government established a new political order within Tibet. Cultural and religious intolerance spearheaded the policies of this new political order. In 1959, the Dalai Llama, considered by many to be the political and spiritual leader of Tibet, fled from China where he sought political asylum in India. The Tibetan Government in Exile was established near Dharamshala in the foothills of the Himalayas in northern India.

Undoubtedly, credibility of information is source-dependent and sources of information can be biased. The online information provided about the history of Chinese-Tibetan relations is largely from a Tibetan perspective; a Chinese perspective can be hard to find on Internet sites published in

English. Little and Hibbard (1993) of the United States Institute of Peace reported "there is a deep-seated ideological hostility on the part of the Communist Party toward religion, and a cultural and ethnic bias against 'backward' Tibetans" (p. 5). Numerous websites hosted by the Tibetan Government in Exile and other pro-Tibetan organizations relay countless facts concerning the policies and practices implemented after the Chinese invasion of Tibet. For example, information on the Government of Tibet in Exile's (2007) official website relays that "Over 1.2 million Tibetans have died as a direct result of the Chinese invasion and occupation of Tibet. Today, it is hard to come across a Tibetan family that has not had at least one member imprisoned or killed by the Chinese regime" (p. 1).

The appropriation of ICTs for political consciousness raising is a powerful tool used to promote pro-Tibetan causes and is part of the initial stages of a much longer process of Tibetan reconciliation with the Chinese government. Numerous informational papers and initiatives are reported on The Tibetan Government in Exile's official website (www.tibet.net). TibetNet provides up to date news concerning Tibetan issues. The Tibetan Justice Center (www.tibetjustice.org), a collaboration between international lawyers and numerous other professionals, provides factual information regarding human rights abuses, the environment, immigration, democracy building, and other issues for both Tibetans inside China as well as those in exile. Tibet Online, Tibetan Information Network, and the Tibetan Youth Congress are among numerous other organizations that utilize ICTs to promote awareness about Tibetan issues to the English-speaking world.

Education, Healing, and Consciousness Raising toward Reconciliation

In order for reconciliation to occur, dialogue between affected or afflicted parties as well as information dissemination about the conflict aimed at larger global audiences needs to be part of the process. Power and voice walk hand in hand. The Internet is a powerful educational tool used by numerous groups to give voice to Tibetan issues and initiatives. The Tibetan Justice Center's 2001 online document, *A Generation in Peril: The Lives of Tibetans Under Chinese Rule* reported the following: inequalities and inequities in access to education for Tibetan children; a political curriculum content focuses on Chinese language indoctrination and political history (rather than Tibetan) that violates China's international legal obligations and represses Tibetan culture, history, and religious expression; and discriminatory treatment and harassment within schools that serve Tibetan children inside the Tibetan Autonomous Region (International Committee of Lawyers for Tibet, 2001). A politically charged, nationalist motive spearheads the implementation of educational policy within Tibet. To borrow from Althusser (1970), education is being used as an ideological state apparatus according to these claims: the indoctrination of Tibetans inside China ensues. According to the report, the patriotic education programs that are being implemented in Tibetan Buddhist monasteries are aimed at dissuading support for the Dalai Llama. The Tibetan Centre for Human Rights and Democracy (2000) reported that "one of the core objectives of this campaign has been to combat the deep devotion of the Tibetan populace to the Dalai Llama and the influence of the 'Dalai Clique'" (p. 3). Such online reports by various NGOs that support the Dalai Llama and other Tibetans in exile provide a powerful voice for the Tibetan autonomy cause.

Part of the healing process for Tibetan refugees displaced by the 1949 military takeover by the Chinese Government has been the provision of adequate housing, healthcare, and schooling by the Government of India, the Tibetan Government in Exile, and multiple international donors. The Central Tibetan Schools Administration (CTSA) (www.tcewf.org) (2007) has a strong, informative Internet presence. The CTSA, an arm of the Government of India, oversees the schooling of some thirty thousand Tibetan children in exile. The website provides a database for schools established for Tibetan children in exile, a summary of education policy related to these refugee children, and ways that organizations and individuals can donate to the Department of Education/Tibetan Children's Educational and Welfare Fund. This schooling fosters Tibetan language and cultural survival alongside the adaptive skills of multilingualism (Hindi, English, and Tibetan) and a broad knowledge base necessary for successful functioning in India's diverse democratic society. Tibetan language and cultural survival are being supported through various schooling efforts. This education aims to heal. The Internet is proving to be a medium to raise awareness about this education and to gather financial support for this critical step in the process of reconciliation.

The Internet is being used as a powerful means for consciousness raising via information dissemination about the Chinese-Tibet conflict. When in Dharamsala, India in 2000, Edward and his college-age American students personally met Bagdro, a refugee Tibetan monk. Bagdro emotionally shared his story of torture in Chinese prisons inside Tibet, his escape from Tibet, and his current activism toward political and culturally autonomy for Tibet. An example of his testimony and call for political mobilization can now be found on YouTube. In a video posting entitled, "Free Tibet: Boycott Olympic Games in Beijing in 2008," Bagdro provides a historical context of Chinese invasion in Tibet, recalls his personal physical and mental torture when imprisoned by the Chinese inside Tibet, and asks for the international boycott of the 2008 Olympic Games in Beijing (http://www.youtube.com/watch?v=zqEmHSAVbHo). In this example, using ICTs for consciousness raising and political mobilization are critical steps in a much longer reconciliation and conflict transformation process.

Constraints for ICTs for Peace and Reconciliation

A component of conflict transformation is consciousness-raising (see Table 13.2) and the exposure of truths from multiple perspectives involved in a given conflict. For example, for the Truth and Reconciliation Commission to have positive and wide impact in South Africa, saturation via radio broadcasts of the public truth recovery processes was pivotal. Free flow of information is not so easy in other contexts.

Inside of Tibet, pro-Tibetan independence and pro-Dalai Llama radio broadcasting is heavily censored and radio broadcasts are frequently jammed by the Chinese Government. In fact, Radio Free Asia (2007a), a U.S. government sponsored, non-military radio broadcast venue, provides specific instructions how to build anti-jamming antennas for short wave radios in order to circumvent Chinese government jamming technologies. The point here is that control of pro-Dalai Llama and pro-Tibetan independence information inside Tibet is essential for continued Chinese occupation and control. Radio Free Asian news briefs such as "China Replaces Local Tibetan Officials in Lithang after Protest" and "China Moves to Control Tibetan Reincarnate Llamas" are difficult for Tibetans inside Tibet to access (Radio Free Asia, 2007b, 2007c). Control of information is powerful. The squelching of political mobilization and authentic dialogue concerning Tibet is essential for continued Chinese Government dominance. Given this heavy censorship, reconciliation seems a long way off, though dialogue seems to have started just recently.

Since 2002, multiple envoys of the Dalai Llama have met with officials in China to engage in dialogue about the Tibetan Autonomous Region. Persistence and dedication to a nonviolent approach to political change seems to be paying off. Dialogue is beginning to occur between Chinese officials and representatives of the Tibetan Government in Exile. This diplomatic dialogue was not occurring prior to 2002. Recent diplomacy measures seem hopeful for future prospects of Tibetan political and cultural autonomy. Given the Olympic Games in Beijing in 2008, more ICT-based global publicity about the Tibetan situation will surely impact these diplomatic dialogues.

TOWARD CLOSURE

The brief case studies examined here provide snapshots that represent how ICTs are being used to embark in various acts toward peaceful conflict transformation. ICT's provide opportunities for governments and their respective people to engage in consciousness raising activities and in dialogues that help to rebuild social capital in the aftermath of political and military conflicts. ICTs continue to provide a potential means to foster connective relationships that may eventually contribute to deeper consciousness raising, political mobilization, reconciliation, and renewal domains in peaceful conflict transformation processes (see Table 13.2).

For both Cambodia and Tibet, ICTs are giving voice to the historically marginalized and voiceless citizens who were most impacted by conflict. The power of voice in the truth recovery processes is essential for peaceful conflict transformation. The transformative feature of technological globalization is that ICTs help obviate the challenges of space and time formerly encountered in a horse and buggy world. In essence ICTs can potentially create a world without borders that empowers the historically oppressed and marginalized. Although Tibet and Cambodia are bonded by their violent pasts, each is in a unique situation today.

We learn from the brief analysis here that considerable constraints such as access to ICTs and censorship on the free flow of information within Cambodia and the Tibetan Autonomous Region hamper a purely hopeful portrait of the power of ICTs for peaceful conflict transformation. As mentioned previously, technological access and knowledgeable, effective use are vital in harnessing the power of ICTs. Bridging the information divide remains paramount to securing fundamental human rights for the historically marginalized and oppressed. It is a matter of social justice at the grassroots level but it includes global players. Arendt (1968) noted:

> Equality, in contrast to all that is involved in mere existence is not given to us, but is the result of human organization insofar as it is guided by the principle of justice. We are not born equal; we become equal as members of a group on the strength of our decision to guarantee ourselves mutually equal rights. (p. 301)

As a global community and local actors in this community, educators and policy makers have a decision to make about guaranteeing ourselves and others mutually equal rights. Part of that process is to provide access to ICTs in order to reconcile, to rebuild social capital, to re-connect ourselves to one another through dialogue and knowledge generation. ICT's provide a nonviolent means for building a culture of peace through unique and individual forms of forgiveness—be that negotiated or unilateral.

We learn from the brief analysis here that the Cambodian government is using ICTs to promote national renewal, unity, and solidarity among the general populous that is healing from the aftermath of oppression and violence. ICTs are used to raise consciousness, build connective relationships, and renew a positive sense of national solidarity. The government does control the flow of information dissemination to a small degree and this will continue to present a challenge of ideological domination. Thus, access to and unrestricted use of ICTs is not yet an undeniable human right in Cambodia. The unique feature of the Cambodian case study is that although formal reconciliation efforts have yet to formalize, ICTs have spurred the nation to move on and to forge a new culture and foster renewal of a brighter future. ICTs are thus being used for renewal and nation-building.

ICTs, in particular the Internet and radio, will continue to be a powerful means to promote the Tibetan Government in Exiles agendas aimed at consciousness raising, political mobilization, dialogue, eventual reconciliation, and renewal. NGOs have successfully appropriated ICTs to raise consciousness about the Tibetan situation in Tibetan diasporas. The struggle continues for the free flow of information within the Tibetan Autonomous Region. Powerful State interest can guide censorship operations that help to ban information that is counter-hegemonic to state ideological discourse and propaganda machines. In this ongoing struggle, however, ICTs have given voice to Tibetan people amid exile and occupation—a voice that would not be heard globally without ICTs.[1] ICTs are effectively being used for consciousness raising and political mobilization, though dialogue has historically been one-sided with unilateral forgiveness on the part of the Tibetan ruling elite in exile.[2] Reconciliation and renewal seem to be on the distant horizon.

Call for Future Research

Our call for further research here in regards to ICTs for peace and reconciliation is rooted in the fact that ICTs hold tremendous potential for fostering connective relationships in post-conflict reconstruction processes. They provide a unique means for dialogue, truth recovery, forgiveness, trust-building, and healing: all essential ingredients for transformative peacemaking and conflict transformation. Dialogue is at the heart of the reconciliation and renewal processes while ICTs are the means to facilitate these processes. ICTs thus provide the means for healing and restoring the physical, psychological, and social-psychological damage that occur from both direct and indirect forms of violence.[3] The descriptive and prescriptive model presented here on *Domains of ICTs for Catalyzing Peaceful Conflict Transformation* could be used to explore peace, conflict transformation, and reconciliation processes of other nations and subgroups within their populations.

When all is said and done, it is not ICTs that ensure peace and the promise of reconciliation. It is the ability and willingness to make peace and justice a priority. Individuals, societies, institutions, and governments need to garner the courage and will to engage in authentic dialogue about past and present atrocities and future potentials for peace. Although lack of ICTs need not be a barrier to this process, the presence of ICTs can be a catalyst to make meaningful, scalable, and sustainable peace. Peace is centered in individuals and societies; ICTs are our arms, extended to embrace one another in hopeful acts of forgiveness, reconciliation, and renewal.

REFERENCES

Althusser, L. (1970). *Ideology and ideological state apparatuses.* France: La Pensee.

Andrews, M. (2000). Forgiveness in context. *Journal of Moral Education, 29*(1), 75–86.

Arendt, H. (1968). *The origins of totalitarianism.* San Diego, CA: Harcourt.

Bourdieu, P. (1983). Ökonomisches Kapital, kulturelles Kapital, soziales Kapital (R. Nice, Trans.). In R. Kreckel (Ed.), *Soziale ungleichheiten (Soziale Welt, Sonderheft 2* (pp. 183–198). Goettingen: Otto Schartz & Company.

Brantmeier, E. J. (2005). *Constraints and possibilities for intercultural peace curricula: A critical case study of teacher involvement in multicultural change at a Midwestern high school.* Unpublished dissertation, Indiana University.

Calavan, M. M., Briquets, S. D., & O'Brien, J. (2004). *Cambodian corruption assessment.* Washington, DC: USAID.

Chon, G. (2001). Bernard Krisher: Healing the killing fields, *Asia Week.*

Cole, R. S., & Crawford, T. (2007). Building peace through information and communication technologies. Retrieved September 21, 2007, from http://www.idealware.org/articles/peace_through_ICTs.php

DC-Cam. (2007). About DC-cam. Retrieved May 17, 2007, from http://www.dccam.org/Abouts/index.htm

Emmison, M., & Frow, J. (1998). Information technology as cultural capital. *Australian University Review, 1,* 41–45.

Etcheson, C. (2005). *The Khmer Rouge tribunal: Options for the United States and the international community*: Fund for Reconciliation and Development.

Gibson, J. L. (2006). The contributions of truth and reconcilation: Lessons from South Africa. *Journal of Conflict Resolutions, 50*(3), 409–432.

The Government of Tibet in Exile. (2007). *Human rights.* Retrieved June 17, 2007, from http://www.tibet.com/WhitePaper/white5.html

Hattotuwa, S. (2004). Untying the Gordian knot: ICT for conflict transformation and peacebuilding. Retrieved September 21, 2007, from http://www.ict-4peace.org/view_files-1-v-43.html

Hattotuwa, S. (2006). ICTs creating hope. *Peace IT,* 3–4.

Hong, S. (2005). New political tool: Text messaging. Retrieved September 21, 2007, from http://www.usatoday.com/tech/news/2005-06–30-politics-text-tool_x.htm?csp=34

International Committee of Lawyers for Tibet. (2001). A generation in peril: The lives of Tibetan children under Chinese rule. Retrieved June 17, 2007, from http://www.tibetjustice.org/reports/children/index.html

Little, D., & Hibbard, S. W. (1993, September 28–29). *Tibetan co-existence: Creating space for Tibetan self-direction.* Paper presented at the Tibetan Co-Existence, Washington DC.

MoEYS. (2004). *Policy and strategies of information and communication technology in education in Cambodia.* Phnom Penh, Cambodia: Ministry of Education, Youth and Sport.

National Public Radio. (2007). Myanmar locks down monastaeries, cuts Internet. Retrieved September 30, 2007, from http://www.npr.org/templates/story/story.php?storyId=14793352

NIDA. (2006). Cambodia: The road to e-governance. Retrieved June 7, 2007, from http://www.apdip.net/projects/e-government/capblg/casestudies/Cambodia.pdf

PREL. (2003). Cambodia: ICT use in education. In G. M. Farrell & C. Wachholz (Eds.), *Meta-survey on the use of technologies in education in Asia and the Pacific* (pp. 73–77). Bangkok, Thailand: UNESCO.

Radio Free Asia. (2007a). *Anti-jamming antenna.* Retrieved October 5, 2007, from http://www.rfa.org/english/support/antijamming/

Radio Free Asia. (2007b). *China moves to control Tibetan reincarnate lamas.* Retrieved October 5, 2007, from http://www.rfa.org/english/news/2007/08/31/Tibet_lamas_reincarnate/

Radio Free Asia. (2007c). *China replaces local Tibetan officials in lithang after protest.* Retrieved October 5, 2007, from http://www.rfa.org/english/tibetan/2007/09/04/tibetan_protest_update/

Reuters. (2006). *3G phones banned in anti-porn drive.* May 26. Retrieved June 24, 2006, from http://news.yahoo.com/s/nm/20060526/tc_nm/cambodia_phones_dc_2

Royal Government of Cambodia. (2004). *Rectangular strategy for growth, employment, equity, and efficiency in Cambodia.* Retrieved March 10, 2007, from http://www.phnompenh.um.dk/NR/rdonlyres/FB448000-1A59-4AB9-A352-477F16525778/0/RGCRectangularStrategypassw.pdf

Surman, M., & Reilly, K. (2003). *Appropriating the Internet for social change: Towards the strategic use of networked technologies by transnational civil society organizations.* Retrieved Sept 21, 2007, from http://programs.ssrc.org/itic/civ_soc_report/

Tibetan Centre for Human Rights and Democracy. (2000). *Enforcing loyalty.* Retrieved June 17, 2007, from http://www.tchrd.org/publications/annual_reports/2000/

Tibetan Children's Educational & Welfare Fund. (2007). *Introduction.* Retrieved June 17, 2007, from http://www.tcewf.org/introduction/index.html

Tutu, D. (1999). *No future without forgiveness.* New York, NY: Doubleday.

UNESCO. (2006). *Establishing the effective use of information and communication technology in education for all in Cambodia: Draft final report.* Phnom Penh, Cambodia: United Nations Educational, Scientific, and Cultural Organization.

United Nations. (1992). *An agenda for peace: Preventative diplomacy, peacemaking and peace-keeping.* Retrieved June 7, 2007, from http://www.un.org/Docs/SG/agpeace.html

Voices of Reconciliation. (2007). *About us.* Retrieved September 29, 2007, from http://radio.voicesofpeace.lk/?1/v/0

World Bank. (2006). *Further misprocurement declared.* Retrieved June 22, 2006, from http://web.worldbank.org/WBSITE/EXTERNAL/NEWS/0,c.078~pagePK:34370~piPK:34424~theSitePK:4607,00.html

Zembylas, M., & Vrasidas, C. (2005). Globalization, information and communication technologies, and the prospect of a "global village": Promises of inclusion or electronic colonization? *Journal of Curriculum Studies, 37*(1), 65–83.

NOTES

1. The Dalai Llama, arguably the most powerful voice of the Tibetan community in exile, argues continuously for political autonomy for Tibetans in the Chinese government occupied Tibetan Autonomous Region. His approach has not been that of seeking Tibetan independence, but a state of autonomy. The Dalai Llama, aware that his international diplomacy affects the lives of Tibetans who live under Chinese rule, pushes for the protection of Tibetan people, religion, and general ways of life. In the eyes of the Dalai Llama, independence from China seems hopeless while he remains optimistic about autonomy. The Tibetan Government in Exile uses the Internet to disseminate this information around the world, gaining support from multiple leaders of nations as well as multiple celebrities who promote human rights for Tibetans inside China as well as Tibetans in exile.
2. It should be noted that the Dalai Llama and followers were/are considered a powerful ruling elite within Tibet prior to Chinese invasion and currently in exile in India. This asymmetrical political and economic power hierarchy has been critiqued as anti-egalitarian and un-democratic because of disparities in resources and decision-making power between the commoners and the ruling elite.
3. Direct violence can be understood as physical harm such as war, fighting, bullying, etc.... Indirect violence can be understood as forms of violence such as psychological harm, intimidation, fear, etc.... Indirect violence should also be understood in relation to structural violence—political, social, economic, and environmental arrangements that privilege some at the expense of others (Brantmeier, 2005).

CHAPTER 14

SOCIAL NETWORKING APPLICATIONS, SOCIAL JUSTICE, AND MULTICULTURAL UNDERSTANDING

Carrie O'Connor
Teach for America

Rebecca Skulnick
Ursinus College

College students are some of the most fervent users of the Internet, a space for college students to connect with each other internationally, across universities, and within their own institutions. This case study seeks to explore how a small liberal arts college utilized a semi-public Internet forum to resolve problems of diversity following an incident involving inappropriate use of facebook.com, a social networking website. We will highlight some of the ways in which tensions and challenges to community building are enacted and exacerbated in online spaces. In discussing technology in a global environment, online communication is an essential piece of our conversation since research has affirmed that "we do not yet fully understand how diverse views play out in electronic discussions; we do not know much about how the Internet facilitates or obstructs rational agreement on social issues" (Rehm, 2000, p. 154).

ICT for Education, Development, and Social Justice, pages 237–253

The Internet brings research into students' dorm rooms, but it also brings their dorm rooms into the classroom. We focus here on a case study of an incident at a liberal arts college[1] in the American Midwest, which might be seen as a miniature global space. This college shifted from that of a college made up of students and faculty from a local, rural Midwest community to a global and multicultural population within ten years. The college and the incident in question interested the authors of this piece as they both are members of a small college, which has shifted from a local to a global community. We believed that if such incidents are happening in one community, they are also happening in others. Therefore, this "developing" space might be seen as a microcosm for global developing spaces that are trying to engage with a more multicultural population. In such a population, identity struggles are publicized in dorm rooms and on the Internet.

The objective of this study is to better understand what happens when a group of students take it upon themselves to have a difficult conversation online. It can be very powerful for students to have the space to create alternative venues, unmonitored by adult supervision, so that they can talk freely about controversial issues. However, online conversations provide an additional freedom in that students seem, as exemplified in the findings section, free to express themselves in a direct manner that they might not otherwise use when conversing with their peers. The question this study asks is whether such a conversation led to better understanding of diverse cultures or did such conversations strengthen a faulty dichotomized belief system.

A decade after its introduction to the public, the Internet has managed to infiltrate the American and global home, office, and university. The Internet has been widely applauded for its ability to connect people across the globe rapidly and for the promises it creates in terms of increasing interaction between diverse peoples. "Virtual communities enable individuals to express their ideas to countless others, promote relationships among diverse individuals across the world, and offer a new venue for setting goals and resolving pertinent issues" (Rehm, 2000, p. 155). Because the Internet is so widely used and promises so many avenues for connection and dialogue, it is necessary to investigate the ways in which people interact and converse in this type of medium. In light of a lack of understanding regarding exactly how the Internet harms or helps diverse dialogue, it is most often posed as an opportunity and positive influence in bringing diverse individuals from around the world together. This sentiment, however, fails to recognize many of the complications inherent in connecting diverse individuals over controversial issues in such a space.

Although the Internet provides spaces for a variety of activities from information gathering to conducting international business, "one of the most crucial aspects of humans' growing use of the Internet is how they have embraced it as a community-forming device—a space where they can meet and interact with one another" (Fox, 2004, p. 48). As the Internet becomes an increasingly popular outlet for social connection, the promises and pitfalls associated with communicating through the Internet and utilizing it as a space to create community must be explored and understood in order to capitalize on the most practical benefits and most dangerous challenges to these goals. Only applying the idealistic and exciting promise of the Internet to allow communication between and across cultures, values, beliefs, and institutions results in a failure to address how and why these interactions may be complicated by the rapid and often anonymous character of Internet communication.

The Internet is not a neutral space but is often considered to be more pluralistic than other types of media. "Power goes to those to can control the flow of information. But when all information, all music, all art, all images, all ideas are digitized, then everyone can access, alter, create, and transmit anything, anywhere, anytime" (Durgin & Sherif, 2003, p. 203). Thus, as compared to print media, the news, the radio, and the like, which are owned, filtered, censored, and controlled by certain (and often powerful) institutions and organizations, the Internet gives power and voice to any individual with access. This freedom and opportunity for self-expression makes the Internet an essentially multicultural space where expression of opinions and ideas is not limited to those of the mainstream or dominant culture. "Multicultural education maintains that all students should have equal opportunities to learn" (Banks, 1995, p. 391) and universal Internet access at a collegiate institution provides not only equal access to information but open access to spaces to vocalize.

The promises of the Internet cannot completely overshadow the potential downfalls and challenges present in creating dialogue and community among diverse individuals interacting in virtual spaces. Although the Internet is often applauded for acting as a space which offers a more democratic and egalitarian canvas for interaction it can also become a space characterized by contentious struggle for power and voice when exploring pockets of dialogue in separate communities. Unfortunately a variety of potential pitfalls are likely to occur in contentious online discussions including "extreme individualism, presentation of fantasy selves, manipulation of others, self-assertion over dialogue, and self-indulgence over responsibility" (Rehm, 2000, p. 159). The sense of physical safety and anonymity provided by the Internet, as opposed to face-to-face meetings and confrontations between individuals, allows for irresponsibility toward sensitivity as well as hostility with little more than verbal comebacks as consequences. If a virtual community is not founded on reciprocal principles, use of this medium opens a door of possibility for relaxation of social consciousness ultimately resulting in its inability to operate as a space where diverse opinions and ideas are actually heard.

SOCIAL NETWORKING

Dispersion of information on the Internet is increasingly achieved using a variety of social networking applications available to all Internet users. The most widely used of these applications are online communities such as MySpace, Facebook, and Friendster, where individuals create profiles including photographs and information about themselves and their interests. The social network is built through the adding of "friends" to one's profile, be they acquaintances, colleagues, friends-of-friends, family members, or strangers acquired through a search engine on the site. "Teens and young adults have flocked to so-called social-networking sites, to the extent that kids who don't have a profile are becoming the exception to the rule" (Internet Education Foundation, 2003). In recent years such sites have received increased publicity because of their unmonitored use by children and adolescents who publicize information about themselves in the seemingly safe environment of Internet communication and the increased role of social networking sites in allowing older strangers to contact impressionable and vulnerable teens. Other social networking applications such as blogs, wikis, webshots, and Youtube provide vast opportunities for individuals to share files, stories, videos, and photos for free. A blog or wiki is a Web site to which an individual shares stories, news, information, images, and links of their lives and interests. Blogs serve as online diaries or as forums for information on various topics. They are typically frequently updated and are easily used as they are managed by a template into which the user simply types and submits information. Finally, web sites such as Webshots, Photobucket, Snapfish, and Youtube provide Internet space for individuals to post photos and videos either homemade or found on other Internet sites.

METHODS

Setting: Facebook

Facebook.com is a social networking web site. Sites such as MySpace are similar, but Facebook is generally considered the most widely used site of its type among college students. To create an account on Facebook.com, users, be they current students, alumni, or faculty members, must have an email address in the domain of an organization that is registered and affiliated with Facebook. When Facebook was created, access was limited to colleges and universities but has since expanded to include high schools, corporate organizations, and geographic regions. Thus, in a matter of years Facebook expanded from a collection of institutional communities to a global community accessible by anyone with an email account. A number of privacy settings were ushered in with this expansion; however, the choice to make information private to only certain users is at the discretion of the owner of the profile. Once the account is established, individuals create profiles that describe their personal and academic interests, club and organization affiliations, and pictures—virtually any information a user wants to post. An additional feature of Facebook is the ability to post blog-like entries linked to one's profile called notes (EDUCAUSE, 2006, p. 1).

Facebook is a particularly relevant virtual community in that it is different from many other online communities; its users are not faceless or anonymous. Nothing that is posted on Facebook can be done so anonymously. "Each virtual community exists in a unique relationship with physical communities within imagined spaces" (Fox, 2004, p. 55). This is particularly relevant when a virtual community is simply an extension of a physical community, such as a small college campus, as opposed to a community that is created around a hobby or an interest and is participated in by a variety of individuals across geographic space. The implications of this relationship between the virtual and physical are heightened when users are identifiable and particularly when the physical community is relatively small.

The Faebook website boasts 12 million registered users since its creation in 2004 and is the seventh most visited site on the Internet (About Facebook, 2006). Although access to Facebook is limited to those affiliated with the network, it is essentially a public forum. "Concerns about Facebook center on its being public even though it feels like a private forum. [...] Although some students understand how and when to separate private from public content, many lack the discretion to present themselves—and others—appropriately online" (EDUCAUSE, 2006, p. 2). The resulting ambiguity of privacy on Facebook contributes to the decline of social consciousness present in other forms of Internet communication. As is commonly understood, what one is willing to expose, say, or express in email is often less censored than what an individual is likely to say in a face-to-face conversation. Additionally, the likelihood of misinterpretation and misunderstanding across Internet communication such as email is also heightened. In this lies the danger in usingg Facebook as a space in which to interact with others. The nature of Facebook is forcing colleges and universities nationwide to consider its impact on free speech, harassment, and the classroom.

Similar to the Internet at large, Facebook creates a promising yet challenging space for individuals to interact with each other. "Any technology that is able to captivate so many students for so much time not only *carries implications for how those students view the world* but also offers an opportunity for educators to understand the elements of social networking that students find so compelling and to incorporate those elements into teaching and learning" (EDUCAUSE, 2006, p. 2). Facebook is important to examine because it not only brings academics and interests into the dorm room, it also brings the dorm room into the classroom, particularly when it houses tensions and problems pertinent to the academic arena and the college community.

PARTICIPANTS

This exploration of virtual communication was catalyzed by an incident at a small liberal arts college in which four male students posted inappropriate pictures on a Facebook account that anyone associated with the college could access. Sixty photos were uploaded onto Facebook and depicted "one student with discriminatory writing all over his torso, face, and arms. This writing included swastikas and various ethnic and sexist slurs with 'Jew' appearing amidst a Star of David" (Editorial, p. 2). The photos remained posted on the site for two weeks before they were brought to the attention of the college administration. It was at this time that the photos were removed and apologies were posted on Facebook by two of the students involved. A series of conversations revolving around the incident and larger issues of diversity ensued following the posting of these apologies, both on and off the Internet.

DATA COLLECTION

The data for this study consist of publicly available conversations, comments, and writings by students of the college collected over a six-week period. These include Facebook notes (essentially blogs embedded in the Facebook network and linked to one's account), comments posted on those notes by students of the college and in some cases students of other institutions, and discussion boards in Facebook groups formed around the issues. The notes of one outspoken student in particular were utilized as a starting place for the collection of other notes and conversations. Her notes attracted the most attention of all notes posted and quickly became infamous among the students. Subsequent notes were collected by exploring the profiles of students who commented on her notes and successive notes posted. The conversations analyzed consisted of thirty-two Facebook notes written by fifteen individuals, 173 comments made on those various notes, three Facebook group discussion boards, amounting to a total of 113 pages of data. The data were analyzed by extracting themes from the conversations available online in order to examine both what students were talking about and how they were attempting to make their points to each other.

RESULTS

Data analysis resulted in the extraction of a number of themes from the conversations students had with each other. The two most pertinent and common discussions revolved around a) what constitutes racism or makes someone racist, and b) how the students, administration, faculty, and community should react to the Facebook incident. Rhetorical analysis helped to identify three significant barriers to successful communication and community building. These elements comprise the most salient ways in which students communicated with each other: a) choosing to speak or remain silent, and b) "us versus them" posturing.

What Constitutes Racism?

A large degree of contention was present throughout the online dialogue because there existed no agreed upon judgment whether or not the Facebook incident constituted "racism" or meant that the students involved are "racist." A total of 34 statements addressed to this issue or providing various interpretations of "racist" and "racism" were counted. Statements were included if they asserted that the students involved were or were not racist, if the acts committed were or were not racist, or if they provided a reason as to why the students were or were not racist, as seen below. This side of the debate insisted that the incident was a "mistake," and was not reflective of the "true character" of those involved. These students argued that if the perpetrator was sorry and did not intend to harass, discriminate, threaten, or offend, then they were not necessarily racist. The students who chose this side of the debate were predominantly white.

> "you can call them ignorant, but you can't just peg them racists." (White male)

> "Your friends know that what happened doesn't represent who you really are." (White female)

> "I know you well enough to know that you are truly sorry and would never mean harm to anybody.[…] Anybody who knows you understands that this is just a mistake you made." (White male)

> "This week began with a disturbing issue. A minority student was framed as a racist. The irony in this was too much.[…] I know the true character of the persons involved. Can you say you know him for his true self? Can you say the same? NO." (Latino male)

The most frequent defense of the incident's "racist" intent was the character of the students involved; most students believed that these students were good people who did not mean harm and implied that their actions happened out of ignorance rather than hurtful intentions.

The other side of the discussion provided a variety of opinions revolving around the assertion that the act was racist, the students were racist, or both. Many were quick to explain that ignorance is no excuse for using or misusing discriminatory, prejudiced, or racist terms in seriousness or in jest.

> "There is no reason for anybody with an education to not know that promulgating discriminatory—no, misanthropic 'terms n symbols' is harmful to everyone involved." (White female)
>
> "Saying 'I'm not racist' or 'I was raised a Christian' does NOT take away the racist comments. They were there, being Christian or a good person doesn't make you not racist." (White female)
>
> "'I'm not really racist,' they think, as if racism was an extinct dinosaur, despite everything they say and do." (White male)
>
> "I don't believe they think that using N' Lover and Jew is racist. I'm sorry, but when you use that word, you are evoking racism." (White female)

As seen above, sentiments ranged from frustrated to enraged and reflected the degree to which individual students felt the perpetrators intended harm. Ultimately the students participating in these discussions never came to an agreement on whether the acts and postings meant the students involved were racists. This was a significant obstacle to further discussions about what should be done about the incidents and agreement on the severity of the situation because individuals were not approaching the discussion from a common understanding. What is more, the divide between the students escalated racial and cultural tensions in the Facebook comments rather than acted as a mode of communication that might lead toward understanding of both sides.

What Do We Do?

The four students involved in the Facebook incident faced a judiciary hearing to receive punishments from the school but were not charged with or found guilty of harassing the community. This decision caused great uproar and disagreement among the community both online and offline. As a result, the community was faced with deciding what should be done about the escalating issues of diversity and racial tension. Sixty-two comments appeared throughout the data regarding what students felt should be done about future controversies and why this one was not handled effectively. The following comments illustrate students' frustration with the administration's lack of action immediately following the incident. The race of students is given only when students self-defined as belonging to a particular culture. In addition, the culture students identify themselves with is the one used in the subject description below the quotation:

> "When did the racism begin, and why is it only being announced now as unacceptable? Why can't the fricken admin take it upon themselves to acknowledge it, and why does it take student anger to actually have an impact?" (Black female)

The major dispute students had, as seen above, is that the administration did not respond to the incident in a public manner that seemed adequate to the students. Of course, this might also be why students managed such a volatile discussion regarding the incident on Facebook. They felt that they had no mechanism to discuss the incident on campus in a way that their notion of the administration would listen.

The other point of contention surrounding this issue involved the punishment given to the students involved in the incident. Those students who did not believe the acts were racist or did not believe the students involved were racist also felt that the students should not be punished. Another group of students felt that the students involved in the incident should be more severely punished. In addition, they again repeated the notion that those who were offended by the incident were not being listened to:

> I'm sick of being told that everything will be all right if we just ignore it. For f... sake, we did just like they told us and shit got worse. Frankly, I don't want to find out how far someone has to go before the administration stands up and punishes their behavior. (Black female)

> "It does not matter if one forgets what these words and symbols mean and accidentally uses them in some sad attempt to be funny, or something. They mean what they mean, and yes, we are free to use them, but you have to be prepared to accept the consequences." (White female)

These students accused the administration of being too lax with the students' punishment and were offended and disappointed with the judiciary ruling. The following comment was written trying to explain to the community why she believed the judiciary ruling happened as it did:

> "What I am understanding from the administration's understanding of racism is that things like writing 'n[...] lover' on one's self is equivalent to an 'artistic expression.' Yes, that previous quote was a professor at [__________] College! [Professor's name]... Enjoyable." (Biracial female)

In addition to conversations specifically about punishment of the four male students involved in the incident, individuals also discussed other possible and necessary reactions to the escalating racial tensions on campus throughout the community. What is most unfortunate is that the judiciary board issued a public statement in the school's newspaper explaining that the student handbook stated that in order for language to be defined as hate speech it must show "intent to harm."

The students did have a distinct conversation about the notion of intentionality, but never cited the public statement as evidence for why the students were punished in the way that they were, nor did the students offer any plea to change the student handbook. Instead, as with previous discussions, two groups also formed; one was largely ambivalent and apathetic and called for peace or accused those passionate about the issue of being too angry. This group of students was largely composed of white males. Examples of such comments are listed below:

> "I know you and i know those pictures don't represent you or your friends. that said putting you on J-board is total bullshit and I got your back, if they do anything to you as a result of this then I don't know what should happen but some sort of protest or something cause its f... horse shit" (White male)

> "[he] does not deserve as much shit as he's been getting. he took a pic n posted it, mad dumb and ignorant but does he deserve to b kick'd out? I don't think so, he should be reprimanded however, yes." (Black male)

> "It's an opportunity to educate, not ruin people's lives because of misjudgments..." (White female)

> "The white people acting up confuse me as much as they do you, man. If you cant get them to understand, I don't know ho w the hell I can reach them. I think they look at me as a lost cause." (White female)

> "What category you are missing which hurts the most is the category of minorities who are fine and actually believe a mistake was made and that the perpetrators could still be their friends and care about them. [...] SO the minorities who aided in this event, or stand by them are those that are doing the most damage, because they are making it seem as though it ok to hurt others like this as long as you claim it to be a mistake and say 'sorry'" (Biracial female)

> "Here's my input: f... all those white pigs that made the mistake of publicizing the contents of their diseased minds. You go on and fight, [author of note]. They mad now because you're a strong blacky who ain't gonna shut the f... up" (Black female)

The other used more aggressive words, seeming to create a hostile barrier dividing the two sides. This group of students wrestled with their own racial identities based on their reactions to the incident as well as the Facebook comments regarding their reactions.

> "THEY DON'T CARE ABOUT YOU, THESE WHITE PEOPLE DON'T LOVE YOU, and now they are tricking you into thinking they do so they don't get in trouble...ALL OF YOU ARE A GREAT MINSTREL SHOW, AND I AM SORRY I BOUGHT TICKETS TO IT. . . ." (Biracial female)

> "On your wall you referred to us as racist white boys and retards, well I'm not racist or retarded, I'm of Caucasian descent but what does that matter. Color doesn't matter and that should be how we act. If you want to hate on people for racist comments then you have every right, but hate the individual person." (White male)

> "I try aiming for unity and peace and get taken as someone negative from the people that I expected from least." (Black male)

Of all the discussions pursued on the Facebook website, those between individuals who were angered by the incident seemed the most constructive and supportive because they occurred among students who shared similar sentiments about the incidents and the future of the campus. Although many students were more angry or more confused than others, these students, be they white or students of color, shared common ground in a common goal. They were unsuccessful, however, at rallying any of their peers who initially stood on the other side of the fence to join them.

The last group of comments was most involved in speaking toward suggestions of constructive reactions and solutions:

> "The problem here isn't about pictures posted on Facebook—we all know that we can make private profiles to avoid that whole problem. The issue is that people are using racist terms, whether or not they mean them negatively, and thinking that that's ok. These words are racist . . . they have long, painful histories. People should respect that and not play around with slurs."

Listed under "self help" the following poem was the only comment listed that makes explicit reference to multicultural ideologies as learned at the institution:

> we wanna posture about racism
> the elimination of oppression
> attitudinize about the need to
> be held accountable for actions
> yet we laugh at others and their ignorance
> giggle at stupidity and spew hateful words
> without trying to educate.

Spew hateful words without trying to comprehend.
wat Sanchez said about laughin at others?
we claim to understand
the actions and motives of others
well its time we take a stand
and start trying to overstand.
overstand SYSTEMS and INSTITUTIONS and
Ask questions like "who's holdin the paint brush?" "who's controlling the big picture?"
instead of simply standing judgmentally over individuals.
overstand the real reasons behind
ignorant actions instead of spewin hateful words
we sit and gossip/gossip and sit/gossip and sit/chit chat and out wit
as we sip on ___ soda
spewin witty remarks covering hateful words
instead of speaking life
ha but look at me getting behind myself... "judge not least ye be judged? right?
i've decided to take a stand and start practicing what i preach.........
instead of spewin hate imma be about change
instead of spewin hate imma speak life cause life speaks

In general, the Facebook suggestions represented a variety of possible solutions to diversity issues campus wide including educating the community, changing the curriculum, and alerting the news by writing press releases. Other students contributed vague but encouraging sentiments commanding their fellow classmates to take action. The small number of requests for conversation by students who felt that the conversations were too angry never resulted in constructive dialogue and the conversation and subsequent postings always reverted to name calling and hostility.

To Speak or Not to Speak?

The data collected over the six-week period exhibit interesting patterns in who chooses to speak and who chooses to remain silent and for how long. The first week there were 12 notes posted including the apology and 95 comments made by 56 individuals. The second week there were 9 notes posted and 57 comments by 35 individuals. The third week 4 notes were posted and 9 comments were made by 8 individuals. Over the last three weeks only 6 notes were posted and they were commented on 16 times by 14 individuals. These numbers exhibit a sharp decline in participation over the course of the first half of the period (see Figure 14.1).

After the first week of discussions, none of the students involved in the incident chose to contribute to the online forum, nor did any of the indi-

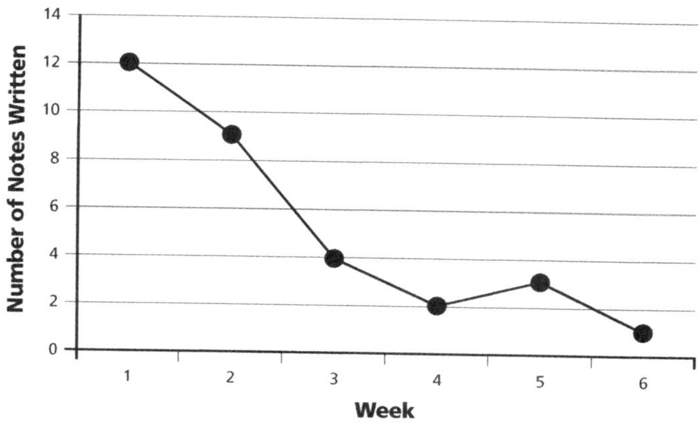

Figure 14.1 Patterns of online commenting over a six week period.

viduals who posted supportive comments on the apology. Additionally, by the third week the white students who were apathetic about the situation stopped participating. The minority students perceived to be sympathetic or apathetic by those minority and white students who were angry were absent from the conversation with the exception of one poem written by a black male. Across the fourth through sixth weeks the only students conversing where those who were angry and attempting to find solutions. It is not possible to tell from the data if the students who stopped participating online were still having conversations offline but the decline of the community is relevant because it reflects the inability to create a space in which everyone feels their voice is heard and can be contributive. It is particularly significant that certain groups of students dropped out of the conversation, not just numbers of students, which demonstrates a lack of community building across the groups and signifies a failure of the use of this application to blend ideas from various groups and sides of the issue.

Us versus Them

The participants in online discussions surrounding the issue of diversity and the incident on Facebook in this forum were divided in a number of ways. Students were quick to demarcate a variety of groups that they felt arose from the situation. These groups included a) angry students, b) apathetic students, c) sympathetic students, d) and a small group of students who were "confused" or "on the fence." Students were categorized as angry (by their peers and for the purpose of this study) if they felt passionately about the wrongness of the incidents. Students were categorized as apathetic if they did not think that the situation was a "big deal," sympathetic if they felt bad for the students involved in the posting of pictures, and "on the fence" if they did not know whose side they were on.

The process of dividing groups was done by peers, as various individuals accused others and groups of being in one category or another. The categories were talked about abstractly in that particular students were not called out by their "enemies" as being in one group or another. The only concrete designation occurred when students identified themselves or their allies explicitly. Nevertheless, the differentiation of groups is relevant because it created and reflected a great deal of hostility.

DISCUSSION AND CONCLUSION

The data provide a wealth of knowledge pointing to a variety of interesting patterns and challenges that occurred throughout the six week period of conversation regarding racial issues. First, the students talked about a handful of issues, but the most prominent ones and those talked about the most were those which could not be agreed upon. In neither of these strands of conversations was agreement ever reached and those students who did not believe that the perpetrators were racist, that they should not be punished, and that the conversations were inflammatory dropped out of the forum by week three. These students comprised the white apathetic and sympathetic groups and those students who identified themselves as confused. The hostility present in demarcation of groups and the sarcastic and hostile tone of the forum were likely factors in this regression. It appears that these students participated in the forum because they were upset by negative reactions to their friends and wanted to vent their frustration. If they were interested in genuinely discussing diverse solutions to the problem it is not clear from the data available, whether as a result of the hostility in the forum or a lack of this desire in the first place. When they discovered, for whatever reason, that the forum was not an appropriate or ample space to express themselves, they left and the conversation turned toward being more constructive and positive among those who remained.

The students who remained active in the forum throughout the six weeks were those initially most angered by the events. These individuals posted notes and comments prolifically in the beginning of the conversations. As the sympathetic and apathetic students dropped out or were driven out of the dialogue, the anger of the students who remained was somewhat assuaged. This led to the more constructive conversations of what to do about the situation and the sharing of tangible possible routes to take. Thus, for these students it appears that the forum served two purposes: initially to vent anger and attempt to educate the community of the wrongdoings and eventually to collaborate and come up with solutions. Unfortunately, it can be extrapolated from the data and the lack of participation by the group who disagreed with these students that they did not successfully reach or obtain dialogue with students who disagreed with them. Thus, the conversations that were occurring by the end were not representative of a diverse perspective, nor the interaction of dominant and transformative opinions and knowledge. This fact, however, should not undermine the conclusion that Facebook did provide students whose voices are typically unheard a space to communicate with each other and provide information publicly to those willing and desiring to read it.

A limitation of this study is that there was no way to obtain all Facebook notes posted by individuals associated with the college without seeking them individually and some Facebook profiles are visible only to those with permission; thus, it is not likely that every note posted on the topic is included, although the notes included in this study represent the most widespread and continuous online conversations regarding the issue. It is possible, therefore, that conversations between apathetic and sympathetic students did continue in an online space and they were not uncovered. It is additionally possible that these students, and other students, are talking about these issues face-to-face or in other online mediums that are not public in order to avoid the scrutiny of their peers.

The most pertinent information uncovered from this study was that the online Facebook forum did not successfully function as a space in which to bring opposing viewpoints together and constructively involve diverse perspectives. These occurrences mirror the findings of another case study focused on online anonymity. In both studies

agreements were short lived and generally unsympathetic to opposing views, giving only terse acknowledgment to others' feelings before quickly devolving into divisive harangues:

> [...]Such posturing made it difficult, if not impossible, to see the common ground that existed between the different members' stances. Polarizing rhetoric made community issues a matter of personal pride and ultimately closed off the discussion despite each side's stated desire to promote a more democratic vision." (Jordan, 2005, p. 216)

These two situations suggest that engaging in debates about divisive and difficult issues online is challenging and in the case of this study largely unsuccessful. This is not to say, however, that there were no positive effects of the online community. It does say nevertheless, that an un-moderated online space is not necessarily the best space to solve issues when diverse perspectives were involved and emotions are heightened.

Even so, in this case the Internet provided students who did not feel "heard" at the college, to express their beliefs. In this case, the primary benefit of the Internet is it acted as a multicultural space in that it provides an opportunity for individuals to create and disperse transformative knowledge. "Transformative academic knowledge consists of the concepts, paradigms, themes, and explanations that challenge mainstream academic knowledge and that expand the historical and literary canon" (Banks, 1995, p. 394). The students challenged each other and, while offending and sometimes isolating the controversy into two distinct and opposing arguments, they made their reading available to the public. One would suppose that having this knowledge consumed coerces an institution into transforming the way in which it approaches and views the status quo and "intellectual justifications for institutionalized stereotypes and misconceptions about groups of color" (Banks, 1995, p. 394). No longer is the control of information and ideas limited to those who hold power in the traditional sense of controlling mass media. Thus, the use of the Internet as a forum for discussion of diversity issues provides vast opportunities to empower students whose voices are commonly unheard in the typical structure of the institution.

REFERENCES

About Facebook. (2006). *Facebook.com.* Retrieved November 15, 2006: http://www.facebook.com/about.php

Banks, J. (Autumn 1995). Multicultural education and curriculum transformation. *The Journal of Negro Education, 64*(4), 390–400.

Durgin, J., & Sherif, J.S. (March 2003). The effects of the virtual community on changing worldwide business and culture. *Journal of Academy of Business and Economics, 2*(1), 202–212.

EDUCAUSE. (Sept. 2006). Seven things you should know about Facebook. *EDUCAUSE Learning Initiative.* Retrieved November 15, 2006: http://www.educause.edu/ir/library/pdf/ELI7017.pdf

Editorial: A call to responsibility. (October 12, 2006). *The watershed.* p. 2.

Fox, S. (Jan 2004). The new imagined community: Identifying and exploring a bidirectional continuum integrating virtual and physical communities through the Community Embodiment Model (CEM). *Journal of Communication Inquiry, 28*(1), 47–62.

Internet Education Foundation. (2003). Risks by technology: Social networking sites. *GetNetWise.* Retrieved June 13, 2007: http://kids.getnetwise.org/safetyguide/technology/socialnetworking

Jordan, J. W. (Spring 2005). A virtual death and a real dilemma: Identity, trust, and community in cyberspace. *The Southern Communication Journal, 70*(3), 200–219.

Rehm, M. L. (Dec 2000). An aesthetic approach to virtual community. *Family and Consumer Sciences Research Journal, 29*(2), 153–172.

NOTE

1. All indicators of the college's name has been changed in order to preserve anonymity.

ABOUT THE CONTRIBUTORS

Abreu-Ellis, Carla, Ashland University
cellis1@ashland.edu

Carla Abreu-Ellis earned her PhD at Bowling Green State University in Higher Education Administration. She is an assistant professor in the Dwight Schar College of Education at Ashland University in Ohio. Her research interests include college experiences of students with learning disabilities, technology use in higher education, and university retention.

Bekerman, Zvi, Hebrew University of Jerusalem
mszviman@mscc.huji.ac.il

Zvi Bekerman teaches anthropology of education at the School of Education and the Melton Center, Hebrew University of Jerusalem. He also serves in the faculty of the Mandel Leadership Institute. His main interests are in the study of cultural, ethnic, and national identity, including identity processes and negotiation during intercultural encounters and in formal/informal learning contexts. He is the Editor (with Seonaigh MacPherson) of the refereed scholarly journal *Diaspora, Indigenous, ad Minority Education: An International Journal.* Among his recent books is Mirror Images: Popular Culture and Education edited with Diana Silberman-Keller, Henry A. Giroux, and Nicholas Burbules (2008).

Brantmeier, Edward J., Colorado State University
edward.brantmeier@colostate.edu

Dr. Edward J. Brantmeier is an Assistant Professor in the School of Education at Colorado State University. His research interests include multicultural peace education in the context of teacher education/educational leadership as well as cultural conflict and change. He teaches multicultural education and other foundations courses at the undergraduate and gradu-

ICT for Education, Development, and Social Justice, pages 255–264

ate level. He has authored or co-authored articles in the following select journals: *Theory and Research in Social Education; Journal of Peace Education; Journal of American Indian Education; & International Education.* His co-edited book, *Transforming Education for Peace,* is available from Information Age Publishing. http://mycahs.colostate.edu/Edward.j.Brantmeier/

Cohen, Rebecca Skulnick, Ursinus College
rskulnick@mac.com

An Assistant Professor at Ursinus College, Rebecca Skulnick Cohen holds a PhD in Curriculum Studies and American Studies from Indiana University. In addition to teaching lower and upper level courses in the Education Department at Ursinus College, Dr. Cohen works with secondary education students to prepare them to teach in Philadelphia's charter and comprehensive schools as the director of the college's Philadelphia student teaching experience. By involving new teachers in her research, Cohen also supports new teachers' interest and involvement in academic research. Dr. Cohen's research interests are informed by her former students and new teachers. As a former high school English teacher in Michigan, Cohen's work focuses on language and identity. From adolescents to college age students, Cohen is interested in how individual students assert themselves and how schools can create spaces in which productive and positive social and intellectual development can develop from students' passions. In this vein, her work has two main foci: 1) how urban school reform and policies affect students' and teachers' schooling experiences; 2) how individual students succeed and flourish in particular reform-based settings.

Daniel, Sir John, Commonwealth of Learning
jdaniel@col.org

After obtaining degrees from the Universities of Oxford and Paris, Sir John Daniel then took 25 years to complete a part-time Master's degree in Educational Technology at Concordia University. During this time he worked in conventional and distance-teaching universities in Canada and the UK, including 17 years as a university president at Laurentian University, Ontario and the UK Open University. More recently his work has focused on the role of education and learning in development through his appointments as Assistant Director-General of UNESCO and President of the Commonwealth of Learning.

Dede, Chris, Harvard University
Chris_Dede@harvard.edu

Chris Dede's fields of scholarship include emerging technologies, policy, and leadership. His funded research includes four grants from NSF and the US Department of Education to explore immersive and semi-immersive simulations as a means of student engagement, learning, and assessment.

In 2007, he was honored by Harvard University as an outstanding teacher. Chris has served as a member of the National Academy of Sciences Committee on Foundations of Educational and Psychological Assessment, a member of the U.S. Department of Education's Expert Panel on Technology, and International Steering Committee member for the Second International Technology in Education study.

Ellis, Jason Brent, Ashland University
jbellis@ashland.edu

Jason Brent Ellis is an Assistant Professor at Ashland University. He earned his PhD from the University of Windsor, Canada. His instructional area is education and assistive technologies. His research includes such topics as assistive and adaptive technology use by students with disabilities in higher education and ways of leveling the digital divide through grass-roots community approaches.

Fischman, Gustavo E., Arizona State University
gustavo.fischman@mac.com

Gustavo E. Fischman, is an Associate Professor in the Mary Lou Fulton College of Education at Arizona State University. His areas of specialization are comparative education, gender studies in education, and the use of image-based methods in educational research. He teaches and collaborates on research projects in Argentina, Brazil, Mexico, and the US. He is the Associate Editor of *Education Review* and *Education Policy Analysis Archives*, and the author of several books, articles and chapters about education policies.

Glass, Gene V, Arizona State University–CARDET
glass@asu.edu

Gene V Glass is Regents' Professor in the Mary Lou Fulton College of Education at has Arizona State University, where he has served as a member of the faculty since 1986. Trained originally in statistics, his interests broadened to include psychotherapy research, evaluation methodology, and policy analysis. He coined the term "meta-analysis" in 1975 and illustrated many of its techniques in a series of books and papers in the late 1970s and early 1980s. He was elected President of the American Educational Research Association in 1974. In 1993, he created one of the first open-access, electronic, peer-reviewed scholarly journals in education, the *Education Policy Analysis Archives*. In 2006, he was honored with the Distinguished Contributions to Educational Research Award of the American Educational Research Association. He is also Director of Research and Policy at CARDET. His latest book, *Fertilizers, Pills & Magnetic Strips: The Fate of Public Education in America*, argues that basic economic and demographic forces have determined the history and will determine the future of public education in America.

Grafton, Lee, Palm Springs Unified School District
lgrafton@psusd.us

Dr. Lee Grafton is the Instructional Technology Specialist at Palm Springs Unified School District (PSUSD) and an adjust faculty member in the College of Education at California State University, San Bernardino teaching research methods. She currently manages instructional technology staff development and technology planning programs for PSUSD's twenty four schools in California where she has facilitated, administered, and written several technology grants, totaling over $8.4 million. Dr. Grafton has delivered more than twenty professional presentations at national and state conventions. Her research interests include technology and learning, technology integration, distance learning, and web-based instruction. She serves on the Computer Using Educators (CUE) Conference Planning Committee and is the vice-president of the Cahuilla CUE Chapter. In addition to her current work, Dr. Grafton has taught communication and education courses at three universities, managed instructional technology programs for Fortune 500 companies, and taught in the public schools.

Hedberg, John G., Macquarie University
john.hedberg@mq.edu.au

Professor John G. Hedberg holds the Millennium Innovations Chair in ICT and Education and is Head of the School of Education at Macquarie University, Sydney, Australia. He is well known for his research into learning environments that engage students and employ problem-based learning. He is currently President of the International Council for Educational Media and has worked in several countries exploring how interactive and digital media can be employed as part of innovative pedagogies. In particular, he studies how students can be engaged and motivated in Mathematics, Science, History and Geography learning contexts. For more information, please see his personal homepage at http://www.educ.mq.edu.au/staff_bio.aspx?sid=313

Horenczyk, Gabriel, The Hebrew University of Jerusalem
gabriel@vms.huji.ac.il

Gabriel Horenczyk is an Associate Professor at the School of Education and the Melton Center for Jewish Education, The Hebrew University of Jerusalem. His teaching and research areas include: the psychological study of cultural and ethnic identity; Jewish identity transitions; education and immigration; cultural identity processes during intergroup contact; acculturation and identity processes among immigrants. He has published extensively in various scientific journals, and has co-edited two books: *Language, Identity, and Immigration* (with E. Olshtain), and *National*

Variations in Jewish Identity (with S. Cohen). Some of his current research projects include a multidimensional socio-psychological approach to Jewish identity; stress and coping among teachers working with immigrant students; the acculturative school context and the adaptation of immigrant students; the intergroup encounter: strategies, outcome, and the role of collective identity.

Kayler, Mary A., George Mason University
mkayler@gmu.edu

Mary A. Kayler is an Assistant Professor in the College of Education and Human Development at George Mason University. Research areas include online gaming, teaching and learning with technology, and constructivist pedagogy. She has numerous publications related to teacher development and pedagogy that support constructivist learning and on the use of self-assessment to support learning within online discussion groups and teacher development. She is a strong advocate for the scholarship of teaching and learning as a means to transform educational instructional practices to enhance learning.

Leach, Jenny, Open University, UK

The late Jenny Leach was Professor of Teacher Learning and Development at the Open University. She had published extensively in the area of communication technologies and teacher development and was editor of the international journal *Education, Communication and Information*. Her most recent project was as Director of Teacher Education in Sub-Saharan Africa (TESSA) www.tessafrica.net, a continuing project which creates open content multimedia resources and course design guidance for teachers and teacher educators, funded by the Ferguson Charitable Trust and the Hewlett Foundation.

Leh, Amy S. C., California State University San Bernardino
aleh@csusb.edu

Dr. Amy S. C. Leh is a Professor in Instructional Technology at the College of Education at California State University, San Bernardino. She has taught technology courses to credential students at three universities. She has also instructed in a variety of graduate education technology courses. She has written more than thirty articles and made more than seventy presentations at international/national conventions. Her research interests include technology and learning, distance education, web-based instruction, interaction in web-based learning environments, computer-mediated communication (CMC) and social presence, technology integration, and telecommunication technologies in foreign (second) language acquisition.

Lim Cher Ping, Edith Cowan University
c.lim@ecu.edu.au

Dr. Lim is an Associate Professor of teaching and learning at the School of Education in Edith Cowan University, Australia. He is the director of the Asia-Pacific Centre of Excellence for Teacher Education and Innovations. He has been the chief investigator of four major research projects: (1) Effective Integration of IT in Singapore Schools: Pedagogical and Policy Implications (Ministry of Education/Singapore), (2) Supporting E-discussions and e-sharing with New Technologies in Learning Communities (MobileOne/Singapore), (3) 3D Multi-User Virtual Environments in Schools (CRPP/NIE), and (4) Establishing the Feasibility of Digital Forms for Authentic and Reliable Assessment of Performance in Western Australian Senior Secondary School Courses (ARC Linkage Grant). He has also provided consulting services to the World Bank, World Links, Singapore Armed Forces Training Institute, APEC, UNESCO, Inter-American Development Bank, Microsoft, ACER Computers, schools and the Government of Barbados and Oman. For more information, please see his personal homepage at: http://edresearch.education.ecu.edu.au/chirp.

Makalima, Shumi, DEEP
shumi2@telkomsa.net

Shumi Makalema was the national co-ordinator of the DEEP project in South Africa, between 2002–2007. She led many aspects of training and research implementation with the teachers in South Africa, developing and sustaining relationships with project teachers throughout. She was instrumental in "grounding" the project in the realities of life as experienced by teachers in the Eastern Cape of South Africa. Shumi is currently concentrating her energies on raising three vibrant children, while also working as a consultant in education and development.

McIsaac, Marina Stock, Arizona State University–CARDET
mmcisaac@asu.edu

Born in Trieste Italy, Marina Stock McIsaac holds a PhD in Educational Technology from the University of Wisconsin, Madison, US. She is currently Professor Emerita from Arizona State University, and President of International Training Associates through which she does international work in the field of Educational Technology. She is Past-President of the International Council for Educational Media, the International Visual Literacy Association, and both the International Division and the Research and Theory Divisions of the Association for Educational Communications and Technology. Her teaching and research are directed toward intercultural issues as they relate to teaching and learning, focusing on the pedagogical use of Internet-based technologies and professional development. Her work has taken her to Turkey, Italy, Germany, Cyprus, Taiwan, Hong Kong, Nigeria, Singapore and Portugal.

Moreira, António, Universidade de Aveiro, Portugal
moreira@dte.ua.pt

Born in Aveiro, Portugal in 1957, António Moreira has a PhD in Didactics from the University of Aveiro where he has taught and conducted research since 1982. With several books and papers published in Portugal and abroad, he coordinates the Nónio Século XXI Competence Centre, the Didactic Courseware Laboratory and the Post-graduation Courses in Multimedia in Education of the Department of Didactics and Educational Technology of the University of Aveiro. His main activity is with post-graduate studies, where he supervises various studies in the field of education technology. His main research interests are centred on cognitive flexibility hypertexts, random access instruction, and communities of learning and of practice and, more recently, the educational dimensions of non-formal learning contexts and social web tools.

O'Connor, Carrie, Teach for America
carrieannoconnor@gmail.com

A pre-school teacher in Camden, New Jersey with Teach for America, Carrie Ann O'Connor holds a BS in Psychology from Ursinus College. Interested in issues of social justice and equity, Ms. O'Connor will work toward supporting equity in the public schools.

Porteous, Kimberly, Nelson Mandela Institute, University of Fort Hare
kporteus@ufh.ac.za

Kimberley Porteus is the Executive Director of the Nelson Mandela Institute, based at the University of Fort Hare. Her work has been located on the interface of educational transformation and the process of democratization in South Africa. Through the democratic elections in 1994, she worked with the Congress of South African Trade Unions; then with the Education Policy Unit at the University of the Witswatersrand, in education policy transformation. Since 2004, she has been working with networks of rural school communities in the Eastern Cape, to find ways of confronting the patterns of educational non-performance that cycle from the past. Her research interests include foundation phase teacher development, and the knowledge and systems that connect and disconnect historic oppression with current educational dysfunction.

Power, Tom, The Open University
t.j.m.p.power@open.ac.uk

Tom Power co-directed the Digital Education Enhancement Project (2001–2007 www.open.ac.uk/deep) together with his late friend and colleague, Professor Jenny Leach. DEEP explored the potential of mobile technologies to support teacher professional development and practice, with particular emphasis on the contexts of teachers in schools serving disadvantaged rural communities in the global south. Tom is now continuing the themes of DEEPs research within "English in Action," a large-scale DFID funded project in Bangladesh.

Ramadiro, Brian, Nelson Mandela Institute, University of Fort Hare
bramadiro@ufh.ac.za

Brian Ramadiro is the Deputy Director of the Nelson Mandela Institute for Education and Rural Development (NMI). Having grown up as a youth activist in Soweto in the 1980s, he completed his Masters degree in Sweden, while he simultaneously completed the first translation of the Communist Manifesto in isiZulu. At the University of the Witwatersrand, he coordinated a public research and mobilization campaign toward the elimination of school fees and other barriers of educational access (Education Rights Project). He is currently completing his second Masters in applied linguistics. His research interests include multilingual education programming, the intellectualization of African indigenous languages, education rights, literacy, teacher development, youth studies, and education in the context of rurality. He speaks isiZulu, isiXhosa, sePedi, seSotho, English, Afrikaans and Swedish.

Richardson, Jayson W., University of North Carolina
richardsonj@uncw.edu

Jayson W. Richardson is an Assistant Professor in the Department of Educational Leaders in the Watson School of Education at the University of North Carolina, Wilmington (UNCW). His research interests include global technology leadership, leadership in international contexts, and information and communication technologies for development (ICT4D). He currently teaches education technology and education leadership at the graduate level. At UNCW, Dr. Richardson is actively working to create international experiences for school leaders.

Ricker, Amber, Bowling Green State University
aricker@bgnet.bgsu.edu

Amber Ricker is currently a senior at Bowling Green State University, majoring in education. She is the co-founder and current president of F.I.G.U.R.E. (Finding Intelligent Greatness Uniquely Residing in Everyone). Amber also works with individuals who have cognitive disabilities in the community and assists them in their daily living needs.

Romero, Jose Luis Ramírez, University of Sonora
jlrmrz@golfo.uson.mx

Jose Luis Ramírez Romero holds the Doctor of Education degree from the University of California, Los Angeles and is Professor in the Department of Foreign Languages of the University of Sonora, where he teaches education technology and conducts research on the uses of technology in education. He has worked as faculty developer, curriculum consultant, and guest professor in several Latin American universities, and has published several articles on the topics of faculty development, curriculum, and educational technology.

Sankale, James, Ministry of Youth Affairs and Sports, in Kenya
jimsankale@hotmail.com

James is currently working in the Ministry of Youth Affairs and Sports in Kenya. He heads the Information Systems management team (developing and maintaining databases, and researching on the use of ICT in empowering youth). Previously he worked for more than ten years in the ministry of Education, where he coordinated the design and implementation of Teachers' Inservice Programmes, where use of modern technology was central, specifically using mobile technology which was geared toward enhancing teachers' performance and communication strategies.

Sprague, Debra, George Mason University
dspragu1@gmu.edu

Debra Sprague is an Associate Professor in the College of Education and Human Development at George Mason University. Her research interests focus on the use of technology to support teaching and learning. She currently serves as the editor for the *Journal of Technology and Teacher Education.*

Thomas, Rhodri, The Open University
rhodri.thomas@open.ac.uk

Rhodri Thomas is the Open University's Vitual Learning Environment's Mobile Learner Support, Collaboration and Communications project leader. He is involved in coordinating OU activities with regard to providing course support and materials for a mobile audience. Current areas of interest are Podcasting, Moblogging (user-generated content on-the-move) and widening access (to those with unreliable connectivity via offline approaches). Rhodri has worked on research and development programs, including Educational Technologist for DEEP in the Faculty of Education and Language Studies.

Tshume, Nomakholwa, Nelson Mandela Institute, University of Fort Hare
ntshume@ufh.ac.za

Nomakholwa Tshume has been working for the Nelson Mandela Institute for Education and Rural Development (NMI) since 2004. Her special line of interest is Information Communication Technology (ICT). She started by taking part as one of the passionate ICT team, which was involved in training, technical support, documentation and problem solving in rural school communities; she is currently working as an ICT Coordinator at the

NMI. Her current area of focus is applying relevant and sustainable ICTs to the challenges of rural schooling and community development.

Vrasidas, Charalambos, CARDET & University of Nicosia
pambos@cardet.org

Dr. Charalambos Vrasidas is co-founder and *Executive Director* of CARDET Centre for the Advancement of Research & Development in Educational Technology (http://www.cardet.org), a non-profit research and development centre based in Cyprus with partners around the world. He is also Associate Professor of Learning Technologies and Innovation at the University of Nicosia. He held positions at academic institutions and research and development centers including *Western Illinois University, Arizona State University, Satellite Education Network,* and the *Center for the Application of Information Technologies.* He currently serves on the Executive Committee of the *International Council for Educational Media,* an *UNESCO* affiliated organization. A former *Fulbright* scholar, he holds a PhD from Arizona State University in Educational Media and Computers. He has received grants for projects implemented in more than twenty countries, which were funded by agencies like the National Science Foundation, the Cyprus Research Promotion Foundation, The Pew Charitable Trusts, Microsoft, the US Department of Education, and the European Commission. He has published five books and more than a hundred articles in international journals and edited volumes. He currently serves as Editor-in-Chief for *Educational Media International.*

Zembylas, Michalinos, Open University of Cyprus & CARDET
zembylas@cardet.org

Michalinos Zembylas is Assistant Professor of Education at the Open University of Cyprus and Director of Curriculum Development for CARDET (Centre for the Advancement of Research & Development in Educational Technology). His research interests are in the areas educational philosophy and curriculum theory, and his work focuses on exploring the role of emotion and affect in curriculum and pedagogy. He is particularly interested in how affective politics intersect with issues of social justice pedagogies, intercultural and peace education, and citizenship education. Zembylas is the author of numerous articles in international refereed journals as well as the books, *Teaching with Emotion: A Postmodern Enactment* (Information Age Publishing, 2005), *Five Pedagogies, a Thousand Possibilities: Struggling for Hope and Transformation* (Rotterdam, The Netherlands: SensePublishers, 2007), and *The Politics of Trauma in Education* (New York, Palgrave Macmillan, 2008).

9 781607 520214

Printed and bound by CPI Group (UK) Ltd, Croydon, CR0 4YY
15/09/2026
14962367-0001